The Virtues of Captain America

*To my father, who never lost his love for his country
even when disheartened by the people who ran it.
He will always be my Captain America.*

The Virtues of Captain America

Modern-Day Lessons on Character from a World War II Superhero

Mark D. White

WILEY Blackwell

This edition first published 2014
© 2014 John Wiley & Sons, Inc.

Registered Office
John Wiley & Sons, Ltd, The Atrium, Southern Gate, Chichester, West Sussex, PO19 8SQ, UK

Editorial Offices
350 Main Street, Malden, MA 02148-5020, USA
9600 Garsington Road, Oxford, OX4 2DQ, UK
The Atrium, Southern Gate, Chichester, West Sussex, PO19 8SQ, UK

For details of our global editorial offices, for customer services, and for information about how to apply for permission to reuse the copyright material in this book please see our website at www.wiley.com/wiley-blackwell.

The right of Mark D. White to be identified as the author of this work has been asserted in accordance with the UK Copyright, Designs and Patents Act 1988.

Wiley also publishes its books in a variety of electronic formats. Some content that appears in print may not be available in electronic books.

Designations used by companies to distinguish their products are often claimed as trademarks. All brand names and product names used in this book are trade names, service marks, trademarks or registered trademarks of their respective owners. The publisher is not associated with any product or vendor mentioned in this book.

Limit of Liability/Disclaimer of Warranty: While the publisher and author have used their best efforts in preparing this book, they make no representations or warranties with respect to the accuracy or completeness of the contents of this book and specifically disclaim any implied warranties of merchantability or fitness for a particular purpose. It is sold on the understanding that the publisher is not engaged in rendering professional services and neither the publisher nor the author shall be liable for damages arising herefrom. If professional advice or other expert assistance is required, the services of a competent professional should be sought.

Library of Congress Cataloging-in-Publication Data is available for this book

Paperback: 9781118619261

A catalogue record for this book is available from the British Library.

Cover image: Flag © LoudRedCreative; Star © Moose2000; Wings © Visualgo; Metal background © Pomachka (all images iStockphoto)
Cover design by Simon Levy

Set in 10.5/13pt Minion by SPi Publisher Services, Pondicherry, India
Printed by Courier/Westford

2   2014

Contents

Introduction

This is a book I've wanted to write for years, and I'm very excited finally to share it with you. In these pages, I'm going to explain how Captain America—the fictional World War II super-soldier and modern-day Avenger familiar from comic books, movies, and animated TV series—provides an example of the personal virtues that philosophers since ancient times have put forward as defining personal excellence, as well as the ideals and principles upon which the United States of America was founded. To do this, I will combine my love of superhero comics with my background in moral and political philosophy to show how we can be better people—for ourselves, our family, and our communities—and how we can raise the level of political discussion in America so we can start addressing our problems rather than simply yelling at each other about them.

Not bad for something based on a "funny book," huh?

Captain America—or simply "Cap"—has been one of the premier comic-book superheroes for almost three quarters of a century. Steve Rogers, the scrawny kid from New York who was transformed into a super-soldier by the United States government with super-soldier serum and Vita-Rays, was introduced when Joe Simon and Jack Kirby's *Captain America Comics* #1 hit the newsstands on March 10, 1941, nine months before the attack on Pearl Harbor.[1] The book lasted until the end of the 1940s, suffering the fate of most superhero comics as readers' interests turned to romance, horror, and Western comics. After a short-lived revival in the mid-1950s, Captain America was not seen again until 1964, when *Avengers* #4 told the now-famous tale of how Iron Man, Thor, Giant Man, and Wasp found Steve Rogers frozen in a block of ice, his super-soldier-serum preserving his body in a state of suspended animation.[2] For the last fifty years, Cap has been a central player in the ever-expanding Marvel Universe, both in his own solo title and various *Avengers* books as well as the epic crossover stories that have become an annual event in comics publishing since the mid-1980s. Add to those the *Captain America* and *Avengers* films and his appearances in animated series, videogames, and other media, and it's easy to see why Captain America remains as much a heroic icon today as he was during World War II.

For all their groundbreaking ideas and innovative artwork, the "Golden Age" superhero comics published in the 1940s were never big on characterization, focusing mostly on exciting action and pure heroics. But that changed with the revival of superheroes in the late 1950s and early 1960s, especially when the Fantastic Four and other new heroes were introduced by Marvel Comics. Once simply a patriotic symbol meant to inspire a nation at war, upon his return Captain America became a tragic figure along with his fellow Avengers and other Marvel superheroes. Just as the Fantastic Four's Thing was disfigured by cosmic rays, Iron Man's heart was under constant threat of encroaching shrapnel, and Spider-Man bore the guilt of inadvertently causing the death of his beloved Uncle Ben, Captain America found himself a "man out of time," uncomfortable in the modern age with its new technology, social customs, and values. This sense of displacement, established almost immediately by Stan Lee, Jack Kirby, and Don Heck upon Cap's reappearance in comics like *Avengers*, *Tales of Suspense*, and his own title, came to define the character for years to come. And nothing epitomized Cap's "strangeness" more than his "old-fashioned" values, forged in the Great Depression and World War II and thought by many of his fellow superheroes to be relics of a simpler time.

Ironically, it is this code of ethics, backed by Captain America's steely resolve and careful judgment, that makes his participation and leadership invaluable to the Marvel Universe. Soon after his reappearance, Cap became the moral center of the superhero community, a figure to whom all other heroes would compare themselves and against whom they would argue their own moral positions. This was most obvious during Marvel's "Civil War" when Captain America and Iron Man stood against each other over the issue of superhero registration. (We'll talk about this conflict much more throughout the book, because "Civil War" is a storyline incredibly rich in moral and political concepts.) Soon afterwards, when Cap was apparently shot and killed, the Marvel Universe came under the control of a madman, Norman Osborn (formerly Spider-Man's nemesis the Green Goblin), in what was called the "Dark Reign," which ended only after Captain America returned from the "dead."[3] With the simple command,

"It's time to take back this country," Cap rallied the other heroes to defeat Osborn, launching what was called the "Heroic Age."[4]

While Cap was gone (not dead but rather thrown back in time), the Marvel Universe was literally a ship without its Captain, and without his leadership, Norman Osborn was able to take control of the world. After Cap came back during Osborn's siege on Thor's home of Asgard and helped to set the world right again, the moral center of the Marvel Universe was restored at last. This is not to say that the other heroes—or the readers—always agree with Cap on what the right thing to do is. There are sound arguments to be made against his positions, just as there are against anybody else's. But the strength and constancy of Cap's core moral positions provide a valuable source of debate and disagreement in the comics—and they also give us a lot of material to draw from throughout the course of this book!

In this book, I'm going to present Captain America's personal morality in terms of *virtue ethics*, a type of moral theory originating with ancient Greek philosophers such as Aristotle, Plato, and the Stoics. There are other ways to describe Cap's ethics, certainly, and I'll draw from these other traditions when appropriate. But I chose virtue ethics as my main framework because it has clear intuitive appeal, does not require a lot of fancy philosophical language to explain, and is easily applicable to the personal and political issues of today. Literally speaking, if we look at them this way, Cap's values *are* old-fashioned, dating from about 2500 years ago, but many philosophers (including myself) regard the work of the early virtue ethicists as timeless, and innovative work continues in the tradition today.

The original virtue ethicists incorporated wonderfully perceptive observations about human nature into their prescriptions for behaving morally and promoting the "good life." This allowed them to avoid the strict rules and formulas of the ethical systems that followed, and instead they offered the flexibility of moral judgment that people need to make decisions in complex real-world situations. As advanced as we like to think we are in the modern world, the essential moral problems of respecting each other, getting along, and working together have not changed much in the last several thousand years. In fact, because technology, along with its many gifts, has also expanded the scale and scope of the ways we can hurt each other, the lessons of the virtue ethicists are more important now than ever—and a "man out of time" such as Captain America can see that better than anyone.

Throughout this book, I'll argue that Cap's "old-fashioned" moral code is exactly what we need to restore civility and respect in the twenty-first century in both our personal lives and our political debates. He is what the ancient philosophers—yes, more ancient than Cap—called a *moral exemplar*. Today we'd call him a role model, but both terms refer to a person we can look up to and use as an example of how to act in certain situations. Role models today are often political figures, entertainers, or athletes—all of whom are real people (whether alive or dead). But can a fictional character be a role model? We'll talk about that soon, but obviously I would answer yes, we *can* learn things from fictional characters (while keeping in mind that many of the details or stories we "know" about real-life role models are just as fictional!).

This book starts with an introduction of basic ethics in chapter 1 and discusses several issues with using fictional characters such as Captain America as role models in chapter 2. After that, we start looking at Captain America in detail, using examples and quotations from the last fifty years of his stories in the comics. In chapter 3, we'll discuss several of the individual virtues that Cap exemplifies, such as courage, humility, and perseverance, and show how virtue ethics shows them to be more subtle and nuanced than they might seem. In chapter 4, we'll look at qualities that describe Cap's moral character more broadly, such as honor and integrity, and we'll explore his adherence to principle and duty, both of which influence how Captain America exercises his virtuous character traits—and provide a valuable example for us in the twenty-first century as well.

While these virtues and characteristics describe the basic themes of Captain America's ethics, they aren't much help when it comes to making hard choices in specific circumstances. As we'll see, having the virtue of courage doesn't tell you just how brave you should be in different circumstances; for that, you need judgment, which we'll discuss in chapter 5. We'll borrow some ideas from legal philosophy to show how we can use judgment in moral dilemmas in the same way judges make decisions in difficult legal cases: by balancing our personal principles to arrive at a decision that maintains our integrity. We'll also see how Captain America's judgment regarding some issues like killing and torture may have changed over the years—and why. Did the world change in such a way that Cap had to make moral compromises, or was it his moral character that changed? I'll present the evidence, and you be the judge.

In chapter 6, we'll move from the personal to the political by exploring the "America" in Captain America. We'll see what patriotism means to philosophers and how Cap's particular brand of patriotism is inclusive and cosmopolitan rather than exclusionary and jingoistic. We'll discuss how he consistently puts principle before politics, including the orders of his own government, which is a reflection of his moral integrity and sense of honor. This chapter reinforces the point that Captain America represents the basic ideals of America, not its politics or government, which explains how he can serve as a symbol of these ideals to all Americans, regardless of political orientation, as well as people around the world.

In the final chapter, I'll argue that Captain America's belief in principle over politics can help Americans in the real world to address our current state of political divisiveness. By focusing on what we have in common— the core American principles of justice, equality, and liberty—we can start to realize that our disagreements are largely about how we want to interpret and implement these ideals, with each of us balancing our versions of them in ways that express our individual characters. If we keep in mind what principles we share, we will have a common framework upon which to debate our different approaches to solving the problems America faces, instead of spending our time and energy arguing past each other, demonizing our opponents, and trying to "control the narrative" rather than push it forward. As Cap often says, we need to work together to turn the American dream into the American reality—and I'm just crazy enough to think a comic-book superhero can help us do that.

Most of the examples I use in this book are drawn from the various *Captain America* and *Avengers* comic books published over the last fifty years by Marvel Comics, many of which are available in collected editions in your local comics shop, bookstore, or online. (A complete listing appears at the end of the book.) But I promise, you don't have to be familiar with any of this source material to appreciate the points I make—ultimately, this is a book about philosophy and politics, not superheroes. (You can consider them a bonus!) Just sit back and enjoy the book—and if it inspires you to pick up a *Captain America* comic or a copy of Aristotle's *Nicomachean Ethics*, all the better!

Notes

1 Cap's origin has been retold a number of times since his first appearance, my favorite being *Captain America*, vol. 1, #255 (1981).

2 "A" Captain America (actually the villainous Acrobat in disguise) was seen in a story titled "The Human Torch Meets ... Captain America" in *Strange Tales*, vol. 1, #114 in 1963 (later reprinted in *Captain America*, vol. 1, #216, 1977), to

test the waters and see if readers wanted the real Cap back. (Guess we know the answer to that, hmm?)

3   Death in comic books is rarely what it seems, so I use quotation marks and words like "apparently" a lot. They're not legal disclaimers, but they're very close!

4   *Siege* #2 (2010).

Acknowledgments

I would like to thank Jeff Dean for supporting this project from the beginning, and Allison Kostka, Lindsay Bourgeois, and Jennifer Bray at Wiley Blackwell for helping shepherd it through the process. I'd also like to thank William Irwin, who not only gave me the opportunity to edit and write on superheroes and philosophy for his Blackwell Philosophy and Pop Culture series, but who has also been a wonderful and supportive friend for many years. Speaking of the Blackwell series, I want to thank all the co-editors and contributors I've worked with—including Bill Irwin, who has the distinct honor of being thanked twice—all of whom helped me hone whatever writing style I've got. Many friends provided encouragement and support while writing this book, chief among them Lauren Hale, Lynn Beighley, Carol Borden, Heather Giltner, and Anita Leirfall. (I would mention Bill again, but no one deserves to be thanked three times—he'll start expecting money!)

Finally, I could not have written this book if not for all the brilliant and inventive creators who contributed to the Captain America canon: first and foremost Joe Simon, Jack Kirby, and Stan Lee, but also people such as Brian Michael Bendis, Ed Brubaker, Kurt Busiek, J.M. DeMatteis, Steve Engleheart, Christos Gage, Mark Gruenwald, Paul Jenkins, Dan Jurgens, David Morell, John Ney Reiber, Rick Remender, Jim Steranko, Roger Stern, J. Michael Straczynski, and Mark Waid. Steve Rogers may have made Captain America the symbol of justice, equality, and liberty that he is, but all of these creators (and more) made Steve Rogers who he is, and my gratitude to them is endless.

Notes on Source Material

1. Throughout this book I quote from many comics, and most of these quotes are of dialogue. Comic book dialogue—usually displayed in word balloons arranged throughout the artwork—has a number of unique conventions, including the frequent use of boldface, italics, ellipses, and dashes. Not all of these translate well in the printed word in a book, especially the boldface and italics that spruce up word balloons in comics but look excessive on a staid page of text. By the same token, ellipses and dashes, which help connect the dialogue across multiple word-balloons, look choppy when reproduced in a continuous series of words on a page. So I had to make choices: I omitted the boldface and italic, but I kept ellipses and boldface where I thought they were important to the dialogue. Furthermore, comics writers use a *lot* of exclamation points! Often after every phrase!! *Like this!!!* That's just the nature of superhero dialogue; it can be corny but it's part of the charm of the medium. So the exclamation points stay!

2. Since Captain America has appeared in various forms and media over the years, there are many versions of the character out there. To keep things simple, in this book I use only one: Steve Rogers, the Captain America in the mainstream Marvel Comics Universe, who was introduced in 1941, revived in 1964, and is still appearing regularly in comics books such as *Captain America* and *Avengers* to this day. (An appendix at the end of this book details the titles he has appeared in over the years.) Although I don't draw on them, the versions of Captain America who appear in the *Avengers* and *Captain America* movies, as well as the one seen in animated series such as *Avengers: Earth's Mightiest Heroes* and *Ultimate Spider-Man*, are also very close to what I consider to be the "real" Captain America, based on the character traits reflected in his words and actions (as I'll describe them in chapters 3 and 4).

In terms of the comics themselves, when I discuss Captain America, I am discussing only Steve Rogers, not any of the other men who have served under that name in the mainstream Marvel Universe, including his former World War II sidekick Bucky Barnes. Also, I am not discussing the Captain America in the Ultimate Marvel Universe, who is also named Steve Rogers but sometimes exhibits distinctly different and less virtuous character traits. If you're not a comics fan, none of this means anything to you, so don't worry about it, but for those of you who are, I want to make clear that I am talking about the man I consider to be the one-and-only Captain America, Steve Rogers of Earth-616. (That number is a whole other story in itself!)

About the Author

Mark D. White is Professor and Chair of the Department of Philosophy at the College of Staten Island/CUNY, where he teaches courses in philosophy, economics, and law. In addition to writing dozens of journal articles and book chapters in these areas, he has authored *Kantian Ethics and Economics: Autonomy, Dignity, and Character* (2011) and *The Manipulation of Choice: Ethics and Libertarian Paternalism* (2013) and has edited or co-edited books such as *The Thief of Time: Philosophical Essay on Procrastination* (2010) and *Retributivism: Essays on Theory and Policy* (2012). He is also a frequent editor and contributor to the Blackwell Philosophy and Pop Culture series, having edited or co-edited books on Batman, Superman, Iron Man, Green Lantern, the Avengers, and *Watchmen*, and contributed to many more. Online, he blogs for *Psychology Today*, *Economics and Ethics*, and *The Comics Professor*, and you can follow him on Twitter as @profmdwhite. More details about his work are available at his website, www.profmdwhite.com.

1

Superhuman Ethics Class

Never let it be said that superheroes don't take ethics seriously! After his fellow Avengers engaged in some questionable activities during an interstellar conflict in the "Galactic Storm" storyline, Captain America initiated a "Superhuman Ethics" class; later, the young heroes-in-training at Avengers Academy took the same class as part of their regular curriculum (taught by perennial screw-up Hank Pym).[1]

Even though the situations faced by superheroes may seem extraordinary, often involving aliens, wizards, or time travelers, most of them actually boil down to the same issues each of us face on a regular basis: the right ways to manage our interactions with other people given the various ways we can affect them in good ways and bad. We may not have super-strength or fire energy bolts from our eyes, but we can still use our very human abilities and the tools at our disposal to help or hurt people (including ourselves). Even if we're of a mind to help people—like the heroes we are—questions nonetheless arise regarding when to offer help, how to do it when we decide to, and who to help if we have to make choices or set priorities. We also have to consider that the help we offer may come at a cost, not just to ourselves but possibly to other people, which also deserves consideration. Compared to the complexities of moral decision-making, all of the flying, punching, and mind-reading might seem like the easier part of a hero's day! But these ethical dilemmas are the types of problems that we in the real world face all the time in our ordinary lives, and in the comics they lend an important sense of humanity to even the most super of heroes.

The Virtues of Captain America: Modern-Day Lessons on Character from a World War II Superhero, First Edition. Mark D. White.
© 2014 John Wiley & Sons, Inc. Published 2014 by John Wiley & Sons, Inc.

Before we get into the various schools of ethics, however, I want to clear up a popular misconception about philosophy professors (including myself). Some people think that when we teach ethics courses, we simply tell our students the difference between right and wrong by instilling our own ethical principles in them. But nothing could be farther from the truth. What we do is help students refine their own ethical beliefs by introducing them to the terminology and concepts that philosophers have used to discuss moral issues for thousands of years. We want to help students understand their *own* values better by challenging them to consider their views in light of alternative ones and helping them to describe their ethical positions more precisely. After reflecting on their own ethical views, students may want to adjust or reject them—perhaps if they find inconsistencies or contradictions in the way they think about moral questions—but whether or not they do is entirely up to them. If both the professor and the students do their jobs, by the end of the term the students will have the tools to think about moral questions more clearly so they can express themselves better, engage in rational discussion about ethical issues with other people, and better appreciate other people's points of view (without necessarily agreeing with them). And by discussing ethics with our students, we professors often come out with a better idea of our own morals—and sometimes our students challenge *us* to look at moral issues in new ways. Everyone wins!

In this spirit, I am going to briefly talk about the three basic schools of ethics—utilitarianism, deontology, and virtue ethics. This will not only help us situate Captain America's ethics within moral philosophy more broadly, but it will also help us understand the ethical points of view of other people in the Marvel Universe, especially when they debate moral issues with Cap in the comics. (I'm looking at you, Iron Man—do you think I don't know you're sleeping under that helmet?)

Utilitarianism

The most straightforward school of ethics is *utilitarianism*, which stems from the work of the English philosophers Jeremy Bentham and John Stuart Mill.[2] Utilitarians maintain that the morally best choice is the one that promotes the greatest happiness of the greatest number of people. Another way of saying this is that the best choice will result in the greatest surplus of pleasure over pain, or, as Bentham put it, "when the tendency it has to augment the happiness of the community is greater than any it has to diminish it."[3] These descriptions capture the basic point of utilitarianism, but we need a little more detail to see its benefits as well as its downsides.

To be precise, utilitarianism is a specific type of consequentialism. *Consequentialism* refers to any system of ethics that judges the moral worth of actions based on their outcomes or results (as opposed to looking at the action itself or the person who performed it). Consequentialism is more general than utilitarianism in that it doesn't say what *about* the outcomes of an action should be considered, or how those qualities of outcomes should be combined or weighed against each other, to form a moral judgment of the action itself. It merely says that outcomes are what matters, and philosophers can fill in the details to specify which form of consequentialism— such as utilitarianism—they want to use to evaluate moral choices.[4]

According to utilitarianism in particular, the outcome of an action is assessed according to its *utility*, which can be defined as the happiness, pleasure, or well-being it creates. There are variations of utilitarianism that claim that each of these is the "right" understanding of utility. This is a crucially important issue for philosophers, because the way we define what is morally good affects the judgments we make. If we consider utility to be happiness, we'll do things to promote happiness, but if we define utility as a broader conception of well-being, then we'll focus on that instead, which may lead to different ethical conclusions. For our purposes, however, we can keep things general and say the utility of an action is simply the *good* it produces for people. When Captain America saves a child from a burning apartment building, he increases the amount of good experienced by the child, her parents and other family members, and the firefighters who otherwise would have (willingly) risked their lives to do the same. Actions that produce more good—or less "bad"—are said to have more utility, and actions that produce less good (or more bad) have less utility. (Some would call the latter *disutility*, but I think it's easier to say "less utility." And it's my book.) It doesn't matter if we look at Cap's actions as increasing a family's utility or decreasing its disutility (sounds weird, right?); either way, their utility is higher because of his action, which makes his action ethical according to this simplistic utilitarian judgment. (We'll discuss complications later, even though it usually turns out that saving children from burning buildings is a good thing to do.)

Regardless of how utility is defined in any particular version of utilitarianism, it's the answer to the second question—how should the utilities of various people be combined—that lends the system much of its moral power. In utilitarianism, the utilities of individual persons are simply added up, which implies that each person's utility or well-being counts no more and no less than anybody else's. In other words, utilitarianism is based on the idea that all people have equal moral status. As you can imagine, this was a revolutionary thought in the eighteenth century, not just in terms of race and gender but also socioeconomic class—especially in countries like Bentham and Mill's native England, which had a strict class system. This rebellious streak in utilitarianism suited Bentham, a social reformer who wanted to see the government acknowledge the well-being of the lower classes as well as the rich when making decisions; it appealed to Mill as well, who advocated strongly for women's rights alongside his wife, Harriet Taylor Mill.[5] This moral equality forces us to think of everyone who is affected by our actions, not just those close to us (such as family or friends) or similar to us (in race, gender, or nationality).

Despite its simplicity and intuitive appeal, there are some problems with utilitarianism that are widely acknowledged by philosophers (even those partial to it). First, you have to determine how much utility is produced (or disutility prevented) by an action, which is often difficult to measure. It is one thing to say that helping an elderly neighbor with his groceries is good for him, but it's another thing entirely to say *how much* you would help him. In most cases this isn't necessary; let's be honest, we can all afford to help each other out more, especially at little if any cost to ourselves. But if you can help your neighbor only at the expense of delaying a commitment you made to someone else, you need to be able to determine the utilities of those two actions before you can compare them and choose the best action. This may seem like a simple problem of estimation or measurement, but since the definition of utility—defining what the good is—is an ethical question in itself, any attempt to measure it involves a value judgment as well.

Second, you have to be able to determine a *lot* of utilities—and do a lot of math—in order to know that you have arrived at the best action. To start with, a utilitarian needs to compute the change in utility of every person affected by her action. She also has to forecast all the ripple effects of her action as they spread out in the world and figure out those utilities. But we're not done—the world is an uncertain place, after all, and any action will have many possible consequences, some more likely than others. As a result, the utilitarian has to determine the probabilities of each possible outcome and discount the utilities of those outcomes by their likelihood. (All else the same, more likely outcomes deserve more consideration than less likely ones.) These complications aren't going to be very important when deciding whether to help your neighbor with his groceries, but if you're using utilitarian logic to help make a big decision like what to major in in college, what job to take, or whether to have a child, all of the possible outcomes you will want to consider can be mindboggling. Ironically, the complexities of utilitarian decision-making might suggest that engaging in it sacrifices too much utility, especially with regard to minor decisions, and that you should just make a choice with the information you have. (It makes sense, after all, that you would spend weeks shopping for a house but just seconds choosing a Captain America toothbrush.)[6]

More important from a moral point of view—and perhaps just as surprising—the principle of equality that grounds utilitarianism has downsides too. For instance, some people are what philosophers call "utility monsters" who derive extraordinary amounts of utility (or disutility) from ordinary actions.[7] We all know people who are like this in certain situations: our best friend who lives to see his favorite movie star in her latest film, or our cousin whose eyes roll back in her head in ecstasy when eating Belgian chocolate. Utility monsters can go the other way too, getting incredibly sad or upset at relatively small disappointments, such as missing a cab or watching your cousin take the last piece of Belgian chocolate. True utility monsters get exaggerated amounts of utility, positive or negative, from certain things. The problem is that, even though their utility doesn't count any more than anyone else's, they get so much more of it from things that changes in their utility tend to overwhelm everyone else's. If I'm deciding who to give the last piece of chocolate to, I might decide that, because your cousin would get more pleasure out of it than anyone else, she should get it—and she might get all of it because she loves it so much. But that hardly seems fair, does it? Even though utilitarianism is based on equality, people don't have equal capacities for getting utility from things, and this can bias the results of utilitarian decision-making so that actions are always chosen in utility monsters' favor.

There's a more pressing problem with the equal consideration of utilities: it's not obvious that in every situation, everyone deserves to have his or her utility counted equally, if at all! Certainly we should start from an assumption of equal treatment, but there are circumstances that may lead us to question it. In one story, Captain America and another hero, Nomad (about whom we'll hear much more later in the book), were fighting a villain on a yacht that suddenly burst into flame.[8] While Cap's first priority was to save the unconscious (and massive) villain in front of him, Nomad chose to ignore the villain, telling Cap that he's "not worth the effort of saving," and running to save any (innocent) passengers left on the boat. To Nomad, the villain's wrongful acts made his utility less worthy of consideration than the passengers, while Cap felt that all life is equally worth protecting regardless of any one person's record of wrongdoing. In less extreme—but more realistic—circumstances, we can ask if the disutility of convicted criminals from time spent in prison should count against their punishment, or if that consideration is waived because of their criminal acts.[9] Without taking either side, there is a case to be made that the utilities of every person should not necessarily count equally in all cases, even though the standard version of utilitarianism demands that it does.

Deontology

We left the most significant problem with utilitarianism until now because it leads directly to the next approach to ethics. Because utilitarianism puts the sum of utilities above all other considerations when it comes to picking out the best action, it runs the risk of ignoring other moral factors that some may feel are more important.

One example often used by philosophers deals with a despotic government faced with a growing angry mob of citizens. The ruler thinks that the mob can be scared into submission, saving numerous lives, if he plucks an innocent person out of the crowd and executes him. In essence, the ruler would be sacrificing one life to save many, which makes sense in terms of utilitarianism (assuming all lives are valued equally in terms of utility), but nonetheless seems wrong to many people. A more down-to-earth example could be lying about your education to get a promotion at work, which may be recommended by utilitarian logic if the benefits from the promotion exceed the possible costs of being caught. But this doesn't consider the widespread intuition that lying is wrong regardless of the possibility of good consequences on the whole. But unless there is something about lying that *always* results in less utility for all, then it's difficult to reconcile the wrongness of lying with a utilitarian approach to it.

Another way of stating this problem with utilitarianism is that, by ignoring any moral aspects of an action other than the utility it produces, it implies that the "ends justify the means." In other words, utilitarianism places no limits on what can be done (the means) to produce the greatest amount of happiness for the greatest number of people (the ends). But this flies in the face of common-sense morality, which maintains that some means are simply wrong and should never be used, even when they promote good ends.[10] This phrase is common enough that it's often used in comics when characters discuss ethics, especially considering that Captain America is not fond of the idea! For example, when Cap criticized Iron Man for some extreme actions he'd taken in the past in pursuit of otherwise noble aims, Iron Man told him, "I knew you could never understand that—you don't believe that the ends justify the means."[11] At the end of a recent battle between the Avengers and the X-Men—which resulted in the death of Professor Xavier, the X-Men's mentor—their leader Cyclops told Cap that change always involves sacrifice, to which Cap responded, "if only it was that simple. If only the ends always justified the means."[12]

This aspect of common-sense morality that conflicts with utilitarianism corresponds to our second major school of ethics: *deontology.* Deontology is much harder to define than utilitarianism and consequentialism are. It would be easy to say simply that deontology is the opposite of consequentialism, but that wouldn't be accurate—deontology is both more and less than "anti-consequentialism." Deontologists don't necessary rule out any ethical role for the outcome of an action; they just don't think it's the only factor at play in every situation. If utilitarians say that the ends *always* justify the means, deontologists are the ones in the back of the room pointing out "*not* always." As Yogi Berra might have said, the ends justify the means except when they don't, and the role of deontology is to explain exactly in which cases they don't. So deontology is not as extreme as anti-consequentialism—the "less" part—but it also fills in the gaps that consequentialism can't fill, like the wrongness of lying—which provides the "more."

But … if not consequences, what else is there? In the examples we gave above, something about the means themselves seemed to rule out their use. Regardless of the possible good outcomes, we simply *shouldn't* kill innocent citizens or lie to our employers. There's something intrinsically wrong about such actions that outweighs any consideration of their consequences. That's what deontology contributes: the belief that there are some moral wrongs that sometimes (not always) take precedence over consequences. Another way to put it is that sometimes the "right" comes before the "good," or that principle is sometimes more important than outcomes.[13]

That still leaves us with a question: what are these wrongs and where do they come from? The answer differs from one deontologist to the next, just as utilitarians have different ideas of what utility is. For our purposes, that issue is less important than the fact that principles of right and wrong can take precedence over consequences. Nonetheless, I'll briefly introduce the most developed and influential version of deontology, courtesy of the philosopher Immanuel Kant. Kant's ethical theory is best known for its emphasis on *duties*, moral commands that tell a person what to do or not do, such as "do not lie," "do not kill," and "be kind to others." In fact, Kant's version of deontology has become so influential that sometimes deontology is defined as being a duty-based ethics.[14]

These duties are derived from Kant's *categorical imperative*, his formalization of "the moral law," which can be expressed in several ways. The first version is the most widely known (though perhaps not in the original, exact language): "act only according to that maxim whereby you can at the same time will that it should become a universal law."[15] In other words, if we want to do something, such as lie, we have to be able to let everyone do it (or *universalize* it), and if this results in a contradiction, that means it's wrong to do. In terms of lying, if we allow everyone to lie because we want to lie, it would result in so much lying that no one would believe anyone—which would defeat the purpose of the lie we want to tell! Based on that contradiction, we can derive a duty not to lie.

This seems logical—which Kant claims was the key to its appeal—but it strikes many as morally empty. After all, how can right or wrong be derived from logic? After all, just because something might not work well doesn't make it wrong. The moral content of this version of categorical imperative doesn't come from the logic, however, but from why we universalize in the first place: an attitude of reciprocity based on equal moral status for all. Sound familiar? This is the same principle that motivates the summing-up of individual utilities in utilitarianism, but Kant beat Bentham to it by a few decades. He was the first major philosopher to argue that all persons, by virtue of their *autonomy*—the ability to make moral decisions independent of external authority or internal drives—have an intrinsic and incomparable worth or *dignity*. No one is better than anyone else based on race, gender, or privilege of birth—which is just as radical an idea in Kant's world as it was in Bentham's (not to mention many parts of the world today). The utilitarians adopted this principle as their foundation and built a different moral system upon it, but the central idea of both schools of ethics is the same.

This respect for the dignity of persons is more obvious in another version of Kant's categorical imperative: "act in such a way that you treat humanity, whether in your own person or in the person of another, always at the same time as an end and never simply as a means."[16] This formula results in the same duties as the first—according to Kant, all the versions of the categorically imperative were merely different ways to express the same moral law—but the reasoning behind it is often seen as more direct (if less formal). For instance, the duty not to lie results from this formula also, because when we lie, we use the person we lie to as a means to whatever end we're trying to further by lying, without letting that person in on the ruse (which would show that person the respect owed him or her). This is not to say we can't use people to get things we need—we do that every time we buy coffee, hire a lawyer, or get our shields buffed. What it does mean is that we have to do these things while considering the other person as a end in him- or herself, treating that person with respect and kindness, rather than being rude, deceitful, or violent.

As I said above, Kant's duties represent just one source of deontological rights and wrongs. Another deontological philosopher, W.D. Ross, also held that duties were important to ethics but believed that they were derived from intuition.[17] In his opinion, everyone "knows" that killing and lying are wrong, so we don't need a categorical imperative to figure that out. Other deontologists use the language of rights instead of duties, and just like duties, these rights can take precedence over utility. Consider, for example, the right to free speech that appears in the First Amendment to the US Constitution, which implies that individuals have the right to speak their mind even if it bothers other people (that is, subtracts from their utility). As the legal and political philosopher Ronald Dworkin wrote, sometimes rights "trump" utility—but other times they don't, as in cases of clear and present danger (such as yelling "fire" in a crowded theater), a famous exception to the right to free speech.[18] There is a clear link between rights and duties—for instance, a right to one's property implies that others have a duty not to steal it—so the two approaches to deontology are not so different. The important thing, again, is that they both identify an issue that can be of higher moral importance than utility, an instance of the "right" that can block considerations of the "good."

Notice I keep saying "can" rather than "do"—that's very important, lest we become deontological absolutists. (Worst superhero team name ever.) While deontology has a certain appeal, especially in cases in which issues of right and wrong clearly seem more important than outcomes, there are cases in which it can look extreme. Sticking to your principles and fulfilling your duties are great, even noble, but there are sometimes significant or even enormous costs to doing so, which is a consequence that even a deontologist will find hard to ignore.

One famous example that Kant gave deals with someone trying to kill your best friend.[19] Imagine this: your friend Susan pounds on your door one day. After you answer, she begs you to hide her because someone is trying to kill her. Five minutes after locking her in your bathroom, there is a second knock on your door: it's a burly stranger who asks if Susan is there while he holds what seems to be a large battle-axe behind his back. What's an ethical person to do: tell the truth to the stranger or lie to him to save your best friend?

Kant said that even in this situation you mustn't lie—which is fine for you, but not so great for Susan, who ends up paying the cost for your "clean hands."[20] Are you willing to incur that cost—or, more precisely, have Susan incur that cost—in order to preserve your honesty? I think most people would say no: honesty is important, but not as important as our friend's *life*. No matter how strongly a person adheres to a principle, there is almost always some cost, either to that person or someone he cares about, that will force him to reconsider it.[21] This is not cynicism, such as when people say "every man has his price." It's simply the recognition that there are many things of moral importance, and no single one, whether consequence or duty, always takes precedence over all others. Morality—like life in general—is more complicated than that.

A Civil War ... of Ethics!

The conflict between utilitarianism and deontology took center stage in "Civil War," a storyline which dominated most Marvel comics during much of 2006 and 2007.[22] A series of disasters involving the superhero community—including a battle between a supervillain and a team of teen-aged heroes in Stamford, CT, that resulted in the death of hundreds of people, mostly schoolchildren—led Congress to pass the Superhuman Registration Act (SHRA). The act required all superpowered heroes to register with the government, revealing their identities and submitting to training when necessary. After trying but failing to stop passage of the SHRA, Tony Stark (Iron Man) took charge of its implementation while Captain America led an underground resistance movement, with the rest of the Marvel heroes taking one side or the other (and the X-Men playing Switzerland).

Iron Man justified the SHRA and his involvement with it on utilitarian grounds.[23] He recognized both the tremendous power heroes have and the lack of oversight or accountability for how they use it, especially regarding the consequences when things went wrong. Furthermore, these issues were not simply academic for him. Just before the Stamford incident, a villain took over Tony's mind and forced him, as Iron Man, to kill hundreds of people. Even though a friend assured him he wasn't responsible, that the armor was like a gun and the villain pulled the trigger, Tony replied, "Every super hero is a potential gun ... and the last time I checked, guns required registration."[24] As an alcoholic in recovery, Tony was all too familiar with losing control in other ways as well; as he said to Cap during the Civil War, "You know how dangerous a drunk is behind the wheel of a car? Imagine one piloting the world's most sophisticated battle armor."[25]

Tony Stark saw the big picture and decided to take charge of registration to minimize the harm to his fellow heroes. Even before Stamford, he showed other heroes an early draft of the SHRA and said, "I'm telling you: this is happening. Right now. ... An environment of fear has been created where this can not only exist but will pass."[26] As he told Cap, "It was coming anyway. I always thought it was inevitable, though I did try to delay it. But after Stamford there was no stopping it."[27] Once the SHRA became law, Iron Man became its public face and chief enforcer, leading a team of other heroes in rounding up unregistered heroes. After the Civil War ended, Tony said, "I knew that I would be put in the position of taking charge of things. Because if not me, who? Who else was there? No one. So I sucked it up."[28] Tony considers himself a futurist, uniquely able to look at everything that's going on and see what's coming, so he took responsibility for managing the implementation of the SHRA using his intelligence and judgment. And as a good utilitarian, he took whatever means necessary to do his job, such as enlisting the help of convicted supervillains to help capture unregistered heroes and building a prison in another dimension to detain them indefinitely— using the ends to justify the means, as he had many times before (much to Captain America's chagrin).[29]

Speaking of Captain America, he did not see things the same way his fellow Avenger did. While we'll describe him primarily in terms of virtue ethics in this book, many of Cap's attitudes and actions, especially during the Civil War, can also be cast in terms of deontology: specifically, the way he favored principles over consequences. Throughout the Civil War saga, he maintained that registration sacrifices the liberty and autonomy of heroes trying to help people, that heroes have to stay above politics unless they want the government telling them who the villains are, and that politicians are all too quick to trade freedom for security. To sum up, "what they're doing is wrong. Plain and simple."[30] This isn't to say that Cap didn't also see negative consequences from registration; he often cited the danger to heroes and their loved ones if their identities are leaked. But he tied this to the issue of autonomy: while some heroes have public identities, such as the members of the Fantastic Four, that openness was their choice, not the result of a failure of database security (or government corruption). Cap felt that heroes should have the choice to keep their identities secret to protect their loved ones, and that registration endangered this choice.

More personally, Captain America doubted Tony's ability to consider the countless factors in the situation as well as he thought he could. Cap cited Tony's previous failures of judgment, telling him that "You've always thought you knew best by virtue of your genius. And once you decide, that's it."[31] What Cap may have been implying is that a brilliant mind can process a great deal of information, but moral decision-making takes more than data—especially if it must account for issues of right and wrong, as deontology requires. And even a genius cannot possibly take *every* contingency into account, much less assess the likelihood of each one. As we know, utilitarian decision-making depends critically on these estimations, and one forgotten possibility can turn the "best" decision into one of the worst, as Cap pointed out by recounting some of Tony's past disasters. At the worst, the judgment calls that any utilitarian must make can be warped, even unconsciously, by a person's desires, such as when Cap accused Tony of making decisions in his own interests rather than the greater good.[32] This twisting of moral decision-making is possible within any system of ethics, but the data-driven nature of utilitarianism makes it especially susceptible to manipulation while retaining the appearance of objectivity ("it's just math").

But in the end, even Captain America acknowledged the limits of standing firm on principle. During the epic final battle between the pro- and anti-registration forces, Cap was about to deliver the final blow to Iron Man when several civilians pulled him off. Cap begged them, "Let me go! Please, I don't want to hurt you," but they pointed to the destruction the heroes had left in their wake and asked him, "Don't want to hurt us? Are you trying to be funny?" Cap looked around him, surveyed the damage to buildings and people, and finally realized the cost of fighting for his principles. He asked his supporters to stop and surrender, saying, "We're not fighting for the people anymore … we're just fighting." When Spider-Man told him, "we were winning," Cap replied, "everything except the argument."[33] In the end, Captain America realized that he wasn't bearing the cost of his principles— they were borne by the very people he had sworn to protect.

Cap didn't give up on his principles, however; rather, he decided that the costs of defending them had become too high in this situation. As he said to Tony after his arrest following his surrender,

> We maintained the principles we swore to defend and protect. You sold your principles. ... Do you actually think the fact that you know how to program a computer makes you more of a human being than me? That I'm out of touch because I don't know what you know? I know what freedom is. I know what it feels like to fight for it and I know what it costs to have it. You know compromise.[34]

When it comes down to it, utilitarians and deontologists both acknowledge the necessity of compromise. The difference is that utilitarians accept it as a component of their decision-making, while deontologists see it as a last resort. (We'll talk a lot more about compromise and judgment in later chapters.)

Virtue Ethics

While many ethical debates (such as those during the Civil War) can be framed in terms of principles versus consequences, we see a much different approach altogether in the third major moral theory—or, historically speaking, the first major moral theory. Instead of focusing on an act itself and asking "is this act right" or "is it the best thing to do," *virtue ethics* turns our attention to the person who performs the act and asks "is this something a virtuous or good person would do?" Virtue ethics looks at a person's *character*, which is understood in terms of his or her traits, dispositions, and behavior, and asks whether he or she is ethical, rather than looking at the person's actions alone. While virtue ethics often comes to the same con-clusions about moral questions that utilitarianism and deontology do, it comes to them by a different path, and that difference gives virtue ethics a distinct flavor compared to the other two moral theories.

Virtue ethics dates back to the ancient Greeks and Romans, and is most often associated with the philosopher Aristotle.[35] We saw that utilitarianism is very easy to define and deontology less clear-cut, but virtue ethics is the most difficult to nail down because it comes in many varieties. However, there are some common themes among them. As with the other moral theories, virtue ethicists are concerned with how people should conduct themselves both for their own benefit as well as the benefit of others. A central theme in virtue ethics is "the good life," although every virtue ethicist has his or her own idea of what this means (as we saw with "the good" in utilitarianism and "the right" in deontology).

For instance, Aristotle used the term *eudaimonia* for his version of the good life. *Eudaimonia* has no precise English translation: it's often sloppily translated as "happiness," but is more properly regarded as "fulfillment" or "flourishing." It doesn't refer to the pleasure of eating a great piece of cake, or even watching your kid score her first basket or goal. Although the feelings of joy in these cases might be significant, even profound, Aristotle was talking about more of a lifelong project: the pursuit of a good life, in which you experience not only great joy but also deep fulfillment, particularly by practicing virtue. Contemporary virtue ethicist Rosalind Hursthouse describes *eudaimonia* as "the sort of happiness worth having," implying a higher standard than merely simple pleasure.[36] Other early virtue theorists, such as the Stoics, had similar ideas; according to philosopher A.A. Long, the Stoics believed that "philosophy should provide its adepts with the foundation for the best possible human life—that is to say, a happiness that would be lasting and serene."[37] This view of a deeper and more complete happiness was shared also by our favorite deontologist Immanuel Kant, who wrote that virtue makes a person worthy of happiness, and the combination of the two represents the "highest good."[38] John Stuart Mill also agreed: in his version of utilitarianism, Mill distinguished between higher and lower pleasures, regarding higher pleasures of greater intrinsic value to a person's life even if they are less satisfied than lower ones. As he famously wrote, "it is better to be a human being dissatisfied than a pig satisfied; better to be Socrates dissatisfied than a fool satisfied."[39]

Another way that Aristotle described virtue and its role in *eudaimonia* was as trying to achieve excellence. "Be the best 'you' that you can be" is how we would put this today: whatever goals you set for yourself, whatever makes up your version of the good life, you should try to be excellent at them. If you want to be a scientist, or a writer, or a super-soldier, do whatever is necessary to be excellent at it. (If you want to be a villain, that's a different story!) But more broadly, we should all try to be excellent *persons*, and that's where we see the importance of general virtues such as honesty, integrity, and courage. Virtue ethicists claim that practicing virtues will make us excellent human beings, promoting our fulfillment and flourishing, and will lead to a good life, not just for ourselves but for our communities.

A virtue is normally understood to be a character trait or disposition that is the middle point between two extremes, or what Aristotle called "the golden mean." Take courage, for instance: while a person should not be cowardly, she shouldn't be foolhardy either. By the same token, while a person should never be dishonest or deceptive, neither should he be always forthcoming or indiscreet; proper honesty lies somewhere in the middle. But where? A virtuous person finds the golden mean by using her practical wisdom (*phronēsis*) or judgment to determine how courageous or honest to be in any particular circumstances. Certainly, courage means a different thing for a firefighter than it does for a business executive or a schoolteacher. They each have opportunities to be brave in their jobs, but in very different ways: the firefighter needs to be brave in the face of physical danger while the others may more often need moral bravery (which is much more useful for most of us in the modern world). But it's important to note that while the golden mean applies to the definition of a virtue, it doesn't apply to its execution. Once a person determines how honest or courageous he or she should be, that person should practice that virtue as much as possible. Put it this way: while each virtue is a golden mean, there is no middle ground when it comes to being virtuous![40]

To recap, virtue ethicists consider that good acts are those performed by good people (rather than the other way around), so the emphasis is on virtuous character traits instead of the actions that result from them. But simply saying that someone (like Captain America—remember him?) possesses virtues like honesty and courage doesn't tell us what that person is going to do in any particular situation. Even if a person is generally honest or brave, there can be many factors in a given circumstance that will affect how a person reacts to it. The virtuous person has to sort through these factors, using his or her practical wisdom or judgment to come to an ethical choice that expresses his or her character. On occasion, an honest person may lie and a brave person may flee danger—but if they are truly honest or brave, we can assume there were important considerations that steered their judgment elsewhere. (We will discuss judgment and compromise a lot throughout this book.)

To be sure, utilitarianism and deontology are nuanced and complex as well, requiring judgment in their own ways, such as anticipating contingencies and balancing duties or rights. Nonetheless, they are too often understood as issuing simply rules as such "do not lie." Such rules are useful as guidelines and frameworks for moral decisions: for example, if a person is faced with a situation involving lying, he'll probably start with the assumption that lying is wrong and then ask himself if there are any circumstances in this case which may outweigh that rule. But the rule is never the final word, and this is often lost in discussions of deontology and utilitarianism, both of which focus on determining the right or best action to take in any situation—a focus that would seem to lend itself to following rules. Virtue ethics puts the complexity of moral decision-making and the need for judgment front and center by taking the focus away from action and turning it to people and how they make decisions, rather than the decisions they make.[41]

As we've seen, philosophers describe virtues themselves—as well as their opposite, *vices*—as character traits or dispositions that a person possesses.[42] We say that John is kind or that Joan is reliable; Peter is mean or Patty is dishonest. What virtue ethicists mean when they say these things is that, for instance, one of John's character traits is kindness, which means that he is disposed to be kind in situations in which it's appropriate. Virtuous character traits should be cultivated, preferably at an early age, so that they become an integral part of who we are. Furthermore, they must never be engaged in for other purposes, such as self-interest. We wouldn't think John is truly kind if he acts that way just to impress people and get praise, and most of us can sense when a person's virtuous behavior is insincere. That's why a virtue must be ingrained in us, a part of who we are, rather than simply a role we play or a mask we wear when it serves our interests.

Furthermore, while virtues, once learned and truly embodied, are intrinsic parts of a person's character, they are meaningless if they don't reveal themselves in action. We wouldn't think of John as kind if he never lifted a hand to help anyone, would we? How would we know he was kind in the first place? This doesn't mean that a virtuous person has to be kind, honest, or courageous every chance he or she gets, but that the person exhibits these character traits in most of the cases that call for them, and when judgment given the circumstances dictates it. If John fails to help someone in a particular instance, we can't conclude that he isn't kind after all; there may be other circumstances or considerations that prevented him from being kind in that case, or maybe he simply forgot and didn't notice.

If none of us is born with a full set of virtues implanted in our heads, how are they learned and ingrained? Many virtue ethicists, especially Aristotle, emphasize the importance of role models or *moral exemplars*, people who demonstrate good behavior for others to emulate. If a kid looks up to a political figure, athlete, or celebrity and asks himself or herself, "what would my role model do in this situation I'm in," that kid is using his or her hero as a role model. In the comics, Bucky Barnes—Captain America's sidekick during World War II—often thought about what Steve Rogers would do, especially after Bucky found himself filling Steve's shoes after his death following the Civil War. When facing a mob scene, Bucky thought to himself,

> How am I supposed to help these people? ... How can one man hold back this much chaos? Steve would find a way. I know that. And he wouldn't stop to question it. He'd just do it. Somehow. Whatever it took. He'd do the impossible. Which is what I have to do now.[43]

Of course, moral exemplars can't be just anybody—ideally they would exemplify many if not most of the virtues that we value.[44] And no one moral exemplar has to cover all the virtues: someone can have one role model in her work life, exemplifying professional virtues like hard work and dedication, and another role model in her personal life, stressing values such as loyalty and kindness. These moral exemplars may even be fictional characters, like Captain America is to us—we'll talk about issues pertaining to this in the next chapter.

Finally, a point on which many virtue ethicists disagree is whether having one virtue implies having others—or even all of them! The *unity of the virtues* refers to the position that, while we refer to distinct virtues like courage and honesty because they reveal themselves in different kinds of behavior, they are merely different facets of a good person who embodies *all* of the virtues.[45] In the Marvel Universe, Captain America is the paragon of general virtue, but in this respect he stands almost alone; most Marvel characters, by design, have at least one serious character flaw. For instance, Tony Stark (Iron Man) is an arrogant womanizer susceptible to addiction, and Henry Pym (Ant-Man, Giant Man, and many more identities) lacks self-confidence and has violent tendencies. Peter Parker is almost like a Steve Rogers in training, generally regarded as possessing all the virtues but still learning how to balance them in making moral decisions. Captain America is an example of mature virtue, a role model for the rest of the Marvel heroes—but not without imperfections, as we'll see as we discuss his virtues in later chapters.

Virtuous Deontology ... No, Deontological
Virtue ... Maybe "Deontovirtue"?

When virtue ethics was "revived" in the mid-twentieth century, many philosophers hailed its benefits compared to deontology and utilitarianism, citing those two schools' rule-oriented focus that missed the boat as far as personal character and broader context were concerned.[46] Recently, however, there has been an explosion—well, a very mild explosion, but this *is* academic philosophy, remember—of work by scholars pointing out the similarities between Kantian deontology and virtue ethics, especially the writing of the Stoics (who were a strong influence on Kant).[47] Commitment and dutifulness are obvious candidates for virtues, after all, as are the essence of most of Kant's duties, such as honesty and courage. This is most obvious with those duties that Kant called *imperfect* or *wide*, duties that don't specify particular actions or inactions but rather require attitudes that must be held at all times and expressed when possible, such as beneficence or kindness. The flexible nature of imperfect duties has obvious similarities to virtues— and even perfect duties such as "do not lie" can easily be translated into virtues such as honesty (although the Kantian version emphasizes the negative "thou shall not" rather than the positive "thou shalt").

Kant also shared with the virtue ethicists a concern regarding character and motivation, emphasizing that to be a good person you had to "follow duty for the sake of duty," not simply as a means to some other end. The virtue ethicists' focus on character is also reflected in Kant's emphasis on the "good will," which he regarded as the only thing in the world that could be purely moral and would reliably lead to good behavior.[48] Sounds a lot like virtue ethics, right? In practice, it would be very difficult to tell a virtuous person from a Kantian. We would have ask people why they behave morally: if they said things like "to be a good person" or "because it's what my mother would do," they probably lean to the side of the virtue ethicists, but if they replied "to do my duty," or "because it was the right thing to do," that's a good sign they think more like Kant. But for our purposes, duty and virtue seem very compatible, as we will see when describing Captain America's ethics later in this book.

Another aspect that virtue ethics and Kant's deontology have in common is their emphasis on practical wisdom or judgment. As we saw before, judgment refers to the ability to make hard moral choices when the standard ethical rules, such as "do not lie" and "be helpful," do not provide a clear answer. Judgment cannot be captured by rules or formulas—rather, judgment is what you use when rules and formulas don't tell you clearly what to do. Judgment is integral to virtue ethics, of course, because virtue ethics provides no rules at all. Certainly you should be honest, brave, and generous when the situation calls for it, but that determination requires judgment, especially when deciding where the golden mean falls in any particular circumstance. Likewise, deontology provides a number of rules, principles, or duties that help you decide what you should *not* do, but they are little help in deciding what you *should* do. This is especially true with Kantian duties, whether negative (such as "do not lie") or positive (such as "help others"), because neither type tells us exactly what to do, but only what not to do (the duty to help others can be understood as "don't stand by while others suffer").

The essential role of judgment is even more clear when obligations conflict; for instance, you may feel a tension between loyalty and honesty if your brother asks you to lie for him to his partner or boss. One famous case of conflicting obligations is Kant's "murderer-at-the-door" example described above: you have obligations not to lie and also to help your friend, but you cannot fulfill both. Since there is no higher-level rule or duty to tell you which obligation is more important, you need to use judgment to arrive at a choice. What's more, not everyone's judgment will result in the same answer in any given circumstance, even if they feel the same obligations, because they may attach different weights to them. In such cases, people need to arrive at the judgment that they feel comfortable with, the one that expresses their moral character or who they want to be.

Even utilitarianism requires judgment, but in a different way. Once all the effects on individual utilities are added up, the best decision is a simple matter of math: the action with the greatest positive effect (or smallest negative one) is the best action. But as Cap explained to Iron Man—albeit in different terms—the difficulty of measuring and calculating all the utilities and probabilities makes utilitarian decision-making nearly impossible to carry out perfectly in complex situations. Therefore, the utilitarian has to compromise upfront and decide *which* effects on *which* people in *which* possible states of the world to focus on. Naturally, he or she will consider the largest and most likely effects, since they will have the most significant effect on the final outcome. Once these decisions are made, the utilities are summed as usual, but the end result is ultimately based on judgment because the utilities themselves were based on judgment (much like adding or multiplying with rounded numbers introduces error into calculations from the get-go). Utilitarianism can appear more "scientific" and impartial if we focus on the final step of adding and maximizing, but this ignores the judgment involved in getting the raw utilities in the first place. In the end, judgment proves to be essential to moral decision-making in every school of ethics.

While all three of the ethical theories introduced in this chapter provide valuable insights, throughout the rest of this book I will describe Captain America using primarily the language and concepts of virtue ethics. My point is to show how Captain America's "old-fashioned" ethics are still of value in the twenty-first century—not in terms of rules, formulas, or moral theorizing, but rather basic moral ideals like honesty and kindness, as well as more general qualities such as determination and sound judgment. Nonetheless, I will be drawing from Kantian deontology from time to time, especially when Cap's virtuous behavior adheres to concepts such as duty, principle, and doing what's right. For Cap, however, duty is not an end in itself, but rather a way to express his virtuous character. Even when he talks specifically about performing his duty and doing the right thing, those can interpreted as exercising his character traits of dutifulness and personal justice. But this is just one way to frame it, and I won't be arguing here that this is the only way or the best way to describe Cap's ethics and behavior—it's merely the most straightforward way to make my point.

In the next chapter, we'll talk about the issues with using a fictional character such as Captain America as a role model or moral exemplar. Is the fact that he's not real a problem in itself? If not, might he be "too good" to be a realistic role model for people in the real world? And to what extent can we say that a superhero such as Captain America has "a" character at all when he's been written by many people in many ways over many years? You might be shocked to hear that none of these questions concern me. In fact, I'll argue that several of these "problems" are more relevant to using real people as role models than using fictional ones. Take that, real people! (Not you, of course—you're wonderful.)

Notes

1 *Captain America*, vol. 1, #401 (1992) and *Avengers Academy* #10 (2011), respectively.
2 See Jeremy Bentham, *The Principles of Morals and Legislation* (Buffalo, NY: Prometheus Books, 1781/1988), and John Stuart Mill, *Utilitarianism* (Buffalo,

NY: Prometheus Books, 1863/1987), both widely available as e-texts online as well. For an excellent discussion of the pros and cons of utilitarianism, see J.J.C. Smart and Bernard Williams, *Utilitarianism: For and Against* (Cambridge: Cambridge University Press, 1973).

3   Bentham, *Principles*, p. 3.

4   For more on the varieties of consequentialism, see Walter Sinnott-Armstrong's "Consequentialism" in the *Stanford Encyclopedia of Philosophy* (http://plato. stanford.edu/entries/consequentialism/).

5   John Stuart Mill's 1869 essay "The Subjection of Women" is widely believed to have been co-written with Harriet Taylor Mill; in any case, she was extremely influential on his thinking on this issue, as well as others.

6   In the theory of decision-making, this is known as *satisficing* (as opposed to optimizing), which is considered to be a more realistic model of choice. See Herbert Simon, "Rational Choice and the Structure of the Environment," collected in his book *Models of Thought* (New Haven, CT: Yale University Press, 1979), chapter 2.

7   This was first suggested by Robert Nozick in his classic *Anarchy, State, and Utopia* (New York, NY: Basic Books, 1974), p. 41.

8   *Captain America*, vol. 1, #325 (1987); this incident is discussed more in chapter 5.

9   For instance, see Adam J. Kolber, "The Subjective Experience of Punishment," *Columbia Law Review* 109 (2009): 182–236.

10   You might be asking, "why do we care how common-sense morality compares to what philosophers in all their wisdom say about it?" Philosophers do this more than you might think, actually; any system of ethics that permits murder, rape, or theft would fall under intense scrutiny solely because those actions are thought to be undeniably immoral. Nonetheless, you would have a good point: in principle philosophers shouldn't test their theories against common intuition. But for practical purposes, if philosophers want to influence how people make moral decisions, they can't stray too far from people's basic moral intuitions.

11   *Captain America*, vol. 1, #401 (1992). Also, after Iron Man used the villain Mentallo's technology to erase all knowledge of his secret identity from people's minds, Cap told him that "your ends didn't justify your means as neatly as you say" (*Iron Man/Captain America Annual 1998*). (We'll discuss this story more in the final chapter of this book.)

12   *Avengers vs. X-Men* #12 (2012).

13   For example, in 1930 the deontological philosopher W.D. Ross wrote a book titled *The Right and the Good* (Oxford: Oxford University Press, 2003 edition), setting deontology (focusing on the "right") against consequentialism (focusing on the "good") in a battle that certainly rivals *Avengers vs. X-Men* for sheer excitement.

14 Kant's ethical theory is contained mostly in three books: *Grounding for the Metaphysics of Morals* (1785), *Critique of Practical Reason* (1788), and *The Metaphysics of Morals* (1797), all available in different editions and translations from several publishers. A fantastic and concise introduction to his ethics is Roger J. Sullivan's *An Introduction to Kant's Ethics* (Cambridge: Cambridge University Press, 1994).

15 Kant, *Grounding for the Metaphysics of Morals*, trans. James W. Ellington (Indianapolis, IN: Hackett), p. 421. This page number reflects the standard pagination for Kant's work, based on the "official" edition of his collected works, and is included in all reputable editions of his work.

16 Ibid., p. 429.

17 Ross, *The Right and the Good*.

18 Ronald Dworkin, *Taking Rights Seriously* (Cambridge, MA: Harvard University Press, 1977)—remember that name, because we'll hear it many times throughout this book.

19 Kant, "On a Supposed Right to Lie Because of Philanthropic Concerns," included as a supplement to the Hackett edition of *Grounding for the Metaphysics of Morals*, and originally published in 1799.

20 Many Kant scholars regard this position as absurd, and have felled many a tree in attempts to reconcile it with his broader ethics. I prefer to see it as a simple mistake and maintain that his broader writings about judgment clearly recommend lying to the murderer.

21 This is the point of *threshold deontology*, which recommends sticking to your principles unless the cost reaches a certain level (or "threshold"), after which consequentialist considerations take over; we'll revisit this idea in chapter 5.

22 The main story was told in the 2007 trade paperback *Civil War* (collecting *Civil War* #1–7, 2006–2007), written by Mark Millar and illustrated by Steve McNiven and Dexter Vines (with several other inkers). Important aspects of the story were told also in issues of *Captain America*, *Iron Man*, *Amazing Spider-Man*, and *Fantastic Four*, among others (all collected in trade paperbacks).

23 For more on Tony's motivation regarding the SHRA and the Civil War, see my chapter "Did Iron Man Kill Captain America?" in *Iron Man and Philosophy: Facing the Stark Reality*, ed. Mark D. White (Hoboken, NJ: John Wiley & Sons, 2010), pp. 64–79.

24 *Iron Man*, vol. 4, #12 (2006).

25 *Iron Man/Captain America: Casualties of War* (2007), a sequel to their discussion in *Captain America*, vol. 1, #401 (1992), cited above.

26 *New Avengers: Illuminati* (2006).

27 *Iron Man/Captain America: Casualties of War* (2007).

28 *Civil War: The Confession* (2007).

29 Sound familiar? In many ways, the Civil War storyline was a less-than-subtle allegory for the war on terror following the disaster of September 11, 2001, including the controversy over Guantanamo Bay, with a touch of the gun control debate in the form of superhero registration.

30 *Captain America*, vol. 5, #22 (2006).

31 *Iron Man/Captain America: Casualties of War* (2007).

32 Once, Iron Man defeated a foe by stopping his heart before reviving him. Captain America took him to task for this, arguing, "You could have handled the situation without stopping the man's heart! I can think of at least four ways—" Tony interrupted, saying "—and I can think of seven. But this one was the most expedient," to which Cap responded, "Expedient, Tony? Or interesting?" (*Iron Man*, vol. 4, #7, 2006).

33 *Civil War* #7 (2007). For Spidey's ethical journey during the Civil War, see my chapter "'My Name Is Peter Parker': Unmasking the Right and the Good," in *Spider-Man and Philosophy: The Web of Inquiry*, ed. Jonathan J. Sanford (Hoboken, NJ: John Wiley & Sons, 2012), pp. 37–52.

34 *Civil War: The Confession* (2007).

35 Aristotle's most important ethical work is his *Nicomachean Ethics*, dating from 350 BCE and available in many editions and translations; the translation by W.D. Ross is available at the Internet Classics Archive (http://classics.mit.edu/Aristotle/nicomachaen.html). On virtue ethics in general, see Rosalind Hursthouse's entry in the *Stanford Encyclopedia of Philosophy* (http://plato.stanford.edu/entries/ethics-virtue/) or her book *On Virtue Ethics* (Oxford: Oxford University Press, 1999).

36 Hursthouse, *On Virtue Ethics*, p. 10. For more on the central role on happiness in virtue ethics, see Julia Annas, *The Morality of Happiness* (Oxford: Oxford University Press, 1995).

37 A.A. Long, *Epictetus: A Stoic and Socratic Guide to Life* (Oxford: Oxford University Press, 2002), p. 18. As you can see from Long's title, the Stoics were particularly interested in giving the people of their age practical guidance for living. One of the most popular collections of Cicero's writing, for instance, is titled *On the Good Life* (London: Penguin, 1971), and a contemporary introduction to Stoicism by William B. Irvine is titled *A Guide to the Good Life: The Ancient Art of Stoic Joy* (Oxford: Oxford University Press, 2009).

38 See his *Critique of Practical Reason* (Upper Saddle River, NJ: Prentice Hall, 1788/1993), pp. 108–110. For the strange role this concept plays in Kant's ethics, see Stephen Engstrom, "The Concept of the Highest Good in Kant's Moral Theory," *Philosophy and Phenomenological Research* 52 (1992): 747–780.

39 Mill, *Utilitarianism*, p. 20.

40 For an in-depth look at Aristotle's doctrine of the mean, see Rosalind Hursthouse, "The Central Doctrine of the Mean," in Richard Kraut, ed., *The Blackwell Guide to Aristotle's Nicomachean Ethics* (Malden, MA: Blackwell, 2006), pp. 96–115.

41 Interestingly, some prominent Stoics such as Cicero and Seneca wrote favorably of rules and principles, which was as controversial with their fellow philosophers then as it is today; see Stephen M. Gardner, "Virtuous Moral Rules," in Stephen M. Gardner (ed.), *Virtue Ethics Old and New* (Ithaca, NY: Cornell University Press, 2005), pp. 30–59.

42 We'll see in the next chapter that psychologists have raised important concerns about the existence and stability of character traits.

43 *Captain America*, vol. 5, #35 (2008).

44 And reasonable people can disagree about who makes a good role model—such as the English mum who told her son that Cap was too violent and American to be a good role model for him (*Avengers*, vol. 3, #77, 2004)!

45 For more on this concept, usually associated with Plato, see John M. Cooper, "The Unity of Virtue," in Ellen Frankel Paul, Fred D. Miller, Jr., and Jeffrey Paul (eds.), *Virtue and Vice* (Cambridge: Cambridge University Press, 1998), pp. 233–274.

46 This revival of virtue ethics is usually dated to philosopher G.E.M. Anscombe's 1958 paper "Modern Moral Philosophy" (*Philosophy* 33: 1–19). Michael Stocker's 1976 article "The Schizophrenia of Modern Ethical Theories" (*Journal of Philosophy* 73: 453–466), and Alasdair MacIntyre's 1981 book *After Virtue* (Notre Dame, IN: University of Notre Dame Press) are also central to modern virtue ethics and its contrast with utilitarianism and deontology, especially concerning the issue of motivation.

47 See, for instance, Stephen Engstrom and Jennifer Whiting (eds.), *Aristotle, Kant, and the Stoics: Rethinking Happiness and Duty* (Cambridge: Cambridge University Press, 1996); Nancy Sherman, *Making a Necessity of Virtue: Aristotle and Kant on Virtue* (Cambridge: Cambridge University Press, 1997); Monika Betzler (ed.), *Kant's Ethics of Virtue* (Berlin: Walter de Gruyter, 2008); Anne Margaret Baxley, *Kant's Theory of Virtue: The Value of Autocracy* (Cambridge: Cambridge University Press, 2010); and Lawrence Jost and Julian Wuerth (eds.), *Perfecting Virtue: New Essays on Kantian Ethics and Virtue Ethics* (Cambridge: Cambridge University Press, 2011). (There will be a quiz on Friday.)

48 In fact, the first sentence of Kant's *Grounding for the Metaphysics of Morals* reads: "There is no possibility of thinking of anything at all in the world, or even out of it, which can be regarded as good without qualification, except a *good will*" (p. 393).

2

Captain America as a Moral Exemplar

In the Marvel Universe, Captain America is widely held to be a role model, not just for his fellow heroes but for regular people as well: as Cap thought to himself once, when pondering his various roles and responsibilities, "being Captain America is about setting an example."[1] This is often worded more specifically in terms of being a symbol of America and its founding principles. For example, in one retelling of his origin, Cap said he had become "the embodiment of my nation ... its living symbol," and the narration in another issue described "his mission to give America an enduring symbol of its highest virtues: freedom, justice, dignity, and opportunity for all."[2] Cap has embraced this role and the responsibility that comes with it, saying once that "for years I've strived to be a symbol of triumph over adversity ... it makes it that much more important to remain steadfast to my ideals and keep doing the right thing, no matter how tough it becomes!"[3] This responsibility also leads him to refuse to do things that would compromise his role as a moral exemplar, such as when he declines an invitation to spy for SHIELD: "Despite how I aided them in the past, I feel it's inappropriate for America's most visible symbol to do covert operations for the world's biggest spy agency."[4] We'll talk more about Captain America's responsibility, determination, and adherence to ideals later in this book, but first I want to talk about some of the finer points concerning Captain America and his eligibility to serve as a moral exemplar.

In this book, I'm not claiming merely that Cap serves in this capacity in the Marvel Universe, but that he can also do the same for us in real world. But there are several ways in which these two cases are different, because

The Virtues of Captain America: Modern-Day Lessons on Character from a World War II Superhero, First Edition. Mark D. White.
© 2014 John Wiley & Sons, Inc. Published 2014 by John Wiley & Sons, Inc.

while Cap may be "real" to his fellow characters in the comics, movies, and animated series, he's a fictional character to us. This raises interesting issues—not only with Captain America, but with fictional characters in general, whether they be Buffy Summers, Sherlock Holmes, or the heroes of ancient mythology.

There are three issues I want to explore in this chapter:

1) *Fictional characters are simply not real.* At its most basic, it may seem odd to claim that Captain America can be a role model for people in the real world when he's not real himself.
2) *Fictional characters can be perfect and we can't.* Writers can easily make a fictional character like Captain America perfect rather than flawed. If they do, doesn't this make him even more unrealistic and inappropriate as a role model?
3) *Fictional characters can be depicted inconsistently over the years by different writers.* Since Cap has been around since 1941—or 1964 in his "modern" form—and has been written by dozens of different writers in that time, is his characterization over the last fifty years consistent enough to use as an example of ethical behavior?

Let's tackle them one at a time, beginning with the one at the center of it all: the fact that Captain America is a fictional character.

Can a Fictional Character Be a Moral Exemplar?

Many of us—perhaps most of us—have had role models, even if only when we were younger. They might be relatives, such as parents, grandparents, aunts or uncles, or maybe even older brothers or sisters. They can also be members of your local community, such as teachers, church leaders, police officers, or firefighters. For others, they may be current national or international figures: activists, athletes, actors or actresses, musicians, or political figures. Of course, not all of our role models are living, and instead are drawn from history: presidents such as John F. Kennedy, Franklin Delano Roosevelt, Abraham Lincoln, and George Washington; inspirational people such as Nelson Mandela, the Reverend Martin Luther King, Jr., Mother Teresa, or Mahatma Gandhi; religious figures such as Jesus, Mohammed, or the Buddha; and athletes such as Michael Jordan, Martina Navratilova, or Jesse Owens.

Basically, a role model is anybody we admire and look up to. It may be for the simple reason that they have achieved something in their lives that we aspire to, such as becoming president, promoting social causes, or winning the World Series or Super Bowl. Many people have done such things, however, but few of them become idols to millions. What's different about the few who become true role models, the ones we would suggest to someone who needed some inspiration? Good role models provide not just inspiration to achieve our goals, but also an example of the right way to achieve them. For example, a world-class athlete who trained hard, sacrificed, and overcame obstacles can be a great role model, but one who relied on doping and cheating can't. In general, role models serve as examples of behavior as well as achievement, and what they model for us is *character*, making them moral exemplars as well. This is especially important not just for those young enough to be finding their way in the world, but also for those of us who think we know what we want to do and how we want to do it, but might need a little guidance from time to time. And the popularity of the question "What would so-and-so do?", whether the subject is Jesus or Superman, shows that many of us do crave moral exemplars and that we care about how they behave as much as what they accomplish.

With the exception of Superman, however, the people I mentioned above are real (whether living or dead); even those who don't believe in the divinity of religious figures like Jesus acknowledge that historical figures existed to inspire scripture. With historical and living people, we have evidence of their achievements and how they reached them, whether through movies, books, or stories passed down orally through time, and we say, "I want to be like her" or "he's the kind of person I want to be." We draw something from their lives that inspires us to emulate them, especially the character traits that helped them achieve their goals and affect the world in some positive way.

Fictional characters cannot directly change the world through their actions or behavior, of course, so they cannot inspire in exactly the same way as historical or living real-world figures. But they can still model positive character traits such as honesty, courage, and wisdom—which means more if the actions resulting from these virtues have consequences, even if only in their fictional worlds. For example, superheroes display courage—especially those like Captain America who have no fantastic superpowers—which results in defeating villains and saving lives, often at the expense of their own well-being. On the other side of the coin, when a hero fails to show courage, the villain escapes and people are hurt, both negative consequences that are just as instructive. The best comic-book writers, in my opinion, are the ones who make these connections most explicit, which is often the case in the stories of Captain America just as they were in classical mythology, which were told to children to teach them moral lessons (and to which modern superhero comics are often compared). Of course, many superheroes use fantastic powers or magic in the fight against evil, which we would have a hard time emulating! But at the heart of these stories we find heroism, bravery, and sacrifice, all virtues that we can adopt and practice. Rick Remender, the writer of *Captain America* from the title's relaunch in 2012, listed many of Cap's virtues in a personal column at the end of his first issue, ending with what Cap means to him: "Steve Rogers is a patriotic soldier, directed by a personal ethical compass, belief in the American dream and faith in his fellow man. He's clever, roughish, quick with a sly look and droll comment. He can punch out bad people and jump through glass. *He's the person you wish you were.*"[5]

Above I argued that fictional characters can model virtuous character traits by demonstrating their consequences in an imaginary world that readers identify with. This is a positive, assertive argument, but we can also argue defensively that real-world role models have their own imaginary elements, none of which detract from their value as moral exemplars. I mentioned religious figures like Jesus earlier: the faithful take their scriptural tales to be true, but even those skeptical of the religious aspects can still learn lessons from the stories passed on by the faithful. But consider secular historical figures like presidents, activists, and athletes: do we know *everything* about them? And is everything we think we know about them true? It's tragic when a beloved role model is revealed to have a flaw, such as when a superstar athlete is revealed to have used performance-enhancing drugs or when a president is revealed to have lied to the public. This may diminish their value as role models from that point on, but they still served that purpose before the revelations about their less-than-virtuous behavior disillusioned their early admirers. In fact, I would argue that they were better role models *because* their lives were somewhat idealized. In the real world, no one is perfect; sometimes we can learn from and be inspired by the way our role models overcame their flaws, but in other cases their flaws are fatal to their status as role models. We do tend to idealize our role models, however, and to make this easier we tend to close our eyes to their shortcomings, especially if these flaws interfere with the "narrative" we build around their lives. For better or worse, we often fictionalize actual people in order to make them better role models—and when we do this, they become more like fictional characters than we might realize![6]

Aren't Fictional Characters Liable to Be Perfect?

While real-world people can't be perfect (unless we ignore or deny their imperfections, of course), fictional characters can be: writers just have to write them that way! Ironically, while we tend to idealize our historical and current role models, fictional characters are sometimes criticized for not being "flawed enough" to provide guidance and inspiration to people dealing with real-world problems. In the world of comics, Superman and Captain America are often accused of being *too* good, *too* virtuous—simply put, perfect. They may be, as Remender said, "the person you wish you were," but do we have any hope of actually being like them if they're perfect?

But is this true—is Captain America really perfect? And even if he is, is that necessarily a bad thing? Let's consider the second point first. A perfect role model can serve as an example to emulate, but this can be frustrating because we can never hope to be perfect. Few of us will ever be Olympic athletes, presidents or prime ministers, or Nobel Prize winners—and even these achievements do not represent human perfection but "merely" the pinnacle in each field. Everybody who has achieved any of these goals is imperfect in other ways, and it is these imperfections that help make them relatable and therefore good role models. Creators of fiction know this very well: they have long recognized that perfect characters are usually boring and hard for readers to identify with, even if they never envisioned their creations as being potential role models. Any extraordinary skills, abilities, or achievements in one area of life are often offset by flaws or shortcomings in another.

The creators of superhero comics realize this, especially the people behind Marvel Comics in the 1960s such as Stan Lee, Jack Kirby, and Steve Ditko. One widely cited difference between the heroes of Marvel and their rival DC Comics is that Marvel's superheroes have flaws or failings whereas DC's heroes are perfect and ideal. Marvel's heroes are grounded in the real world, not only literally (most of them operate out of New York City rather than fictional cities such as Metropolis or Gotham City), but also figuratively, in terms of their moral characters.

Most important for our purposes, the early Marvel heroes had pro-
nounced character flaws that, along with individual catchphrases and
speech patterns, really set them apart from each other (as well as from the
heroes of their Distinguished Competition):

Spider-Man (Peter Parker):	youthful insecurity
Iron Man (Tony Stark):	conceit, addictive personality
Ant-Man (Henry Pym):	self-doubt, jealousy, anger issues, prone to mental breakdowns
Wasp (Janet van Dyne):	lovestruck and flighty
Thor (Donald Blake):	vain and arrogant
Hulk (Bruce Banner):	rage, rage, and more rage

Even the Fantastic Four, the flagship superhero group of Marvel Comics,
was made up of four distant individuals defined by their personality traits,
some of them negative:

Mr. Fantastic (Reed Richards):	unemotional and neglectful of his wife
Invisible Woman (Sue Storm Richards):	lacking in self-confidence and assertiveness
Human Torch (Johnny Storm):	rash and impetuous
The Thing (Benjamin Grimm):	self-loathing

The creators at Marvel Comics developed all of these characters tremendously over the years—especially the female ones, thankfully—making
them richer and deeper in terms of their overall personalities. However,
they wisely kept at least a hint of these central character flaws, both to
remind us who these heroes were at their core (a topic for later in this
chapter), as well as to keep them grounded in reality (especially when their
powers pulled them out of it!).

These flaws notwithstanding, all of the Marvel characters mentioned
above (and many more) are true heroes, exhibiting courage and self-
sacrifice to help others. For example, Spider-Man's dedication was motivated by his early irresponsibility and the resulting death of his beloved
Uncle Ben, and the Wasp gradually detached herself from her husband
Hank Pym and proved herself to be a natural leader of the Avengers. And
it's not that these heroes overcame their negative character traits completely—Tony Stark, for example, is still an arrogant playboy who struggles
with alcoholism—but that they learned to control and overcome them,

especially when it mattered most, which makes for powerful storytelling of all-too-human struggles with weakness.

In their own comics during the 1960s, longtime DC Comics heroes such as Superman, Batman, and Wonder Woman weren't written to have significant character flaws (or any distinct personalities whatsoever, for that matter). In later years, DC made many of their heroes more realistic: Batman became obsessively dedicated to his mission against crime, often at the expense of friends, colleagues, and romantic interests; Green Lantern went from being fearless to being able to overcome fear; and Green Arrow became a habitual adulterer and occasional murderer. As you can see, not all of the changes were positive, and some seemed motivated to introduce character flaws in emulation of Marvel's success. But one can argue that, for the most part, Superman and Wonder Woman remained idealized, and therefore remained the most difficult characters to make interesting enough to appeal to a large number of readers, while Batman became the most popular DC character once he was portrayed as almost pathologically obsessed with his mission against crime in Gotham City.

Just as Superman, the "big blue Boy Scout," is often considered boring next to the dark and complex Batman, Captain America is usually criticized as being "too good" for the Marvel Universe, exhibiting few of the negative character traits possessed by his fellow Marvel heroes. He is too noble, too brave, and too honest, often to the point of making other superheroes uncomfortable. As Iron Man told him during the Civil War, "You're the perfect man. You live by ideals and standards that are … more than outdated, they're impossible for anyone but you."[7] This can also alienate readers, of course, and if taken too far it may make him unattractive as a role model. He may be a moral exemplar in an ideal sense, but as an inspiration in the real world, he would fail—and if people can't bring themselves to look up to him, he is not serving as a moral exemplar, no matter how heroic his character may be.

One important point argues against this criticism, however: Captain America is human. He is not a god like Thor or an alien like Mar-Vell, has no superpowers like Spider-Man or the X-Men, and does not use extravagant gadgetry like Iron Man. Of course, he does have enhanced strength and speed due to the super-soldier serum and Vita-Rays to which he was exposed in the early 1940s, but, as Remender wrote, "he's not superhuman; he's just the pinnacle of our natural potential."[8] He does, of course, have his trusty shield, but this is a simple weapon more comparable to Hawkeye's bow and arrows than to Iron Man's technologically advanced armor. If Cap's character traits tend to make him seem perfect, his humanity brings him down to earth.

There is great irony in the fact that the most idealistic of Marvel heroes should be one of the most relatable in terms of his being simply human. After all, this is widely cited as one of the reasons Batman is so popular: even though he is fantastically wealthy and has trained himself to mental and physical perfection, at the end of the day he is "merely" human, and therefore his other achievements seem attainable (even if extremely unlikely!). He shares many other traits with Captain America as well, especially determination and preparation: for this reason it was appropriate that, when the cross-company meeting between the Avengers and the Justice League of America started off with a battle, Cap and Batman did not fight long before recognizing their equals in each other, and then worked together to lead their united teams to defeat their real foe.[9]

It is also often said that Captain America is a great hero not because of his enhanced strength and speed, but because of his character. In fact, it was this strength of character that led the Army to choose him for the super-soldier program, Project Rebirth, in the first place. We see this in the stories of the scrawny, pre-treatment Steve Rogers (as shown so well in the *Captain America* film as well as many retellings of his origin), who was turned away at every enlistment office he applied to—but was still brave, still strong of heart, and still principled. As Cap remembered later about his constant rejections and 4-Fs, "Not strong enough? In my heart, I had all the strength anyone would ever need."[10] In an anti-drug storyline, Cap worried about the role that the super-soldier serum played in his life, and he worked out his anxieties while he slept. In his dream he argued with Professor Erskine, the man who developed and administered the formula (but was killed before it could be replicated), that "the drug may have made me strong, but it did not make me brave! It may have made me agile, but it did not give me skills! It may have made me tough, but it did not give me my ideals! Those are all things I contributed! Those things make up Captain America, not your drug!"[11] We see it also in the many stories in which the effects of the 1940s treatment are reversed, and Steve returns to the feeble young man he once was.[12] Despite losing his strength, Cap remains just as heroic and courageous as ever, and the only thing that changes once he (inevitably) regains his full strength and speed is that he has better tools with which to put his character traits into action.

But in the end, this concern about Captain America's supposed perfection is misplaced. Despite his great heroic virtues, Cap has been written since his return in the 1960s with definite flaws, albeit milder ones than most of his fellow Marvel heroes. Some of these sound like the answers you give on a job interview in which you're asked for your greatest short-coming, things like "I work too hard" and "I take my job too seriously." In fact, Cap *is* too hard on himself, not willing to excuse his own mistakes and shortcomings, and instead holding himself to a superhuman level of perfection. This is seen most vividly in his anguish over the death of his sidekick James "Bucky" Barnes during World War II and his reluctance to put his fellow heroes in danger because of it. But he's too harsh on others as well—after one of Cap's and Iron Man's heart-to-heart talks, when Tony asked for forgiveness for his mistakes, saying "I'm not as perfect as you," Cap answered, "I'm not perfect either. I'm sometimes too quick to judge ... too slow to forgive."[13] Also, he often fails to think of the costs that other people endure in the process of heroism, costs that he takes for granted when he bears them himself. For example, during one Avengers battle he ordered the Scarlet Witch to use her hex magic to summon a dead Avenger, Wonder Man, to whom she was close, and she refused. When another Avenger, Firestar, noticed her distress afterwards, Cap told her, "I'll talk to her, Firestar. This is due to my mistake, not hers ... I should have realized the effect it could have on her."[14] As with Iron Man, Cap comes around eventually, but his rush to judgment threatens to compromise his leadership (which is considered second-to-none among the Marvel heroes).

Finally, like Batman, Captain America all too often ignores his own life, his very human wants and needs, in order to serve as America's sentinel of liberty. A persistent theme in the comics is his desire to live the American dream that he works so hard to protect for others: to have a chance to settle down with a woman he loves, have a "normal" job, and start a family. But he never seems to be able to, either because his sense of duty is too great or, because after so many years of being Captain America, he doesn't know who Steve Rogers is. As he thought after faking his death to restore his secret identity, "Can I truthfully say Steve Rogers was ever more than a name? Did he really have a life—a meaningful identity—to call his own? No! Ever since adulthood—I've lived under the all-pervasive shadow of Captain America!"[15] We'll discuss the conflict between Cap's duty and his private life later, but I mention it now as an example of a flaw that only committed workaholics would think to emulate.[16]

Even if Captain America were perfect, however, I still maintain (as before) that he has value as a moral exemplar and a role model. Perfection is unattainable in most things, but it gives you something to strive toward—as long as you remember that you will never reach it and you don't beat yourself up when you don't. As Bucky said after Cap's death following the Civil War, "he was like that sainted, can-do-no-wrong big brother. The guy you can't help but look up to ... because you just know you can never be that good ... that graceful under pressure ... or that strong in the face of horror."[17] Soon after saying those words, Bucky became the new Captain America for several years, and he never felt that he lived up his predecessor's example—but he also never stopped trying. And the original Cap never stopped trying either, never saying "I'm good enough" but instead saying things such as "I'm just a man ... can't live up to my ideals all the time" and "recently I realized that despite all the good things I've tried to do, I have fallen short of being the champion the American people deserve"—showing that even Captain America thinks he can improve on "perfection."[18]

In the end, maybe Cap *is* a little "too good." But isn't that what we want in a moral exemplar? We certainly don't want to aim down! We want to be like the best, and with all due respect to Wolverine, whose catchphrase is "I'm the best at what I do," Captain America *is* the best at being a hero, even if that ideal seems out of reach to most of us. But once again I stress his humanity and the fact that his virtues are not really so out of reach—we just have to practice them in more down-to-earth circumstances. As a kid once said about Cap, "he's not super, just a hero—we could do what he does," to which a nearby adult responded, "if we cared so much—and tried as hard."[19] And that's really the point—we *can* care that much and we *can* try that hard.

Fifty Years, Dozens of Writers ... One Captain America?

If we accept that a fictional character can serve as a moral exemplar, there still may be a problem. Starting from his "de-thawing" in 1964 (rather than his first appearance in 1941), Cap has appeared regularly in comics for fifty years, not only in his own comic book but regularly in the Avengers titles, major Marvel events (such as *Civil War*), and various miniseries, not to mention guest appearances in countless other Marvel comics. Even if we only look at his own title and *Avengers*, his two most regular ongoing titles, Cap has been written by dozens of different writers over the last five decades, each with his or her own approach to his character—the same singular "character" that I'm claiming can serve as a role model or moral exemplar.

But what reason do we have to believe that Captain America has been written consistently enough over the last five decades to count as one "person" with stable character traits and behaviors? As I did when I discussed fictional characters as moral exemplars above, I will use two arguments to support my view that Cap can be considered a singular character: by showing that fictional characters are more consistent than we think, even after being written by a number of people, and that real-world people are less consistent than we think, even if their "authors" remain the same throughout their lives. If I do my job well, you might consider the possibility that fictional characters written by dozens of writers over time can be *more* consistent in terms of character than real-world people are!

Let's take the second point first. While it's common to think of people in terms of character traits—John is honest, Karen is brave, Joe's a jerk—we know that no one fits his or her description all the time. (Well … maybe Joe.) John may be honest most of the time, but people who know him well enough can remember times he was less than honest or perhaps even outright dishonest. Are these simply lapses in an otherwise consistent character, or signs that his character isn't as consistent as his friends thought? This question applies to all of us, of course: given that none of us is perfectly consistent in all of our behaviors, does this mean that we're imperfectly consistent or that the idea of consistent character is just a myth?

According to psychologists and philosophers known as *situationists*, the idea of a consistent, unified character *is* a myth. In recent years, researchers have conducted numerous experiments showing significant changes in people's ethical behavior as a result of relatively insignificant changes in their environment. For example, one experiment studied people's helping behavior after checking a payphone for change. (If you don't know what a payphone is, just Google it on your smartphone. Oh, the irony.) Researchers found that people were more likely to help a stranger in need if they had found a coin in the payphone seconds earlier, compared to those who found the payphone empty. If individuals' degrees of kindness were as stable as virtue ethicists like to think, then willingness to help a stranger shouldn't be as closely related to something as trivial as finding a coin in a payphone. Based on research such as this, situationists claim that decisions and actions are more closely linked to particular details of the current situation than to persistent, stable character traits, which poses a problem for our traditional understanding of character—and, by extension, for the relevance of virtue ethics itself.[20]

But this is less damaging to virtue ethics and the concept of character than it might seem. We know from our discussions of virtues in the previous chapter that they aren't directly related to particular actions, because they must be filtered through judgment to accommodate the numerous other factors in a decision. If we think of John as generally honest but then observe him behaving dishonestly in a particular situation, there are many possible explanations other than doubting his honesty. For instance, there may have been other factors at play and John's judgment told him that honesty was not the most important virtue or duty in that particular situation. He may have even lapsed in his general honesty due to moral weakness, or was in fact influenced for some reason by a minor occurrence like finding a coin in a payphone—both of which do not necessarily make him dishonest but simply imperfect. When we describe a person with a particular character trait, we're not saying that that person exhibits that character trait in *every* situation without fail—just that their behavior reflects a certain virtue more often than the behavior of the average person does, or in extraordinary circumstances that would make the average person behave less virtuously.[21] This is not perfect consistency, of course, but virtue ethicists' understanding of character does not demand perfection; in fact, virtue ethics is well known for its accommodation of human imperfections.[22]

Furthermore, not only are people's actions in any one particular instance not a direct result of any one character trait, but, at the risk of stating the obvious … people change! Most of us change too gradually for us or those who see us frequently to notice, but when we see long-lost friends or relatives at class reunions or weddings, it's not uncommon to be told we're different (and not just physically). We may develop more or less tolerance, patience, generosity, or honesty. We may be more open-minded to new points of view or less forthcoming with our own. We may be more guarded to new experiences or more welcoming to them. Age and experience change us, which is natural and often for the better, but it does mean that in important ways we are different people than we were five, ten, or twenty years ago—our characters are hardly consistent over that time. Nonetheless, we continue to see real-world people as role models, although sometimes we may refer to a person at a certain age, saying "he's a great example of dedication now, but he sure wasn't when he was younger." And if a person changes too suddenly or abruptly, behaving much differently today compared to yesterday, it's not uncommon to tell that person, "I hardly recognize you" or "what did you do with the Susan I know?" We say things like this in jest, but there's a glimmer of truth behind them: to the extent people change behavior abruptly, they seem like different people to us, or reveal to us how little we actually knew them in the first place. To the extent that we define people by their character traits, there is a very real sense in which someone who exhibits an abrupt change of behavior is a different person.[23] This also holds for people we regard as role models: we may consider them very admirable and virtuous at certain times in their lives but not others. But we know that nobody's perfect, and we choose which aspects of a person to emulate, even if that person does not consistently embody those character traits over his or her entire life.

So far I've argued that real people's characters are not as consistent as we might think: their actions do not always reflect their traits clearly and consistently, and these character traits may change over time, either gradually or abruptly. So how do fictional characters compare? They have a clear advantage on the first front, especially if they are written by only one author (or a collaborative team of authors) with a deep understanding of the character and for an extended period of time. Depending on how they are written, fictional characters don't have to experience difficult choices or moral weakness, and they can stick to their principles come what may. One could argue that this would be a case of poor writing or unrealistic characterization—and that may be the author's intent, to show how unrealistic moral simplicity and perfection are—but this would make the character a poor candidate for a role model, especially if the consequences of difficult choices and moral weakness are not shown. Even in the best cases, however, fictional characters are necessarily written as much less complex than real people, if only because we see only a small slice on their lives, a glimpse of behavior and perhaps a snippet of internal monologue, compared to real-life people we know well. (And this is true even for soap opera characters that may appear on TV five days a week.) In this small time we "see" a character, the writer can focus on the character's most prominent qualities and show just the right amount of imperfection. While crafting and writing a compelling fictional character is incredibly difficult, a writer can easily make one behave consistently over time simply because there is so little behavior to account for. In other words, the possibility for consistency is much greater for fictional characters simply because we see so little of their lives and the writer is in complete control of the character's behavior, thoughts, and words.

Of course, Captain America appears regularly not only in his own title but also in one or more Avengers books; other heroes like Spider-Man and Wolverine often appear in several of their own books simultaneously, plus team books such as *Avengers* and *X-Men*. If several writers are crafting the stories of a character at the same time, there can be a problem with consistent characterization, although good editors usually keep track of this. Over time, however, this can become more of a problem as writers (and editors) change and the characters "drift" from one creator's interpretation to another.

Fictional characters can change just as naturally as real people do, of course. To the extent we in the real world change, however, we tend to change gradually over time, leaving most of our complex personalities the same. But unless the core attributes of a character are well-defined, new writers can change key aspects of a character too abruptly to make him or her recognizable over time, especially given the small glimpses of them we see at all. This is a potential problem with any type of serial fiction, including long-running TV shows, movie franchises, and book series, as well as comic books. Think of all the people who wrote episodes of *Law & Order* or *Days of Our Lives*, screenplays for James Bond movies, novels in the worlds of *Star Wars* or *Star Trek*, or any comic book featuring a beloved superhero, be it Spider-Man, Wonder Woman, or Captain America. All of these examples involve multiple writers over time interpreting characters in their own ways, but ideally keeping faithful to the key aspects that define the characters in their fans' minds. No writer should make Spider-Man cynical, Wonder Woman weak, or Captain America brutal, because that's not how these heroes have come to be known over the decades. This is not to say that characters can't grow, develop, and change, but like real people they should do so gradually and organically, in a way that makes sense given the story and their history. If Spider-Man does become cynical, there should be a reason grounded in the story, and it should be significant enough to overwhelm his well-established good nature. And if Captain America becomes a savage killing machine … well, the writer better have a *very* good reason for it!

Happily, one thing that Marvel Comics' superheroes are well known for are their well-defined character traits, as we saw before. This allows each successive writer on a series to write a character similarly enough to the way his or her predecessor did, while developing or changing the character within certain bounds. Ideally, a new writer on a character like Captain America will study and absorb what was written previously and then build on that, so any changes he or she does introduce seem gradual and seamless.[24] If a new writer changes Cap's status quo too drastically, making him brutally violent, impolite, or flip—all flying in the face of his reserved and respectful nature as established in decades of stories—then fans won't recognize the character and will wonder "what happened to Cap?" They'll suspect possession by an evil psychic villain, replacement by a shape-shifting alien race like the Skrulls, or some other extraordinary event, because "Cap just doesn't act like that." In other words, an explanation will be sought within the story to explain why a character who is so well-defined is suddenly behaving so differently—and fans wouldn't question the character's behavior in the first place if multiple writers hadn't portrayed him or her so consistently over the years.

This doesn't mean, however, that some writers don't make "mistakes" in characterization. Even though the dozens of writers responsible for Captain America's adventures in his own title and the Avengers books over the last fifty years have been amazingly consistent, there have been aspects of his depiction that some fans have taken issue with (originally in letters columns, now in online discussion forums and Twitter). And it's not just Cap, of course, but all long-running characters. Thor, the Asgardian god of thunder who normally speaks in faux Shakespearean language with lots of "verily" and "thou doth humor me," has been written occasionally saying things like "pain in the ass."[25] Daredevil, that tireless crusader for justice both in the courtroom and on the streets of Hell's Kitchen, has been shown standing by while other heroes tortured a person—a colleague, no less—for information.[26] Examples like this bring fans to outrage, accusing writers of misunderstanding the characters with whom they've been charged.

Readers have two choices in such cases: try to reconcile the odd behavior with the character as they understand him or her, or write it off as a mistake. But who's to decide when a certain "odd" characterization is a mistake or just a matter of interpretation? Matt Fraction, the writer who made Thor sound like a normal guy from Earth for the one line quoted above, defended his choice, arguing that the change in dialogue reflected the apocalyptic situation that the Marvel heroes found themselves in (an event called "Fear Itself") and, more fundamentally, that every writer voices Thor differently: "The characters grow. There are no 'thees' and 'thous' and 'verily' anymore. It's a growing, changing thing. In the heat of that particular moment, 'Thou art a pain in mine arse' would have read stupidly. ... The language grows. The characters change."[27] But many fans weren't convinced, regarding this language as being too far from Thor's normal speech.

So who's right? Does the writer have the final say, or does the character "belong" to the fans, who ultimately judge the writers with their comics dollars? In the end, it's each person's choice, writers and fans alike, to decide if a certain action or behavior "fits" in with their understanding of the character. Writers can and should defend their choices, but fans are free to disagree—and so can Cap himself! When Steve Rogers—an artist whose pencil is mightier than his shield—was hired by Marvel Comics to draw their *Captain America* comic, he told his editor that "the writer may have lost sight of Cap's basic character," later complaining to himself that "this new *Captain America* plot I'm supposed to illustrate really has me stuck. The guy who wrote it just doesn't seem to understand Cap's motivation at all. And I ought to know."[28]

Let's cast this issue in a different light—a very different light, courtesy of legal and political philosopher Ronald Dworkin, whom we met in chapter 1. Dworkin wrote that in "hard cases," those that aren't easily settled by written law and past judicial decisions (or precedents), judges' decisions should be made in much the same way that writers make their contributions to long-running fictional storylines and characters.[29] Judges need to assess all of the existing legal materials at their disposal and make a decision in the case at hand that is consistent with the totality of the legal system as they understand it. In other words, judges need to make decisions that maintain the *integrity* of the legal system, just as new writers on a TV or comic-book series have a responsibility to maintain the integrity of the key characters as they add their own contribution to their ongoing tales. (This holds for our own moral characters as well, as we'll see when we discuss personal integrity later in this book.)

Of course, each judge will have his or her idea of how the various constitutional clauses, statutes, and judicial precedents fit together, which explains how judges come to different decisions despite hearing the same facts and knowing the same laws. Similarly, every comic-book fan and writer will have his or her own idea of who Captain America (or any other superhero) is, and they don't always agree. Some see him primarily as a super-soldier and others as a superhero; some emphasize the persona of Captain America as a symbol of the American dream, while others focus more on Steve Rogers, the man behind the shield. But regardless of his or her individual interpretation, every writer charged with writing Cap's adventures should try to keep the core aspects of the character consistent with the work that preceded him or her in order to maintain a stable characterization that fans new and old can point to and say "that's Cap—and I want to be like him."[30]

We can also apply Dworkin's ideas about integrity in the law to mistakes in characterization. Each judge's unique personal interpretation of the legal system leads to a similarly unique theory of mistakes in the law, which allows him or her to have an opinion on when statutes or precedents should be followed and when they should be overturned. Each judge will see different aspects of the law as inconsistent with the rest—and sometimes they agree, as the Supreme Court did when they overturned *Plessy v. Ferguson* (the case that endorsed segregation) in *Brown v. Board of Education*. In the same way, each writer and each fan will have a personal conception of a character like Captain America that leads them to regard certain behaviors as mistakes, aberrations caused by writers who did not share their idea of the character. For example, Ed Brubaker, who began writing *Captain America* in 2005, felt that it was a mistake for earlier writers to say that Cap had never killed anyone in World War II, and he changed that facet of Cap's backstory when he started to write the character.[31]

Accordingly, on the rare occasion that I identify mistakes in the way Cap is written, I ask you, the reader, to understand that they are mistakes from my point of view only, not necessarily accepted as such by anybody else. You may disagree on things I identify as mistakes, and you may feel that things I identify as core aspects of Cap's character are better regarded as mistakes. As we'll see by the end of this book, disagreements are wonderful, as long as they acknowledge also what we agree on—such as the fact that Captain America is a character worth arguing about!

If you accept that a fictional character can serve as a role model or moral exemplar, then the next step is to explain why Captain America in particular deserves to be held in this high regard. In the next chapter, we'll discuss many of the personal virtues that Captain America embodies, including courage, humility, and perseverance, and explain why they're much more complex than people often think—but still valuable character traits to adopt.

Notes

1 *Captain America*, vol. 5, #616 (2011), "Spin."
2 *Captain America*, vol. 1, #215 (1977) and #312 (1985).
3 *Captain America*, vol. 1, #428 (1994).
4 *Captain America*, vol. 1, #324 (1986). We'll see in chapter 5 that Cap has sometimes had his colleagues do "dirty work" in order to keep his image unsullied for the purpose of serving as a symbol and role model.

5   *Captain America*, vol. 7, #1 (2013) (emphasis added).

6   For more on this topic—in the context of Batman rather than Captain
     America—see Ryan Indy Rhodes and David Kyle Johnson, "What Would
     Batman Do? Bruce Wayne as Moral Exemplar," in Mark D. White and Robert
     Arp (eds.), *Batman and Philosophy: The Dark Knight of the Soul* (Hoboken, NJ:
     John Wiley & Sons, 2008), pp. 101–113.

7   *Iron Man/Captain America: Casualties of War* (2007).

8   *Captain America*, vol. 7, #1 (2013). For a time in the mid-1970s, Cap's powers
     were increased so that he had true super-strength and speed, beginning in
     Captain America, vol. 1, #157 (1973) and revealed to have ended in *Captain
     America*, vol. 1, #218 (1978). This was short-lived and never repeated (wisely,
     in my opinion).

9   *JLA/Avengers* #2 (2003).

10   *Captain America: The Chosen* #4 (2007).

11   *Captain America*, vol. 1, #377 (1990).

12   For example, the anti-drug storyline in *Captain America*, vol. 1, #377 (1990);
     Captain America, vol. 3, #16 (1999); *Steve Rogers: Super-Soldier* #2 (2010); and
     the "Powerless" storyline beginning in *Captain America*, vol. 6, #6 (2012). In
     Captain America, vol. 1, #355 (1989), Cap asks his fellow Avenger Sersi to
     transform him into a teenager so he can infiltrate a cult, not realizing it would
     predate the Project Rebirth treatment ("good grief!").

13   *Captain America*, vol. 1, #401 (1992); see also *Iron Man/Captain America
     Annual 1998*, when Cap told Tony that while he disagreed with what Tony did,
     "I also think I tend to be a little judgmental at times … particularly when it
     comes to issues of independence and personal rights."

14   *Avengers*, vol. 3, #8 (1998).

15   *Captain America*, vol. 1, #114 (1969). Later, Cap was lost in thought, remem-
     bering looking in the mirror and thinking "when I saw the face of Steve
     Rogers staring back at me, younger than it had a right to be after all these
     years … it was always the face of … a stranger!" When the Falcon roused him
     from his "mumbling," Cap told his friend that he felt lost and then shouted
     "who is Steve Rogers?" (*Captain America*, vol. 1, #215, 1977). Finally, see the
     letter from future comics writer Kurt Busiek in the back of *Captain America*,
     vol. 1, #239 (1969), in response to the "who is Steve Rogers" question, in
     which he discussed not just Cap's but Steve Rogers' role as symbol of America
     as well.

16   Hey, why are you looking at me?

17   *Captain America*, vol. 5, #25 (2007).

18   *Captain America*, vol. 1, #295 (1984) and #312 (1985).

19   *Captain America*, vol. 4, #4 (2002).

20   For the most exhaustive treatment of situationism from one of its leading fig-
     ures, including details of experiments such as the payphone one, see John M.

Doris, *Lack of Character: Personality and Moral Behavior* (Cambridge: Cambridge University Press, 2002).

21 This connects back with my earlier point about real-life historical characters: even though George Washington is well known for his honesty, for example, we don't actually know that he was honest *all* of the time. Most likely he wasn't, but he may have been more honest than most people, or remained honest in situations that would tempt other people to lie, which then became exaggerated in the legends that surround him today. But even if we were to discover that George Washington did lie in some situations, that should not compromise his reputation as honest or his value as a moral exemplar.

22 For a very readable and critical perspective on the situationist argument, see Kwame Anthony Appiah, *Experiments in Ethics* (Cambridge, MA: Harvard University Press, 2008), particularly chapter 2. For a more detailed critique, focusing on the nature of virtues and character traits and the degree to which situationists' experiments address them, see Gopal Sreenivasan's papers "Errors about Errors: Virtue Theory and Trait Attribution," *Mind* 111 (2002): 47–68, and "Character and Consistency: Still More Errors," *Mind* 117 (2008): 603–612.

23 To take this argument even further, some philosophers maintain that there is no necessary consistency to a person over even short periods of time. Just as Heraclitus said that you can't step twice into the same river, you cannot meet literally the same person twice; the Steve Rogers on July 15 is a different person than the Steve Rogers on July 14, even if only for the fact that the former has had one day's more experiences. While there can be some measure of continuity across these "time-slices" of a person, the possibility of these being different persons raises important issues of moral responsibility. For example, is the July 15 Steve responsible for the actions of July 14 Steve? What if Steve suffers massive brain trauma or amnesia between the two days? For more on these issues, see David Shoemaker's "Personal Identity and Ethics" at the *Stanford Encyclopedia and Philosophy* (http://plato.stanford.edu/entries/identity-ethics/) and the references therein.

24 Sometimes a writer will draw on one predecessor in particular. For example, Ed Brubaker said that Jim Steranko's three classic issues (*Captain America*, vol. 1, #110, #111, and #113, 1969) inspired his approach to the book (*Marvel Spotlight*, vol. 3, #18, 2007, "The Man Who Killed Captain America"). Also, in his comments at the end of *Captain America*, vol. 7, #1 (2013), Rick Remender similarly credits Jack Kirby's run as both writer and penciller (*Captain America*, vol. 1, #193–214, 1976–1977) as influencing his own.

25 *Fear Itself* #5 (2011).

26 *New Avengers*, vol. 2, #22 (2012).

27 Albert Ching, "Facing Fear: Q&A with Fraction & Brevoort on *Fear Itself* #5," *Newsarama*, August 17, 2011 (www.newsarama.com/8205-facing-fear-q-a-with-fraction-brevoort-on-fear-itself-5.html).

28 *Captain America*, vol. 1, #314 and #315 (1986). As "meta" as this may seem, it still doesn't rise to the level of John Byrne's work on *The Sensational She-Hulk* (the first eight issues of which are collected in *The Sensational She-Hulk, Vol. 1*, 2011), in which he wrote and drew She-Hulk responding to the choices he made in depicting her—all in the same comic. (For more on this topic, see Roy T. Cook's essay "I Am Made of Ink: She-Hulk and Metacomics" in Mark D. White (ed.), *The Avengers and Philosophy: Earth's Mightiest Thinkers* (Hoboken, NJ: John Wiley & Sons, 2012), pp. 57–70.)

29 Ronald Dworkin, "How Law Is Like Literature," in his collection *A Matter of Principle* (Cambridge, MA: Harvard University Press, 1985), pp. 146–166. On his theory of judicial decision-making in general, see his books *Taking Rights Seriously* (Cambridge, MA: Harvard University Press, 1977) and *Law's Empire* (Cambridge, MA: Harvard University Press, 1986), or Stephen Guest's cunningly titled *Ronald Dworkin*, 3rd ed. (Stanford, CA: Stanford University Press, 2013).

30 For similar ideas applied to Spider-Man, see my chapter "The Sound and Fury Behind 'One More Day'" in *Spider-Man and Philosophy: The Web of Inquiry*, ed. Jonathan J. Sanford (Hoboken, NJ: John Wiley & Sons, 2012), pp. 231–242.

31 See the interviews with Brubaker in *Marvel Spotlight*, vol. 3, #9 (2006) and #18 (2007).

3

Five Basic Virtues

In this chapter, we'll start our investigation into what makes Captain America a great role model by describing some of his basic virtues, including ones we most often think of, such as courage, and others that might not spring to mind as quickly, such as humility. These are character traits we immediately associate with Captain America and other heroes—as well as people we know in real life whom we think of as virtuous. The fact that many of these virtues are "ordinary" is not a failing, because this emphasizes both that Captain America is not "too good" to serve as a role model and that each of us can aspire to—and possibly exemplify—these same virtues ourselves.

You might be asking, "why is he going to tell us what virtues like courage are and why they're important?" Of course you already know these things, so to some extent I'm going to take this for granted and not spend too much time on defining them. But they are worth mentioning, because in practice they're not as simple as they seem: a person needs a good deal of judgment to know when and how to be brave, for example. As we saw in the previous chapter, virtues such as courage and humility may describe a person's general character, but they don't provide much guidance regarding what to do. By looking at how Captain America embodies these virtues, we can see that he serves as a role model not only in terms of the virtues themselves but also in how he puts them into practice. In the process, I will also reinforce a major argument of this book: namely, that Captain America's supposed "black-and-white" ethics are anything but. They weren't simplistic in the

The Virtues of Captain America: Modern-Day Lessons on Character from a World War II Superhero, First Edition. Mark D. White.

1940s or 1960s—and neither was the world—and they're just as applicable now as they were then.

Courage

Obviously, one of the characteristics of Captain America that immediately comes to mind is courage, not only for readers but also for the other heroes in the Marvel Universe. For example, after one of their occasional team-ups, Daredevil exclaims about Cap, "and they call *me* the man without fear!"[1] Hercules, Olympian god and Avenger, went one step farther when he said, "the gods measure courage against Cap."[2] Scenes of Cap's bravery in the comics are endless. Most clearly there are the acts of sheer physical bravery, such as running into the path of enemy fire during wartime, rushing into dangerous situations to save lives, and—my personal favorite—jumping out of planes without parachutes.[3] There are also acts of moral courage, such as when Captain America has to pass sentences on his fellow Avengers who have let down the team, including Yellowjacket and Warbird.[4] And then there are the many times that Cap stands up to threats that would frighten all but the most courageous of heroes, whether leading the Avengers against overwhelming odds, facing down a monstrous alien tyrant like Thanos, or standing up to the Asgardian all-father himself, Odin, after Thor was defeated by the Midgard Serpent:

> Odin! That monster my world is killing itself to fight on your behalf just sent two of his thugs to break your boy in two. Well, he fought 'em back with all he had. So now you fix him. … I can't fight and die in your war on my damn feet without Thor out there fighting with me. And if you want your serpent dead we all know there's only one guy who can do it.

When Odin objects, Cap simply says, "Save it. Is that your army, big man? … You're gonna need more guys."[5]

But Captain America is careful to point out that courage is not the same thing as being rash in the face of danger. Aristotle thought the same, of course, maintaining that courage was the golden mean between cowardice and recklessness or foolhardiness.[6] According to him, courage, like all virtues, must be exercised in the pursuit of excellence, and practical wisdom or judgment is needed to do this well. As he wrote in his *Nicomachean Ethics*, "whoever stands firms against the right things and fears the right things, for the right end, in the right way, at the right time, and is correspondingly confident, is the brave person."[7] In this passage, Aristotle practically beats you over the head with the idea that, in order to exercise the virtue of courage, judgment is crucially necessary to determine the "right" way to do so—one cannot simply "be brave." Even for those to whom courage comes naturally, like police officers, firefighters, and soldiers, their instinctive actions are based on their training and experience, all of which help to make their judgment more intuitive than deliberate. As Cap faced a gigantic fire creature that made even the mighty Thor hesitate, the narration read, "Some would call the living legend's actions foolish. How could one man with no powers beyond his all-too human strength and will succeed where a god has failed? Luckily, Captain America has never been one to ponder the odds!"[8] Cap wasn't being rash; rather, he relied on his years of experience to bolster his natural courage and join battle with his foe.

Captain America also realizes that courage does not mean lacking or denying one's fear, but rather overcoming it.[9] Soon after the Scarlet Witch joined the Avengers with her brother Quicksilver, she asked Cap, "do you never know fear?" to which he replied, "only a fool is never afraid."[10] When trying to inspire a young soldier in Afghanistan to find his own strength and courage, Cap told him that "everyday I felt afraid ... The fear never stops."[11] At its essence, "courage can't exist without fear," because a person with no fear does not need courage.[12] In a story set in World War II, we are introduced to Bobby Shaw, whom Steve Rogers met in basic training at Fort Lehigh. Private Shaw reminded Steve of himself before he was transformed into Captain America: a scrawny, timid young man who nonetheless felt the call of duty. At the end of the story, Private Shaw made the ultimate sacrifice, and at his funeral sixty years later, in front of superheroes and military personnel alike, Cap said, "I have been to the end of the skies and back. I have been in the company of heroes. Of all those heroes, he was the bravest I have ever known," specifically because he had such great fear but managed to overcome it anyway.[13]

One might think that, while Captain America acknowledges that fear is normal, he nonetheless doesn't have any—that he is indeed fearless. But this mysterious "one" would be wrong: not only does Cap have normal phobias like a fear of heights,[14] but he regularly experiences fears of failure as well, tied to his exaggerated sense of responsibility (which we'll discuss later in this chapter). In *The Chosen*, a near-future tale in which a dying Captain America used new technology to project his image to those he felt could carry on his mission, he reached out to a young Corporal Jimmy Newman and tried to inspire him to embrace his courage and other heroic virtues. As Cap explained to Jimmy,

> [Bucky] died on one of our missions. And it continued. So many friends. So many people I cared about. I kept fearing who else would die. I pushed myself to the limit, trying to keep them safe. Strangers, too. So many strangers depended on me. The country depended on me. A lifetime of trying. That's why I was afraid ... of failing.[15]

But fear of failure can be taken too far also, paralyzing a person into inaction. As Cap told a sergeant who accused him of not knowing fear, "I know fear ... You know what I fear? Doing wrong. But I don't let it stop me from doing anything."[16]

Sometimes, however, in his rush to do something, even Captain America can act recklessly. Consider what is perhaps his greatest fear: getting his colleagues, especially his young sidekicks, hurt or killed. Starting with his very first solo story in 1964 and continuing for several years—and never really going away, as we heard him tell Colonel Newman—Cap was haunted by the memory of losing Bucky in World War II.[17] When Rick Jones became Cap's new sidekick and was (inevitably) captured, Cap flew off the handle:

> Like a man possessed, the costumed Avenger hurls himself thru the sitting room window ... heedless of the danger ... heedless of the odds against him ... one aching thought raging over and over in his anguished mind ... his partner must not die again![18]

In this case, Cap lost control of his fear and acted rashly, providing an instructive example of foolhardy behavior—as well as further evidence that Captain America is not perfect!

In most cases, however, Captain America handles his fear much more appropriately; as he told the sergeant who asked him about fear, "it's one thing to know fear. Something else to let it control you."[19] In the best cases, Cap uses fear to motivate him, such as when Mr. Hyde planned to blow up a super-tanker docked in New York City. Chained to the front of the tanker, the narration told us that "fear and outrage well up in this man's soul," giving Cap the strength he needed to free himself.[20] Other times, he just doesn't let the fear stop him, keeping in mind all of the people counting on him. When Jimmy Newman asked him, "You felt afraid like this all the time, every day since you became Captain America?", Cap answered, "Every day, every second." Jimmy then asked, "How on Earth did you bear it? Why did you keep going?", to which Cap replied, "So many people needed me … I didn't have a choice."[21]

Of course, you might say "sure, it's easy for Captain America to be courageous—he's got the super-soldier serum running through his veins, plus years of training and experience behind him!" Believe me, no one knows that more than Cap, who has always recognized the superior bravery of those without his special advantages. As he told Jimmy about his early days on the front in World War II, the other soldiers "didn't have super-powers. They were the true heroes," the truly courageous ones.[22] After the war with the Midgard Serpent ended—with the help of Odin and "some more guys"— Cap delivered a eulogy for his former sidekick Bucky, who fought bravely under the name of Captain America and was (apparently) killed by Sin, the daughter of the Red Skull and mastermind of the entire battle. As Cap said, "He was braver than me, because he didn't have any serum making him stronger and faster … but he never hesitated, never faltered."[23] As Cap reminisced about his experiences during World War II, he admitted he never saw himself as a hero, and that "the real heroes were the boys I once knew who feared for their lives, yet fought for freedom anyway, even though they didn't have the benefit of a super-soldier serum to help them dodge a bullet."[24]

Finally, it is important to note that Captain America also exemplifies an often neglected aspect of courage, one that has little to do with his super-soldier serum: standing up for what's right, as when Cap had to remove Hank Pym, one of the original Avengers, from the team for reckless behavior.[25] In *The Chosen*, Jimmy asks Cap why he chose him, and Cap said he was looking for someone who "understood that only cowards turn their back on a righteous task. Someone who looked fear in the face but still did the right thing."[26] Sometimes, to stand up for what you believe in when everyone else disagrees with you is the bravest thing a person can do, as Captain America famously told Spider-Man during the Civil War when Spidey was considering joining Cap's resistance against superhero registration: "This nation was founded on one principle above all else: the requirement that we stand up for what we believe, no matter the odds or the consequences."[27]

Interestingly, courage was the first virtue Aristotle wrote about in his *Nicomachean Ethics*, and one on which he seemed to put tremendous emphasis, but he didn't discuss moral courage, which many philosophers today regard as a more important virtue.[28] It's also the type of courage that the average reader—and author!—have the most need for, as well as the one that is most demanded of us. While the average person isn't expected to rush into a burning building to save a screaming child, everyone can be expected to stand up for what's right. This isn't always easy, of course—but that's exactly why courage is so important. It's also why Captain America serves as a great role model for it, especially since it doesn't involve any super-soldier serum or Vita-Rays, but "only" the brave person he is underneath.

Humility

A subtler virtue than courage, humility is often exemplified by Captain America despite his tremendous achievements, time-honed skills, and his many virtuous character traits. While physical courage is made somewhat irrelevant by Cap's enhanced speed and strength—and moral courage has nothing to do with either—humility becomes essential *because* of them. We know that every virtue is a balancing act between two extremes, but humility requires a particularly delicate one: on the one hand, a person shouldn't be boastful about his or her achievements or talents, but neither should he or she lie about them.

Captain America shows his humility by downplaying his own good qualities and praising those of others. These sentiments often go hand in hand, such as when he claims that "I'm no more of a hero than anyone else" and that "I never felt like a hero … I have been in the company of heroes, and in the company of heroes I remain."[29] Cap is particularly sensitive to hero worship, which he feels is neither earned nor appropriate. After returning from a year's absence in a pocket dimension (during the "Heroes Reborn" episode in the late 1990s), there was an outbreak of "Capmania" (secretly manipulated by the Skrulls, an alien race that periodically invades the Earth). The degree of media attention and hype made Cap uneasy; as he told Thor, he'd earned people's trust but he never wanted to be a celebrity.[30]

Years earlier, as he prepared for a press conference to announce his new national telephone hotline, the narration read:

> The applause that greets the flag-splashed figure is thunderous. As Captain America strides deliberately to the podium, he grins uneasily, concerned that the cheering crowds do not see him as a celebrity like a movie star, pop singer, or sports figure. For his fame is a mere byproduct of his mission to give America an enduring symbol of its highest values—freedom, justice, dignity, and opportunity for all. He hopes that the acclaim is for the things he represents, not the man who represents them.[31]

At the end of the day, Cap simply wants to serve the American people and the American dream; as he thought to himself later, "it's almost funny how other people see me. To some, I'm a living legend. ... I just think of myself as a man who's doing the best he can to make this world a safer, happier place. A simple man who's trying to make a difference."[32] In fact, when a university professor called Cap a living legend, he replied, "I'm living, but I won't admit to the legend part!"[33]

With Captain America, it isn't even a matter solely of how he represents himself to others: he sincerely thinks he's just a normal guy trying to help out. But this doesn't mean that he denies his abilities, virtues, or accomplishments altogether, nor does humility demand this. True humility doesn't require that people refuse to recognize their own positive qualities—this can risk self-deception, which is hardly virtuous! It does require, however, that they remain sensitive to other people's feelings about them.[34] One way to do this is to refocus attention on other people's talents, which Cap does almost by reflex. During an Avengers mission, Hawkeye marveled at Cap's skill with his shield, and when he asked Cap how he did it, Cap answered, "Practice and patience, Clint. Just like you."[35] After Cap's death following the Civil War, Spider-Man remembered one of their early team-ups when Cap helped him face the Hulk. When they were finished, Cap thanked Spider-Man for his help, to which Spider-Man replied, "Whoa, Captain America, thanking me?! I'm just a nobody." Cap answered, "Not to me. I couldn't have taken down the Hulk without you."[36] Finally, when the Avengers arrive on a scene, even if he's serving as team leader, he lets others take the spotlight, such as when he referred reporters to Luke Cage instead of taking the attention on himself.[37]

Captain America's humility shines brightest when it comes to fellow men and women in uniform, whose courage he praises as being far above his own (as we saw above). During World War II, when Steve Rogers and Bucky Barnes watched a newsreel featuring their costumed exploits, Bucky appreciated the cheering crowd, but Steve reminded him that no one was cheering for the rank-and-file soldiers who died during those battles.[38] Whenever Cap meets current or former soldiers—especially ones from his World War II days—he never fails to ask them about their family and thank them for their service, making sure to acknowledge if they specifically helped Cap out during the war.[39] For instance, after defusing a hostage situation, Cap met Stanley Klein, a private from the war—whose name Cap remembered, of course—and to whose sickbed Cap was called not long after. As he faded into death, Cap told his family and others gathered there that "this GI can teach us all about heroism."[40] Most poignantly for longtime comics fans, when Captain America met Peter Parker's Aunt May, he told her, "it's an honor to meet you, ma'am," and praised the way she raised Peter. In return, she told him how much it meant to her late husband Ben to meet him during World War II. When Cap noticed that she was clutching a photo album (which she had recently saved from her burning home), he asked, "Are those pictures of your husband? Perhaps you can show me sometime."[41]

True humility is a fine line to walk, and even Cap doesn't get it right all the time. During the Capmania episode, he told Thor that "I'd be lying if I said it wasn't flattering … it's actually becoming a strain not letting it go to my head."[42] After defeating the Skrulls who perpetrated the Capmania, Cap gave a press conference during which he accepted responsibility for succumbing to the hype:

> Even I was seduced by Capmania. It's not hard to believe your own press when there's so much of it. I let it make me cocky … even arrogant … and that gave the Skrull an advantage. For that, I am sorry beyond any measure this country will ever know.[43]

There are occasions, too, when he does focus on his own superlative abilities; for example, soon after his 1960s revival, he wondered why Nick Fury hadn't invited him to join SHIELD yet, thinking "nobody can be better qualified for the job than I!!"[44] He has also been known to go too far in the other direction and lapse into false modesty at times. When Sharon Carter asked him how he dodged bullets, and he replied, "Oh, that's nothing … I just see faster," Sharon said, "You see faster? And that's nothing …? I have mentioned how infuriating you are, right?"[45] He seemed to take this skill for granted and minimized it—which would be fine if not for his word "just" that failed to appreciate that being able to "see faster" is not exactly a common skill to have!

But usually Captain America finds the right balance between telling the truth about his abilities and virtues without boasting or bragging. After telling a World War II story to the rest of "Cap's Kooky Quartet," an early line-up of the Avengers featuring Cap and three fairly new heroes, Hawkeye said, "To hear you tell it, the Nazis would have won the war if not for your dauntless courage, and your matchless skill, Wing-head!" Cap replied, somewhat defensively, "I didn't mean it to sound that way, Hawkeye! I just told it as it happened!"[46] While recording his part for an Avengers documentary years later, Cap told the interviewer, "I have to tell you … this kind of thing makes me uncomfortable. It always has. There's a fine line between reporting and outright bragging."[47] Cap has even made this point to the president of the United States, who wanted Cap—whom the president regarded as "charming"—to talk to the press after Norman Osborn had stirred up popular sentiment against the Avengers.

CAP: Sir, I'm uncomfortable doing that.
PRESIDENT: Uncomfortable? You wear the flag as clothes.
CAP: Yes, sir, but bragging about what we do is a little—
PRESIDENT: It's not bragging if it's true.[48]

Cap eventually complied with the order from his commander-in-chief— which, we shall see later, he does not always do—but clearly he was concerned with crossing the line between reporting the facts and bragging about them.

Cap shows his humility in other ways as well. We'll talk about judgment in more detail in chapter 5, but I'll simply mention here that Cap shows humility in his decision-making. After he decided to shut down a group of teenaged heroes known as the Young Avengers, he asked his fellow (Old) Avengers, "We're doing the right thing ... aren't we?"[49] While pencilling the *Captain America* comic, Steve Rogers even told his editor at Marvel Comics that "Cap should occasionally have doubts about what he does."[50] What's more, despite his normally sound judgment, he regularly takes responsibility for his mistakes, as he did after Capmania. As he told the Scarlet Witch when he suspected the Thunderbolts, a team of reformed villains, in Hawkeye's latest disappearance, "If I'm wrong, Wanda, I'll apologize."[51] And he does apologize quite a bit, including to a SHIELD agent to whom he had earlier been rude and lost his "sense of diplomacy," a band of lava men whom he wrongly assumed were enemies, and the entire country after he took a life (as well as for his role in the Civil War).[52] Most pointedly, he apologizes to those who are affected by his battles, even those as slightly harmed as bystanders whose clothes get damaged.[53] Often the harm is far more serious, however. For instance, in a story set in Iraq, Cap made a decision that inadvertently resulted in a young Army sergeant losing three of his limbs. Years later, at a welcoming party for the return of the sergeant's comrades from another tour of duty, Cap approached him and apologized, saying he'd doubted that decision every day since making it.[54]

Can we hope to be as humble as Captain America—and do we have to be? After all, his super-soldier serum and advanced training actually make it both more difficult and more necessary for him to be humble compared to most of us. Unlike courage, which becomes more important the more you have to fear, humility becomes more important the greater your accomplishments and virtues. We can't lay claim to all of the abilities and experiences that Captain America has. Each of us does, however, have something to our credit, whether it's skill, talent, intelligence, or virtue, and it falls to each of us to be considerate of others' feelings when talking about them. All it takes is the awareness that, despite our differences in terms of strength, smarts, or talent, when it gets down to it we are all the same, dealing with life's ups and downs the best we can.[55] Look at it this way: if Cap can be humble in the face of who he is, it shouldn't be that hard for us!

Righteous Indignation

This is a virtue that may not strike you as one at first glance. Righteous indignation refers to a virtuous person's natural reaction to injustice and wrongdoing, and like humility, it requires delicate balancing, especially because its extreme—rage or hatred—is so very easy to succumb to.[56] Aristotle uses similar wording to describe the practice of righteous indignation as he did in the case of courage: "the person who is angry at the right things and towards the right people, and also in the right way, at the right time and for the right length of time, is praised."[57] A person who does not feel any anger when witnessing or hearing about injustice is insufficiently sensitive to it, but neither should a person fly into an uncontrollable rage and do something which may well be just as wrong as the event that prompted it (such as in cases of vigilante justice).[58]

We've all felt this type of anger, whether it's when we see someone cut in line at the tollbooth, get a promotion based on someone's else work, or perform a horrific act of violence. These things justifiably make us angry, but we must be careful not to let that turn into hatred. Being an extreme, all-consuming emotion, hatred is very difficult to contain or keep focused on the wrongdoing that caused it, and all too often ends up being applied to large groups of people instead of the individuals or small groups responsible for the injustice. It's no accident that rage-fueled hatred is often used as a tool by Cap's enemies such as the Red Skull and the Hate-Monger (whose name is just a bit on the nose) to destroy American society from within.

Captain America, of course, has been witness to some of the worst atrocities that human beings have subjected each other to in the real world, from the Holocaust and World War II to the terror attacks of September 11, 2001. In the comics, Cap's worst enemy and opposite number, the Red Skull, is portrayed as the very embodiment of hatred and evil (perhaps more so than any other villain in the Marvel Universe). Once Hitler's right-hand man, the Red Skull has been relentless in his fight to spread fascism, destroy liberty, and weed out the "inferior" races.

Once, after he had captured Captain America, the Red Skull told him his life story including all of its gruesome details, with the goal of defeating Cap's virtuous spirit and making him feel true hatred—but Cap refused. The Red Skull fumed,

> What do you think of my story ... my little plan? Does it make your blood boil with rage ... with hate? Speak! Or lash out at me! No ...! I see in your eyes—you have naught but pity and compassion in your heart, for even so vile and venomous a creature as me! So ... even I cannot drag you down from your contemptible ideals and make you hate! And thus, you claim one last victory over me![59]

That's not the end of the story, though; Cap is not perfect, after all. After the Red Skull apparently killed not only several of Cap's friends and partners but also Skull's own family, Cap snapped:

> I have fought hundreds of foes in my career, Skull—criminals, madmen, tyrants—! And never have I been moved to truly hate a man because he was my enemy! But you—! You revel in atrocity! Bask in evil! Delight in depravity! I—hate you, Skull! I hate what you are, what you've done to my friends, what you've done to the world! I hate you with a passion that frightens me![60]

To his credit, Cap recognized that the hate the Skull forced him to feel was dangerous. Furthermore, Cap stopped short of killing the Red Skull, refusing to let even his newfound hate push him to an action he'd regret for the rest of his life. He may have been driven to feel hatred, but as he told the Skull during a later battle involving the Hate-Monger, "hate doesn't motivate me."[61]

In his time as the sentinel of liberty, Captain America has seen entire racial and ethnic groups become the target of hate based on the actions of a few individual members (and sometimes nothing at all). This is how hatred becomes a blunt tool, causing people to act out blindly against anyone who looks like or sounds like those who attacked them. After the terror attacks of September 11, 2001, Steve Rogers joined the first responders at Ground Zero who tirelessly worked to find survivors, while wondering "How could this happen here? We've got to be strong ... stronger than we've ever been. If we lose hope here ... bury our faith in this darkness ... then nothing else matters."[62] Later, he had similar thoughts while protecting an Arab American youth from a grieving man, explaining to him, "You've lost someone. I understand. You want justice. This isn't justice. We're better than this. Save your anger for the enemy."[63] In another example of focusing anger, during World War II Cap accepted a German doctor into the US camp, ordering the other American GIs to treat him as a German soldier rather than a Nazi SS officer and lecturing them on the proper rules of engagement regarding prisoners of war. To Cap, Hitler and the Nazis were the true enemy, and the German soldiers were merely fighting for their homeland; this distinction was confirmed both when the German doctor helped wounded American soldiers and when he was immediately shot for treason upon being returned to the Nazis.[64]

Cap also finds things outside of war to be angry about. One persistent wrong about which Cap expresses righteous indignation is prejudice towards minorities.[65] In the *Man Out of Time* miniseries, which places the story of Cap's revival from the ice closer to the modern day (at the time, 2011), Tony Stark introduced Cap to the national events he missed while frozen, including the civil rights movement and women's fight for equality, both of which pleased Cap (and made him wish he had been there to see it and participate himself). When Tony told him about the 1986 explosion of the space shuttle Challenger, Cap asked if all the astronauts onboard were honored—meaning the two women, Judith Resnik and Christa McAuliffe, and the African-American man, Ronald McNair—and was gratified to hear that they were (and that Tony puzzled at the question itself).[66] When he got a chance to return to 1945 to look for Bucky after the war ended, he was upset to see the mistreatment of African Americans and women that he may not have noticed before, such as segregated seating at baseball stadiums and diner patrons slapping waitresses as they walk away.[67]

Years later, Cap was horrified and ashamed when he learned of the treatment of Isaiah Bradley, the only survivor of a super-soldier serum version of the Tuskegee experiments in which black enlisted men were mutilated and sometimes killed in an attempt to replicate the treatment used on Steve Rogers.[68] Bradley's wife Faith explained that her husband served as "the black Captain America" for a brief time before the corrupted super-soldier serum, together with substandard medical care during his seventeen years of imprisonment (for merely stealing Steve Rogers' uniform), "left my husband sterile, and after so many years of confined neglect, his brain slowly deteriorated."[69] When he finally met Bradley, Cap apologized, told Bradley he wished it could have been him instead, and returned the tattered uniform Bradley wore as Captain America. The main focus of the story is on Bradley and racism, not Steve Rogers, but when Rogers does appear he clearly shows his disgust, especially to the racist Merritt who oversaw the program that created Bradley and killed so many other African-American men.[70]

Not all virtue ethicists have the same opinion regarding righteous indignation and anger, however. While Aristotle saw the anger as an appropriate reaction to injustice, the Stoics were more skeptical of its value. In his essay *On Anger*, Seneca dismissed any positive value to anger, regarding it as a disruptive force on reason. He felt that once a person succumbed to anger in even the slightest way, it would eventually subsume his or her reason: "It is easier to exclude the forces of ruin than to govern them … once they have established possession, they prove to be more powerful than their governor, refusing to be cut back or reduced."[71] Steve Rogers discovered this when he fought a number of brutes who had been given a version of the super-soldier serum, which hit particularly close to home: "I try to maintain control … but my anger boils over."[72] As with his fear over losing yet another partner, we see that not even Captain America can keep his anger in check all the time.

Seneca also disagreed with Aristotle when it came to anger as an appropriate response to injustice. Seneca instead believed that anger, being a "force of ruin," was a vice, and "if the wise man's nature is to be angry at transgressions, he will be angrier the greater they are, and he will be angry often," which a person cannot be expected to control for long.[73] As a result, Stoics such as Seneca recommended avoiding anger altogether; indeed, most of *On Anger* offered advice on exactly how to do this, including forgiving wrongs and placing less value on things and circumstances, focusing instead on what is truly important, namely practicing virtue and experiencing joy. In his own version of "you only live once," near the end of the essay Seneca asked:

> What joy is there in acting as though we were born to live forever, declaring our anger and squandering our momentary span of life? What joy is there in turning the days which could be spent in honest pleasure to the pain and torture of others? These things cannot survive the waste, we have not the time to lose.[74]

Ideally, a person can achieve a state of serenity, tranquility, or what Immanuel Kant (drawing from the Stoics) called "moral apathy," which allows a person to rise above inappropriate emotions and allow reason to have the maximum control over his or her thoughts and actions.[75] Cap also realizes this would be best: once, while reminiscing about his World War II days, he thought to himself, "in battle, one learns a certain kind of calm as an alternative to the fear that dominates every moment. I could never find that elusive calm. It hurt too much to watch my brothers ripped apart by fire from a 10 mm cannon, or shrapnel."[76] Despite his reputation for remaining cool under pressure, Captain America finds it difficult to control his emotions all the time, just like everyone else—but this doesn't stop him from trying.

Sacrifice and Responsibility

The willingness to sacrifice is often considered a particularly heroic virtue, depending on to what degree and in what circumstances we see it. Like all virtues, it is valuable only if a person acts on it; it's not enough to feel generous, one must actually *be* generous.[77] The people we typically think of as heroes are those who give or risk much more than the average person, whether it's a one-time event, such as the accountant who rushes into a burning building to save a baby, or a regular activity, such as firefighters who risk their lives on an ongoing basis. Some would say the firefighter is less heroic because it's his or her responsibility to accept risk—which is true—but that simply means the choice to be a firefighter in the first place demonstrates an attitude of heroic self-sacrificing (and the commitment to act on it).

Superheroes are no different (aside from being fictional and covered in spandex). One common theme in comics is that superheroes give up their personal lives and any chance at "normal happiness" to serve the greater good and fight injustice. This is particularly true of Captain America, who found himself with no private life to speak of after being rescued from the ice; in the last chapter we discussed his failure to claim a life of his own as an example of taking a good thing too far. "All my life I've tried to find a place for Steve Rogers," he thought to himself soon after being rescued from the ice, "but still he lives under the more colorful shadow of Captain America ... Perhaps it's Steve Rogers who's the legend—and Captain America who is the reality! Perhaps I was born to be a red-white-and-blue Avenger—and nothing more!"[78]

Later, it seemed he may have found balance, thinking to himself,

for the first time since I was a boy, I really understand what a "normal" life is about. ... I've seen that American dream I've preached about for so long ... come within my reach. I've tasted the same struggles, hopes, agonies, and triumphs as the people I'm sworn to protect. Steve Rogers has made Captain America ... a better man![79]

But this does not last, and as time goes on, he gradually accepts his main identity as Captain America: "the conflict between my duty to the nation and the semblance of normal life got to be too great. I finally had to drop the trappings of normalcy, and give myself fully to my mission."[80] By the time the Civil War started, Cap seemed to be reconciled with this, having largely abandoned the hope of a private life as Steve Rogers. For example, he told Sharon Carter that he had come to embrace the burdens of being a public superhero (while he was fighting for the right of his fellow super-heroes to keep their identities secret):

My identity is public, and what has that meant? People in my life have been targets, some have been killed, just for knowing me. I couldn't live in a normal apartment, because it was too dangerous for my neighbors. I accept these things, not gladly, but I accept them, because Captain America is who I am ... and I understand what comes with that.[81]

Perhaps the best statement from Captain America regarding his sacrifice came after Bucky's second (apparent) death, while he carried the mantle of Captain America. The president of the United States asked Rogers to serve as Captain America once more, but as Rogers told Sharon Carter, he hadn't wanted the responsibility in the first place—at least, not that particular responsibility.

I never wanted to be Captain America. I was just supposed to be a soldier. The first of a whole platoon of men like me. But after Professor Erskine was killed ... and I was the only one of my kind ... I did what my country asked of me. I became a symbol first, and then a soldier. That symbol was a burden I never planned to carry once the war was won. But I wasn't there to see that day. Instead I woke up in a new world, surrounded by other people in masks. And found I was still needed. And being America's symbol had made me a better man. So even though the burden consumed my life ... and nearly cost me everything ... I carried it willingly. I've rarely tried to find a life outside these stars and stripes. But since I came back ... I haven't wanted them. Partly because of things I see coming. Partly because I saw the burden making Bucky a better man, too. But partly because I never wanted to be Captain America ... I just wanted to serve.[82]

Needless to say, he did choose to become Captain America again—no matter what he might say, he regards it as his duty, regardless of the extraordinary sacrifices it demands.[83]

Captain America's issues with identity and sacrifice flare up in a special way whenever Cap tries to get romantically involved with a woman—especially one who isn't a superhero or SHIELD agent! This inevitably results in a conflict between his duties as Captain America and his responsibilities to his partner, and the former usually win (whether it's his decision or hers). With the exception of SHIELD agent Sharon Carter, Cap has had to accept that foregoing relationships is one of the sacrifices he must make in the service of his duties as America's sentinel of liberty. (We'll talk more about this later when we discuss how duties may conflict and why judgment is necessary to reconcile them.)

But these aren't among the most common expressions of Captain America's virtue of self-sacrifice, of course. Just like real-life soldiers, police officers, firefighters, and others who risk their lives to save others, Cap stands ready to sacrifice all for the sake for those he's sworn to protect. In Germany in 1944, he told a Nazi nurse that he misses America because it's his home, "but it's more than that. ... I'm here because I believe in it. Because I love it. I miss my country ... but I left because it needed me to go. We all have duties ... sacrifices we have to make, for the things we love. But I guess that's how we know we love them."[84] In *The Chosen*, while the president of the United States watched Captain America literally kill himself projecting his image to virtuous people around the country, he said that Cap is "selfless as ever, sacrificing himself to the end."[85] Cap regularly puts his life at risk to save others, such as when he was hurt resisting a raging, mind-controlled crowd and then yelled at Tony Stark for taking care of him rather than working to calm down the mob.[86] Cap also sacrifices himself for his enemies: for example, during a period of gradual paralysis due to his super-soldier serum—a condition which progressed more quickly the more he exerted himself—Cap nonetheless risked everything to save his enemy, Super-Patriot.[87] Months later, as Cap and Sharon Carter ejected out of a jet seconds before it exploded, Cap's chute opened but Sharon's didn't—so he ditched his to try to save her instead. "Are you crazy?" she asked, to which

Cap responded simply, "No. Just loyal."[88] He's also surrendered himself on many occasions to save others, whether innocents threatened by a madman or a criminal whom Cap fears will be killed by corrupt authorities.[89] Cap always thinks of others before himself, which is the very essence of heroism—but something it doesn't take a superhero to do.

As we've seen, however, Captain America often takes his attitude of sacrifice too far. While a certain degree of generosity is a virtue, you shouldn't sacrifice to such an extent that you put yourself in need of help as a result![90] Many would say that Cap deserves the private life that he's given up, that his sacrifices in his long career—before and after his long ice bath—would satisfy even the most demanding assessment. Many of his friends, including fellow Avengers, have urged him to take a break and relax, but Cap refuses—mainly because he has no outlet for relaxation given his lack of a private life. And so it continues!

Captain America's tremendous willingness to sacrifice can be traced to his oversized sense of responsibility, and Sharon Carter has often been well placed to observe it. For example, Cap once told Nick Fury that he felt guilty about the people who lost their lives in the space program, that "it should have been me taking those risks. That's what I was built for, after all." After hearing that story, Sharon said, "Boy, talk about carrying the weight of the world."[91] After Cap "died" following the Civil War and then came back, Sharon told him, "I knew you'd come back ... I knew it," to which Cap simply replied, "How could I not? There's so much left to do."[92] Finally, when he and Sharon faced a riot in New York City at the beginning of the war with the Midgard Serpent, Cap was knocked down by a brick to the head. As he got up, Sharon said, "It's not stopping," to which Cap replied, "That's why we're here. That's our job."[93]

Even saving the world isn't enough to fulfill Captain America's sense of responsibility if he can't also help individual people in everyday situations. Once, after failing to stop a woman from running into traffic and being killed, he lamented that the Avengers can stop conquerors from outer space, "but when it came time to help one desperate individual," they failed.[94] No one's perfect and no one can do everything; nonetheless Cap feels he must. But as Immanuel Kant maintained, "ought implies can," meaning that a person shouldn't feel responsible for doing the impossible—even if that person is Captain America.[95] Yet, as he lay dying from his paralyzing adverse reaction to the super-soldier serum, he thought to himself, "Despite all my good intentions and constant struggles, the world is still filled with crime, war, injustice and tyranny. Let my epitaph read: 'He didn't do enough!' "[96]

Not only does Captain America feel a general responsibility to the people of the world, but he also feels a special responsibility to those close to him, such as his friends, lovers, and sidekicks. He also feels a special responsibility for the Avengers, the group of heroes that rescued him from the ice and has provided him a home and a purpose ever since. Whenever something bad happens to the group, Cap takes it as a personal failure, especially when he's charged with leading the team. Just a few issues into his first turn as leader, public sentiment turned against them (due to a villainous plot). Hawkeye ribbed Cap about his leadership, but Cap took it seriously: "When I took command, the Avengers were at the height of their power, their prestige, their fame! And now—look what I've done!"[97] Next, when squabbles between the members broke up the team, Cap said to himself, "Losing a battle is one thing! But to break up a team!"[98] Turmoil within the ranks of the Avengers was a constant concern of Cap's, who struggled to maintain unity and morale in the team: "It's my job—my responsibility to make the Avengers the most effective fighting force possible!"[99] This attitude extends also to periods when he's not leading the Avengers but keeps a close eye on whoever is, whether it's Iron Man, the Wasp, or another member, even as he fights his natural impulse to take charge.[100]

As we mentioned earlier in this chapter, Captain America's responsibility has also included letting Avengers go from the team. When Warbird (Carol Danvers, now known as Captain Marvel) was demoted to inactive status for her unprofessional conduct and problems with alcohol, Hawkeye accused Cap of being "brutal." Cap answered, "I didn't like it, Hawkeye—but I have to safeguard the team, and the lives we defend."[101] And then there was Hank Pym, the original Ant-Man, who in his long career has also gone by the names Giant Man, Yellowjacket, and Goliath, among others.[102] After shooting an enemy in the back after she stopped fighting, Pym—in his Yellowjacket identity—was court-martialed by the Avengers. During the proceedings, Cap acknowledged that Pym used bad judgment and merely made a mistake, but argued that their responsibility as Avengers doesn't allow that luxury:

> One "error" by one of us can cost thousands of lives! We don't dare allow ourselves to think it's ever right to make a mistake. Our responsibility is overwhelming! We've got to judge ourselves harshly! I recommend for Yellowjacket, as I would for myself, the severest possible penalty![103]

Afterward, however, the Avengers' butler Jarvis found Cap in the training room, working out his guilt over Pym's actions and court-martial, and he actually convinced Cap that he wasn't to blame for Pym's ordeal.[104] (Jarvis may be the most impressive "Avenger" after all!)

The incident with Hank Pym shows the breadth of Captain America's sense of responsibility, not just for the team for also for its members. Even though he knows that his responsibility to the team as a unit, and to their mission to protect the world, is greater than any individual member, he doesn't let that obscure the responsibility he owes his fellow Avengers as people. Even after Pym was exonerated—not only of the court-martial but of criminal charges related to (yet) another incident—Cap apologized for not taking into account the pressures Pym was under, especially as group leader (and displaying his humility in the process).[105] In complex situations such as this, with incomplete information and competing priorities, it's difficult to know you're doing the right thing by all of the people involved, which takes an extraordinary amount of good judgment (as we'll discuss later). Cap demands this of himself all the time, but should he? This is just one more example of his excessive sense of responsibility—which is not to be emulated in its degree, though the intent is to be admired.

Finally, not only does Cap embody the connected virtues of sacrifice and responsibility himself, but he stresses its value in others as well (such as when he lectured Hank Pym on the responsibility of an Avenger). When looking for potential successors in *The Chosen*, he told Corporal Newman that he was searching for people with virtues similar to his: "Around the country, there are people with your virtues. Decent, caring people willing to sacrifice. ... [I'm] using the last of my resolve to urge them to reach into themselves ... to muster the generosity and determination that exemplify the best of what people can be."[106] But once again, Cap must remember that the best that people can be does not include the impossible, which he all too often demands of himself.

Perseverance

Growing up in New York City during the Great Depression, young Steve Rogers all too often saw his mother suffer abuse at the hands of his alcoholic father, who had trouble holding down a job. She never backed down, however; she would just get up, look her husband in the eye, and tell him to keep trying (and to do it sober). When Steve asked his mother why she didn't just stay down, she answered, "because, and you listen close, Steven ... you always stand up."[107] Steve remembered this years later, after being captured, beaten, and tortured by his old foe Arnim Zola; as he screamed in agony, he thought to himself, "find the strength—stand up—you always stand up."[108] When Sharon Carter finally found him, spent and almost ready to give up, she played drill sergeant for Private Rogers: "What the hell is this? Are you letting Arnim Zola reduce you to this? I'm not leaving you here! Stand up! I need you to stand up!" This served as a trigger for Cap, who muttered, "always stand up," and rises to fight again.[109] Cap regularly echoes this same advice to others, such as when he told Tony Stark during their debate over superhero registration, "What's right is what's right. If you believe it, you stand up for it."[110]

Holding certain moral values and acting on them doesn't mean much if a person doesn't stand up for them through thick and thin. People may do the right thing, maybe even often, but if they do it only when it's easy or convenient, it speaks little of their devotion to their ideals. The true test of a person's character is how regularly he or she exhibits ethical behavior and under what pressures he or she continues to do so. This character trait goes by many names—perseverance, resolve, determination, conviction, or strength of will—but whatever you call it, Captain America's got it, remarking during one struggle that he must "remain steadfast to my ideals and do the right thing, no matter how tough it comes!"[111] Perseverance is what philosophers call an *executive virtue* because it helps people follow through on their judgment made in light of their virtues and principles. Determination is no good in and of itself, but it enhances a person's ability to exercise his or her general virtues like honesty and courage, helping him or her to do virtuous things better.[112]

When Captain America tried to convince Spider-Man to oppose superhuman registration during the Civil War, he expanded a bit on determination and conviction (after quoting from Mark Twain on the subjects of patriotism, civil disobedience, and personal integrity):

> Doesn't matter what the press says. Doesn't matter what the politicians or the mobs say. Doesn't matter if the whole country decides that something wrong is something right. This nation was founded on one principle above all else: the requirement that we stand up for what we believe, no matter the odds or the consequences. When the mob and the press and the whole world tell you to move, your job is to plant yourself like a tree beside the river of truth, and tell the whole world—"no, you move."[113]

As Spidey thought later, while watching Cap during the climactic final battle of the Civil War, "I can't stop ... won't stop ... until and unless he stops. And he won't. He'll never sacrifice what he stands for. Not as long as he's alive."[114] Even after Cap surrendered (which we'll come back to at the end of this section) and was shot soon thereafter, Spidey continued to marvel at the strength and determination he showed by pushing a cop out of the way of the gunfire: "With these strength-dampening restraints SHIELD had him in, it was probably taking all he had just to walk up those stairs ... But he hadn't lost anything. He was still a hero ... right to the end."[115]

And it's not just Spider-Man: Cap's determination is well-known among his friends and enemies in the Marvel Universe. During one of their few adventures together, Daredevil and Cap were trapped in a burning warehouse. As Cap led their way out, Daredevil thought to himself, "Incredible! Half-blinded by the smoke—probably half-dead as well—he still refuses to give up! The legends don't do this man justice!"[116] SHIELD agents, too, know Cap's legendary perseverance all too well: as Dum Dum Dugan said, Cap's unstoppable, not because of the super-soldier serum, but because "he knows who and what he's fighting for. And he ain't ever gonna back down from that. Not one inch," and according to Sharon Carter, "He made it look easy. Even though it never was."[117] Even Iron Man—perhaps the only Marvel hero who wishes Cap weren't so strong-willed—has to admire him. For example, while using a sonic weapon on Cap during the Civil War, Iron Man marveled at Cap's resolve, saying "this frequency puts the human brain into shutdown, but look at you, you're still getting up."[118]

In conflict and combat, Captain America's determination often displays itself as defiance; as he told Hawkeye during an early Avengers mission, "nobody's licked while he's still defiant ... unyielding!"[119] Just as his courage was most impressive when facing down invincible foes, so is his defiance and perseverance in the face of adversity. During World War II, Cap was captured by Atlanteans and held for days, "chained in a torturous position ... with absolutely no possibility of rescue," according to an Atlantean guard, "and still, whenever we enter his cell ... every time he says the same thing." What did he say to the Atlanteans? "Surrender yet?"[120] In the current day, after the Avengers were captured, stripped, and hung naked by their wrists in the Savage Land (a prehistoric jungle hidden in the Antarctic), Cap demanded to see their captor, a mutant named Karl Lykos. When Lykos appeared, Cap yelled, "Surrender! Surrender now!"[121] Even more recently, while being throttled by a giant robot that continually demanded that Cap "yield," he simply said, "not a chance."[122] Whether being tortured miles under the surface of the ocean, fighting giant robots in

New York City, or hanging bound and naked in a prehistoric jungle, Cap is forever defiant, just one aspect of his indomitable spirit.

The one villain who has come closest to breaking Captain America's will is the Red Skull, who has a particular talent for piercing Cap's defenses and pushing his emotional buttons (regarding Bucky, for instance). In one of his heinous plots, the Skull used the all-powerful Cosmic Cube to switch bodies with Cap.[123] The Skull (in Cap's body) tried to break Cap's spirit by getting close to Sharon Carter, while Cap (appearing to be the Red Skull) went to the Avengers for help but was captured—and almost executed by Sharon! But to the Red Skull's dismay, Cap "hasn't yet lost faith! Why can't I crush his spirit? But, no matter! Not even his indomitable will can save him now!"[124] Of course, the Skull was wrong; with the help of his new partner the Falcon, Cap fought back to defeat him (as always). But the Red Skull has never given up: recently, he tried to co-opt anti-mutant prejudice to his own evil ends, using telepathy stolen from fallen X-Men mentor Dr. Charles Xavier to try to turn even Captain America against mutants. "But this is no ordinary man," the narration read. "This is Captain America, his resolve unwavering. Skull's hatred finds no grip on his noble heart."[125]

As you may know, Captain America is quite the speechmaker, despite claiming "I'm not one for speeches."[126] Many of his speeches are aimed at spurring his "troops" on—whether actual soldiers or Avengers—encouraging strength in the face of adversity as only he can do. During World War II, he inspired soldiers with words like the following:

> We lost some men today ... good men, all ... and we may lose more tomorrow. But we won't retreat, we won't back down ... and we won't let the fear we all feel in our hearts stop us. We'll remember Pearl Harbor and our people who died there ... and we'll remember why President Roosevelt sent us here ... what depends on us ... the free world's survival ... and we will win![127]

After the epic battle with the Midgard Serpent in *Fear Itself*, during which both Bucky and Thor were thought killed and many cities around the world suffered incredible damage, Cap told his fellow Avengers:

> We'll rebuild. Asgard ... Manhattan ... the world. We'll rebuild it all. Like the rest of the world, we'll dig deep and find the strength to get out of bed tomorrow morning and start all over again. The Avengers will bury our dead, mourn our losses ... and then get back to work.[128]

Finally, when Cap appeared to an exhausted and isolated Corporal Jimmy Newman in *The Chosen*, Jimmy wondered how long he could go on. Cap answered, "To fight the enemies of freedom? To fight hate? You want to know how long we can keep doing this? As long as we're able to lift a finger. As long as we can draw a breath."[129]

Captain America may be usually an exemplar of resolve and conviction—having been written that way—but even he has had brief instances in which his resolve failed him. One was after Thor fell to a magically enhanced Hulk during the battle with the Midgard Serpent, and Spider-Man asked Cap for leave to be with his loved ones. When Hawkeye asked where Spidey went, Cap told him, "look around, Hawkeye ... we're going to lose."[130] However, Cap was soon back to his normal self, worrying about the signal they were giving by carrying the body of the fallen thunder god from a battle: "These folks are all scared and tired and they're watching us run. They need reassurance and reinforcements ... and what we're giving them looks like retreat."[131] Perhaps it was that realization, remembering his responsibility as a symbol of perseverance, that inspired him to defiantly face down Odin and inspire Avenger and civilian alike to fight anew—whatever it was, it was just what Cap needed to reclaim his legendary resolve and help win the battle in the end.

Many philosophers, both ancient and modern, have written about determination, perseverance, and willpower in one form or another. Aristotle called it *continence*, Kant called it *virtue* (which, as you can imagine, is confusing), and contemporary philosopher Richard Holton calls it *strength of will*.[132] These philosophical theories are often backed up by psychologists who study people's strength of will under adverse conditions. Working with various colleagues, psychologist Roy Baumeister argues that willpower is like a muscle that can be temporarily exhausted but, in the long run, is strengthened through "exercise."[133] Subjects in experiments who were forced to exercise self-control for long periods of time were more likely to give in immediately thereafter, their "muscles" exhausted, but were likely to show even more self-control once they had a chance to "recover."[134] We see this in Captain America's struggles to remain resolute as well: in yet another battle with the Red Skull, Cap said, "I mustn't panic! Mustn't give way to despair! No matter how awesome the odds—I'll fight as I've lived—I'll never abandon hope!"[135] Baumeister's view of willpower not only inspired Holton's philosophical take on strength of will but also matches Kant's analysis of it. Kant wrote that "virtue can never settle down in peace ... if it is not rising, [it] is unavoidably sinking," and that "the way to acquire it is to enhance the moral *incentive* (the thought of the law), both by contemplating the dignity of the pure rational law in us and by *practicing* virtue"—in other words, by exercising that "muscle."[136]

Captain America's rock-solid conviction is all too often confused with black-and-white ethical thinking or simple stubbornness. Often we're uncertain of our own moral judgments—or hesitant to make them at all—so we are sometimes uncomfortable with people who confidently know where they stand and are ready to defend their position. But having confidence in your judgment does not mean that you came to that decision lightly or easily, or that you will not listen to other arguments and perhaps change your position. As philosopher William Lad Sessions wrote in terms of honor (which we'll discuss in the next chapter), "once an act is determined to be honorable … an honorable person *qua* honorable simply must do the honorable [thing]."[137] Once Cap has determined the best course of action, he carries that decision out—and nothing will deter him from that unless he is convinced that yet another action is even better.

This does happen, even to Captain America: as we saw in chapter 1, for example, Cap surrendered at the end of the Civil War when he realized that his fierce stand against superhuman registration was hurting the people he was sworn to protect.[138] After reflection he changed his judgment (which showed humility) and then stood behind that, even after his fellow superheroes in the opposition, such as Spider-Man, urged him to keep fighting (which also showed moral courage). Judgment and perseverance work together but judgment always takes precedence: there is no virtue in stubbornly following a plan once you realize it's no longer the best thing to do. And when that happens, you come up with a better plan, and then you stick to *that*. Perseverance, determination, and conviction are virtues, but having them does not imply that one is stubborn or closed-minded—that's a matter of judgment (or lack thereof), which we'll talk about very soon.

The virtues we described in this chapter are only the ones most commonly attributed to Captain America in the comics, but there are many more we didn't mention, such as honesty and loyalty. Cap embodies these also, of course, even if they aren't stressed as often. So do all virtuous people to some extent, especially those whom we can describe as having honor or integrity, "supervirtues" if you will, that describe a person's overall character. Captain America is certainly a hero with honor and integrity, but what exactly do those terms mean, and how do they play out in terms of Cap's actions and words? You don't have to wait another second, dear reader—just turn to the next chapter!

Notes

1   *Captain America*, vol. 1, #235 (1979). In the same issue, Daredevil also asked Cap to stop calling him "son." (Not many have the guts to do that—Daredevil truly *is* the man without fear!)
2   *Captain America*, vol. 1, #444 (1995), yet another time when Cap was thought to be dead.
3   Cap's habit of free-jumping out of airplanes was established as far back as *Tales of Suspense*, vol. 1, #74 (1966), "The Final Sleep," and is seen in the 2014 film *Captain America: The Winter Soldier*. In *Civil War* #1 (2006), he jumped out of the SHIELD helicarrier and landed on a jet, "surfing" it to safety, and in the graphic novel *Avengers: Endless Wartime* (2013), he jumped from his own plane to an enemy plane after wedging his shield in its windshield like a grappling hook. (It's a living.)
4   *Avengers*, vol. 1, #213 (1981) and *Avengers*, vol. 3, #7 (1998), respectively.
5   *Fear Itself* #6 (2011). For Cap's stand against Thanos, see *Infinity Gauntlet* #4 (1991), and for an example of Cap's courage in leadership, see *Avengers*, vol. 1, #338 (1991), when he stands before Thane Ector, warrior champion of the alien Brethren, and proclaims, "the Avengers fear no one." (See also the discussion of defiance in the section on perseverance later in this chapter.)
6   See section 4.1 in Aristotle's *Nicomachean Ethics* for his discussion of courage.
7   Aristotle, *Nicomachean Ethics*, trans. Terence Irwin (Indianapolis, IN: Hackett, 1985), 1115b. (This is standard pagination used in all reputable editions of Aristotle's works.)
8   *Avengers*, vol. 1, #218 (1982).
9   Aristotle doesn't have a name for the state of fearlessness, but calls such a person "some sort of madman" (*Nicomachean Ethics*, 1115b25).
10 *Avengers*, vol. 1, #27 (1966).
11 *Captain America: The Chosen* #4 (2007).
12 *Captain America: The Chosen* #5 (2008).
13 *Captain America Theater of War: America the Beautiful* (2009).
14 *Captain America*, vol. 1, #291 (1984). In that issue, Cap chased the acrobatic vigilante the Tumbler across the rooftops of Manhattan. When the Tumbler asked him, "Would you believe I used to be scared of heights?", Cap replied, "I still am, Tumbler—that's why I'm very, very careful," as he crossed a power line balancing on his shield like a wheel!
15 *Captain America: The Chosen* #5 (2008).
16 *Captain America: Dead Men Running* #3 (2002).
17 *Tales of Suspense*, vol. 1, #59 (1964), in a story cleverly titled "Captain America."
18 *Captain America*, vol. 1, #111 (1969).
19 *Captain America: Dead Men Running* #3 (2002).
20 *Captain America*, vol. 1, #252 (1980).

21 *Captain America: The Chosen* #5 (2008).

22 Ibid.

23 *Fear Itself* #7.1 (2012).

24 *Mythos – Captain America* (2008).

25 *Avengers*, vol. 1, #213 (1981).

26 *Captain America: The Chosen* #6 (2008).

27 *Amazing Spider-Man* #537 (2006). For the complete speech, crafted by writer J. Michael Straczynski, see the section on perseverance at the end of this chapter.

28 See, for instance, Christopher Cordner, "Aristotelian Virtue and Its Limitations," *Philosophy* 69 (1994): 291–316.

29 *Tales of Suspense*, vol. 1, #91 (1967), "The Last Defeat!"; *Mythos – Captain America* (2008). See also the quote from *Captain America Theater of War: America the Beautiful* (2009) above.

30 *Captain America*, vol. 3, #5 (1998).

31 *Captain America*, vol. 1, #312 (1985).

32 *Captain America*, vol. 3, #24 (1999).

33 *Captain America*, vol. 1, #402 (1992), "The Prowling."

34 For important work on humility (or modesty) as a virtue, see Julia Driver's papers "The Virtues of Ignorance," *Journal of Philosophy* 86 (1989): 373–384, and "Modesty and Ignorance," *Ethics* 109 (1999): 827–834. On the other-regarding aspect of humility or modesty, see Irene McMullin, "A Modest Proposal: Accounting for the Virtuousness of Modesty," *Philosophical Quarterly* 60 (2010): 783–807.

35 *Avengers*, vol. 3, #75 (2004).

36 *Fallen Son: The Death of Captain America* #4 (2007).

37 *New Avengers*, vol. 1, #17 (2006).

38 *Captain America*, vol. 5, #11 (2005).

39 For example, see *Captain America: Red, White & Blue* (2007), "… they just fade away …," in which Cap visits a GI lying in the hospital to thank him; in return, he thanks Cap for giving the soldiers during World War II "little snatches of peace."

40 *Captain America*, vol. 3, #32 (2000); they'd met several issues earlier in *Captain America*, vol. 3, #25 (2000). As Cap told an Iraq vet, due to his enhanced mental abilities, he can't forget a single name of a soldier he's lost in battle—but whereas some might consider this to be a curse, Cap considers it a privilege (*Captain America Theater of War: To Soldier On*, 2009).

41 *Amazing Spider-Man* #519 (2005).

42 *Captain America*, vol. 3, #5 (1998).

43 *Captain America*, vol. 3, #7 (1998).

44 *Avengers*, vol. 1, #19 (1965).

45 *Captain America*, vol. 5, #17 (2006).

46 *Tales of Suspense*, vol. 1, #72 (1965), "The Sleeper Shall Awake!"

47 *Avengers*, vol. 4, #13 (2011).

48 *Avengers*, vol. 4, #24 (2012).

49 *Young Avengers*, vol. 1, #6 (2005).

50 *Captain America*, vol. 1, #314 (1986).

51 *Avengers*, vol. 3, #12 (1999).

52 The SHIELD agent's name was Gail Runciter, to whom he apologized in *Captain America*, vol. 1, #275 (1982) for his behavior in *Captain America*, vol. 1, #268 (1982), and again in *Marvel Team-Up*, vol. 1, #128 (1983) for his behavior in *Captain America*, vol. 1, #278 (1983). And if you're still interested, the scene with the lava men was in *Avengers*, vol. 1, #236 (1983); he apologized for taking life in *Captain America*, vol. 1, #323 (1986) and *Captain America*, vol. 4, #3 (2002); and he apologized for his actions during the Civil War in *Civil War: Front Line* #11 (2007), "Embedded Part 11."

53 *Marvel Team-Up*, vol. 1, #106 (1981).

54 *Captain America Theater of War: To Soldier On* (2009).

55 This is the *egalitarian* approach to humility or modesty recommended by philosophers such as Daniel Statman ("Modesty, Pride, and Realistic Self-Assessment," *Philosophical Quarterly* 42 (1992): 420–438) and Aaron Ben-ze'ev ("The Virtue of Modesty," *American Philosophical Quarterly* 30 (1993): 235–246).

56 Sometimes the difference between righteous indignation and simple hate is blurred. For example, I assume Cap meant righteous indignation when he told a group of neo-Nazis, "all you have is hate. But I can hate, too. I hate everything you stand for" (*Captain America*, vol. 1, #245, 1980).

57 Aristotle, *Nicomachean Ethics*, 1125b30.

58 I'm looking at you, Frank Castle.

59 *Captain America*, vol. 1, #298 (1984). For an extended look at the Red Skull's background, see the 2012 trade paperback *Captain America: Red Skull—Incarnate* (collecting the *Red Skull: Incarnate* miniseries from 2011–2012), written by Greg Pak and illustrated by Marko Colak.

60 *Captain America*, vol. 1, #300 (1984).

61 *Captain America*, vol. 3, #48 (2001), the culmination of "America Lost," one of the many storylines in which a villain tries to "destroy America with hate."

62 *Captain America*, vol. 4, #1 (2002), a fantastic comic expressing grief, compassion, and resolve in the face of unspeakable tragedy and loss.

63 Ibid.

64 *Captain America: Theater of War: A Brother in Arms* (2009).

65 This includes some that are unique to the Marvel Universe. In *Avengers*, vol. 1, #113 (1973), he reacts angrily to hate mail towards synthezoids (artificial humans like his World War II ally, the original Human Torch) leading up to the Scarlet Witch's marriage to the synthezoid Avenger the Vision. Intolerance towards mutants has been a persistent theme in the X-Men books since their beginning; see the *Uncanny Avengers* series (which started in 2012) for Cap's recent attempt to be proactive on this front.

66 *Captain America: Man Out of Time* #3 (2011).
67 *Captain America: Man Out of Time* #5 (2011).
68 See the 2009 trade paperback *Captain America: Truth*, collecting the 2003 miniseries *Truth: Red, White & Black* #1–7, written by Robert Morales and illustrated by Kyle Baker.
69 *Truth: Red, White & Black* #7 (2003).
70 *Truth: Red, White & Black* #6 (2003). Later, Bradley's grandson Eli joined the Young Avengers, using the codename Patriot.
71 Seneca, "On Anger," Book I, 7(2), collected in John M. Cooper and J.F. Procopé (eds.), *Seneca: Moral and Political Essays* (Cambridge: Cambridge University Press, 1995).
72 *Steve Rogers: Super-Soldier* #1 (2010).
73 Seneca, *On Anger*, Book II, 6(3).
74 Ibid., Book III 42(2). If this sounds as much like modern psychotherapy as ancient philosophy, there's a reason: Stoic philosophy was a significant influence on *cognitive behavioral therapy*, which focuses on helping patients deal with negative thoughts and correct counterproductive patterns of thinking, especially in depression. See Aaron T. Beck, *Cognitive Therapy of Depression* (New York, NY: Guilford Press, 1979) and Jules Evans, *Philosophy for Life and Other Dangerous Situations: Ancient Philosophy for Modern Problems* (London: New World Library, 2013).
75 On where Kant fits into all of this, see Roger J. Sullivan, *Immanuel Kant's Moral Theory* (Cambridge: Cambridge University Press, 1989), pp. 136–137, and Michael Seidler, "Kant and the Stoics on the Emotional Life," *Philosophy Research Archives* 7 (1981): 1–56.
76 *Mythos – Captain America* (2008).
77 This can also be put in terms of *benevolence* (feelings of kindness) versus *beneficence* (acts of kindness), a very important distinction in Kant's moral philosophy.
78 *Tales of Suspense*, vol. 1, #75 (1966), "30 Minutes to Live!" Lest you think these were just occasional moments of introspection on Cap's part, the cover to *Captain America*, vol. 1, #215 (1977), screamed "Who Is Steve Rogers?", announcing a storyline that began in earnest two issues later in *Captain America*, vol. 1, #217 (1978): "The Search for Steve Rogers."
79 *Captain America*, vol. 1, #289 (1984).
80 *Captain America*, vol. 1, #325 (1987).
81 *Captain America*, vol. 5, #22 (2006).
82 *Captain America*, vol. 5, #616 (2011), "Must There Be a Captain America?"
83 A helpful nudge from his old friend Nick Fury didn't hurt (*Captain America*, vol. 5, #615.1, 2011). See the section on duty in the next chapter for more on Steve Rogers' decision to become Captain America after Bucky's second "death."

84 *Captain America Theater of War: Prisoners of Duty* (2010).

85 *Captain America: The Chosen* #6 (2008).

86 *Captain America*, vol. 6, #10 (2012).

87 *Captain America*, vol. 1, #427 (1994). This Super-Patriot was not John Walker (who served as Captain America before becoming USAgent), but Mike Farrell, a former neighbor of Steve Rogers and member of the Watchdog group that killed Walker's parents (see *Captain America*, vol. 1, #439, 1995).

88 *Captain America*, vol. 1, #452 (1996).

89 For examples of each, see *Captain America*, vol. 1, #268 (1982), in which former CIA agent August Masters threatened to blow up a building full of innocent civilians and the superhero team the Defenders, and *Captain America and the Falcon* #5 (2004), in which Cap submitted to arrest rather than hand over a Cap impostor to a corrupt Navy admiral.

90 As Immanuel Kant wrote about his imperfect duty of beneficence, "How far should one expend one's resources in practicing beneficence? Surely not to the extent that he himself would finally come to need the beneficence of others" (*The Metaphysics of Morals*, edited by Mary Gregor, Cambridge: Cambridge University Press, 1797/1996, p. 454).

91 *Captain America*, vol. 5, #1 (2005).

92 *Captain America: Reborn* #6 (2010).

93 *Fear Itself* #1 (2011). Speaking of Sharon Carter, he not only feels responsible for her safety, but also her moral virtue. When his old friend D-Man was mind-controlled and threatened Cap's life, Sharon shot and killed him. Later, when SHIELD agent Rachel Leighton (a former criminal named Diamondback whom Cap briefly dated) said that Sharon had to do it to save his life, Cap said, "But … she shouldn't have had to …." Rachel assured him, "This is not your fault, Steve … none of this. Do not take on this weight," but of course he refused to listen (*Captain America*, vol. 6, #14, 2012).

94 *Avengers*, vol. 1, #340 (1991).

95 See Sullivan, *Immanuel Kant's Moral Theory*, p. 320n6.

96 *Captain America*, vol. 1, #443 (1995).

97 *Avengers*, vol. 1, #20 (1965).

98 *Avengers*, vol. 1, #21 (1965).

99 *Avengers*, vol. 1, #211 (1981).

100 Cap is particularly generous with his praise for the Wasp's leadership, perhaps because he feels it comes less naturally to her than to experienced CEO Tony Stark. (See, for instance, *Avengers*, vol. 1, #227 and #228, 1983, in which Cap noted how well she was growing into the leadership role—especially during her husband Hank Pym's trial following his Avengers court-martial.) And he feels even worse usurping her: "I nearly jumped in and took charge of the negotiations—I have to watch that. Former leader or not, I have no right to interfere with Jan's command" (*Avengers*, vol. 1, #258, 1985).

101 *Avengers*, vol. 3, #7 (1998). And then there are cases when extracurricular activity between Avengers threatened the morale of the team, such as when Tony Stark dated the Wasp after Yellowjacket's court-martial (and was dressed down for it by Cap in *Avengers*, vol. 1, #224, 1982), or later when Hawkeye slept with the Wasp after Hank Pym was back on the team (for which Cap reprimanded him in *Avengers*, vol. 3, #84, 2004, citing Tony's earlier transgression in the process).

102 For Pym's storied history, see the trade paperback *Avengers: The Many Faces of Henry Pym* (2012), collecting stories by various creators.

103 *Avengers*, vol. 1, #213 (1981). And this was before the Avengers noticed that Pym gave his wife Janet (the Wasp) a black eye (earlier in the same issue), which became a defining event in both of their characters' lives.

104 *Avengers*, vol. 1, #214 (1981).

105 *Avengers*, vol. 1, #230 (1983).

106 *Captain America: The Chosen* #6 (2008).

107 *Captain America*, vol. 7, #1 (2013).

108 Ibid. The storyline which follows, in which Cap is trapped in Zola's alternate dimension for over a decade, fighting to protect Zola's son whom Cap had "adopted" as his own, serves as a fantastic example of Cap's incredible perseverance.

109 *Captain America*, vol. 7, #9 (2013).

110 *Iron Man/Captain America: Casualties of War* (2007).

111 *Captain America*, vol. 1, #428 (1994).

112 The reader may remember a television commercial for BASF, the plastics company, that included the line: "We don't make a lot of the products you buy; we make a lot of the products you buy better." Or I may just be very old.

113 *Amazing Spider-Man* #537 (2006).

114 *Amazing Spider-Man* #538 (2007). This is old news to Spidey, of course: during an early adventure with the Avengers, Spidey thought to himself, "no matter how hopeless he keeps on plugging away! Either he's the gutsiest guy I've ever known or the craziest!" (*Avengers*, vol. 1, #318, 1990).

115 *Captain America*, vol. 5, #26 (2007).

116 *Captain America*, vol. 1, #235 (1979).

117 *Captain America*, vol. 3, #40 (2001) (Dugan); *Captain America*, vol. 5, #25 (2007) (Carter).

118 *Civil War* #4 (2006).

119 *Avengers*, vol. 1, #35 (1966).

120 *Captain America: Sentinel of Liberty* #3 (1998).

121 *New Avengers*, vol. 1, #5 (2005).

122 *Avengers*, vol. 5, #1 (2013).

123 *Captain America*, vol. 1, #115 (1969). The Skull didn't fool everybody, though: in *Captain America*, vol. 1, #117 (1969), a bystander who saw "Cap" come out

of a building thought to himself, "strange … I never thought Captain America would swagger so." (This also points to the real Cap's reputation for humility, not "swagger.")

124 *Captain America*, vol. 1, #117 (1969).

125 *Uncanny Avengers* #3 (2013).

126 *New Avengers*, vol. 1, #15 (2006). After one particularly corny speech in *Avengers Assemble*, vol. 2, #1 (2012), Cap asked his fellow Avengers, "Why don't any of you stop me when I get like that in front of the press?" Thor replied, "It is your calling, Rogers, a leader of men," and Hawkeye quipped, "I like when you get all you." In fact, Hawkeye picked up on Cap's propensity to pontificate very early, telling him in *Avengers*, vol. 1, #25 (1966), "You make everything sound like the Gettysburg Address."

127 *Captain America: Who Will Wield the Shield* (2010).

128 *Fear Itself* #7 (2011).

129 *Captain America: The Chosen* #1 (2007).

130 *Fear Itself* #5 (2011). We won't even mention *Age of Ultron* #1 (2013), which depicts a post-apocalyptic world destroyed by the evil artificial intelligence Ultron; the issue ends with a depressing image of Cap, sitting on the floor, his head hung low in defeat.

131 *Fear Itself* #6 (2011).

132 Aristotle, *Nicomachean Ethics*, Book VII; Kant, *Metaphysics of Morals*, pp. 394–395; Richard Holton, *Willing, Wanting, Waiting* (Oxford: Oxford University Press, 2009).

133 See, for instance, Roy F. Baumeister and John Tierney, *Willpower: Rediscovering the Greatest Human Strength* (New York: Penguin, 2011).

134 Cap apparently didn't read this research: as he said during his fight with the Green Skull, "Weeks without a break. But that's the work. You suck it up … you get it done" (*Captain America*, vol. 7, #1, 2013).

135 *Tales of Suspense*, vol. 1, #81 (1966), "The Red Skull Supreme!"

136 Kant, *Metaphysics of Morals*, pp. 409 and 397 (respectively).

137 William Lad Sessions, *Honor for Us: A Philosophical Analysis, Interpretation and Defense* (New York, NY: Bloomsbury, 2010), pp. 33–34.

138 *Civil War* #7 (2007).

4

Honor and Integrity

Captain America exemplifies many virtues, such as courage, humility, and others that we looked at in the previous chapter. These are the simplest virtues, the kind that influence action in a very specific direction depending on the person's judgment in particular situations. Now we turn to more general virtues that describe the overall character of a person: specifically, honor and integrity. These virtues not only describe how well a person practices the more basic virtues, but also his or her general ethical decision-making, which in Cap's case is based on principle and duty (as we saw in our overview of ethics in chapter 1). For that reason, we'll discuss these two concepts in this chapter as well, because they help to flesh out what honor and integrity mean to Cap, and also show why his legendary strength of character and resolve are so important. Finally, we'll see why Cap is sometimes forced to compromise his principles and also how this affects him, which will lead into the next chapter on judgment.

The Honor of Captain America

Captain America is easily the most respected hero in the Marvel Universe, as we see reflected in the authority he wields. As reporter Ben Urich noted as he watched Cap lead Thor and Iron Man in combat with Nuke (one of many individuals warped by attempts to replicate Cap's super-soldier serum), Cap was "a soldier with a voice that could command a god … and does."[1] In a military conflict secretly engineered by Doctor Doom in a

The Virtues of Captain America: Modern-Day Lessons on Character from a World War II Superhero, First Edition. Mark D. White.
© 2014 John Wiley & Sons, Inc. Published 2014 by John Wiley & Sons, Inc.

country bordering his home of Latveria, Cap tried to stop US forces from retaliating against what they saw as Russian aggression. He ordered the troops to "stand your ground," but the commanding officer argued, "I have orders. Direct from the President of the United States. Move out!" Cap firmly shouted, "Stand. Your. Ground." The troops stopped, they considered, and they saluted the man they chose to obey: Captain America.[2]

What grants Captain America this authority and respect? The narration to an issue of *Iron Man* in which Cap appeared may offer a clue:

> It is difficult to say exactly why he is so impressive. There is the physique, of course, and the costume and the way his muscles flex and lock to give him a purposeful lope. But these do not explain why almost everyone regards Captain America with a mixture of respect and awe. Perhaps it is his air of righteousness that stops short of self-righteousness—perhaps it is simply that he is a living legend.[3]

I would argue that righteousness isn't the best word, even though it captures well his conviction and belief in his ideals and principles (which we'll discuss later in this chapter).[4] Instead, I would use the word "honor," for Cap is nothing if not honorable.

We can easily make a case that it is his overwhelming sense of honor that has earned Cap the trust and devotion of the superhero community in the Marvel Universe. After his "death" following the Civil War, the rest of the heroes wandered in an ethical vacuum, which was filled first by Iron Man (a hero but Cap's ethical opposite) and then the psychotic villain Norman Osborn (the opposite of everything good and heroic!). As the president of the United States said to Cap after he returned to help defeat Osborn:

> We've seen the world according to Nick Fury ... We've seen the world according to Tony Stark ... And, Lord in heaven, we've seen the world according to Norman Osborn. Steve Rogers, Captain ... I am asking you to answer the call ... I am saying right now, the world needs you. Maybe even more than the day you first became the super-soldier.[5]

Only Steve Rogers' innate sense of honor can provide a center to the Marvel Universe around which other heroes rotate, each with his or her own perspective and ethical code that is best understood in relation to that of Captain America.

Spider-Man, who can be viewed as the moral barometer of the Marvel Universe, first stood with Iron Man in support of registration during the

Civil War, and then switched sides to join Cap and the rest of the heroes fighting it. After making this last decision, he thought to himself that he was finally "beside the one hero who will never betray his convictions, never betray those who followed him ... it feels good to be on the right side again."[6] Even Magneto, longtime foe of the X-Men and former leader of the Brotherhood of Evil Mutants, said to Cap when facing a difficult moral choice, "Captain America, you are an honorable man. Perhaps the most honorable man on the entire planet," and asked Cap what he should do.[7] When even the villains look up to Captain America, you know he's doing something right!

Honor is central to understanding Captain America and his relationship to virtue, but it's a difficult word to define. Ancient philosophers such as Aristotle wrote about honor, but modern philosophers don't talk about it much—with several notable exceptions which I'll note—and the idea itself seems to have fallen out of favor outside specific segments of society such as the military and education.[8] It is often seen as a relic, a holdover from a time of rigid divisions in terms of class, race, and gender, and a substitute for more nuanced ethical discussion relying on universal moral concepts. In other words, honor is regarded a lot like Captain America himself is regarded by many: a simplistic anachronism in the complex and nuanced moral environment of the twenty-first century. As I have done throughout this book, however, I will argue that this is mistaken. While honor is often associated with outdated attitudes and brutal rituals, there is nothing essential to the concept that links it with these things. In other words, we can rescue what is at the core of honor—virtue, integrity, and character—and shed its less attractive accoutrements.

External Honor as Respect

Most discussions of honor distinguish between two types: internal and external. *Internal honor* refers to a intrinsic quality of a person, part of his or her character, reflecting the person's virtues such as honesty, loyalty, and trustworthiness, plus how he or she integrates them and exercises them in action. In this sense, honor is a sort of "super-virtue," covering the separate virtues and how well a person exemplifies them separately and together. *External honor*, on the other hand, is not something that is embodied but something that is granted or awarded to someone. For example, we give external honor when we award soldiers the Purple Heart or recognize a top graduating senior with the title valedictorian or *summa cum laude*; we give these people "honors." People are often said also to be "honorable," which suggests both senses of honor: we bestow honors on such people because they displayed honor in some way.

We also see both senses of honor in an exchange between Thor and Captain America during Cap's time as simply "The Captain" while refusing to work for the US government (which we'll discuss more in chapter 6). After Cap told his fellow Avenger about his situation, as well as his concerns about Iron Man, with whom he was clashing over Tony's actions to retrieve his stolen armor, Thor thought to himself, "I have never known a mortal as honorable and noble as Captain America!" In this case, Thor was referring to the first sense of honor we cited, a quality internal to Cap and related to his virtues. Later in the same issue, Cap lifted Thor's enchanted hammer Mjolnir, which "only a man or god worthy—pure of heart and noble of mind" can do, in order to save his friend. After winning their battle, Thor saluted Cap for wielding Mjolnir, to which Cap replied, "I hope I'll always be worthy of that honor and privilege, my friend."[9] Here, Cap used the second sense of honor, referring to a tribute, something he is worthy of based on his inherent and internal quality of honor (in the first sense).

Many scholars who study honor stress the links between the internal and external meanings of the word. Aristotle wrote of the virtue of *magnanimity* or "greatness of soul": the magnanimous person "seems to be the one who thinks of himself worthy of great things and is really worthy of them," that is, who deserves to be honored for behaving honorably.[10] Military historian and ethicist Paul Robinson emphasizes that both aspects of honor are present in Aristotle's conception of magnanimity, which

> appears at first sight to be entirely concerned with external honour. It describes a disposition of character which makes the magnanimous man seek the praise of others, without carrying this trait to excess. However, the magnanimous man seeks the acclaim of others not for its own sake but because of the self-respect this external validation gives him. External honour makes him feel, internally, that he is a man of worth.[11]

Some would object to the motivation provided by external honors in Aristotle's definition of magnanimity, especially in passages such as "it would not fit a magnanimous person to run away, swinging his arms, or to do injustice. For what goal will make him do shameful actions, when none is great to him?"[12] To focus so much on praise and rewards seems to diminish the value of one's internal honor itself, since virtue ethicists (and Kant) stress that the motivation for good acts should derive from the fact that they're good acts, not that they result in good consequences (especially for the one performing them!).

According to sociologist Charles E. Cooley, the two sides of honor are inextricably linked because ethical rules and codes ultimately come from a person's community and are reinforced by that community when it grants honors:

> One's honor, as he feels it, and his honor in the sense of honorable repute, as he conceives it to exist in the minds of others whose opinions he cares for, are two aspects of the same thing. No one can permanently maintain a standard of honor if he does not conceive of some other mind or minds as sharing and corroborating this standard.[13]

This is consistent with the emphasis on honor codes and honor groups in the scholarly literature: think of codes of honor in the military ranks, chivalry among the knights of Arthurian legend, and even the code of *omerta* among members of organized crime organizations. These are rules that the members of these groups internalize not simply because of personal integrity, but because the other members of the group expect it of them and stand ready to enforce it. Solidarity, camaraderie, and brotherhood often play a stronger role than personal adherence to ethics in maintaining codes of honor among honor groups such as these.

But this doesn't apply well to Captain America because his sense of honor, as described in the comics, does not depend on the behavior or ethics of those around him. Cap is portrayed as a lone wolf; as the Scarlet Witch thought to herself about him, early in their time as fellow Avengers, "he endures so much … yet walks alone."[14] True, throughout his life he has been a member of the US military, SHIELD, and the Avengers, each of which has its own code of conduct and expectations of its members. But it is hard to imagine Captain America deriving his sense of honor from any of these groups; the content of his character, while having been influenced by the ethics of the men, women, and organizations he worked with over the years, does not depend on any of them.

In fact, it is often said in the comics that Steve Rogers was chosen to be Captain America based on the strength of character he displayed as a young man. In a recent adventure, his foe Machinesmith depowered Cap, reducing him physically to the scrawny kid he was before the super-soldier serum.

That gave Cap occasion to remember getting beaten by neighborhood kids when he was young and how it affected him:

> Machinesmith thinks I've already lost. Thinking I'm that weak little kid I once was. But he's made a big mistake ... see, those beatings ... and that scared, skinny, sickly little Steve Rogers ... that was where the man I became was really born. Not in the fires of war. Not in a secret government lab. But inside a sense of justice.[15]

When, in 1941, a newly minted Captain America met President Franklin Delano Roosevelt for the first time, he was surprised to find his idol in a wheelchair (a fact kept from the wider public at the time to preserve their confidence in their president). As FDR told him, "physical strength isn't an important part of being a leader. Courage and integrity are. You have those in spades. I know the kind of life you've led, Private Rogers. You became Captain America long before they pumped you full of any chemicals."[16]

There aren't many tales of Steve Rogers in his childhood, but those that exist focus on the crucial role his mother and his working-class upbringing played in crafting his character. In one such story, a neighborhood bully named Hutch helped Steve steal from a local store to pay the rent. When his mother wondered where he got the money, Steve told her, "I ... I've been working a new job. ... I promise, I'll do whatever it takes." She easily saw through this, and told him:

> Not whatever it takes, Steve. I don't know where you got this money, but ... You listen to me. Your father let his circumstances change him from a good man to a weak one. You promise me you'll never do the same, Steve. You promise me no matter what you'll be a good and honorable man, no matter the circumstances. It would kill me to see these hard times change you. You are a good person, Steve ... promise me you'll always keep that intact.[17]

When she said "keep that intact" she was imploring her son to maintain his integrity as a "good person" in the face of adversity—something Cap still lives by today, not because it's expected of him as a soldier or an Avenger, but because the man who is Steve Rogers expects it of himself.

This is not to say, however, that Captain America has no regard for bestowing honors—just not on himself. He's very careful to honor his fellow heroes, whether soldiers, Avengers, or civilians, who sacrificed themselves or otherwise behaved with honor. As Captain America sees it, honoring others is a show of respect and acknowledgment for those who have earned it, which he never fails to do (as we mentioned in the last chapter when we discussed humility). The examples are legion, especially ones of Cap honoring his fellow soldiers who gave their lives during World War II and later conflicts, including those from France and Russia, and even Germans who acted honorably and respectfully towards American soldiers.[18] This is not to downplay the sacrifices of civilians; Cap simply feels a special remorse for fallen soldiers due to his survivor's guilt, made sharper due to both his special abilities and the bravery of regular soldiers despite their lack of them. Of course, this holds doubly true with regard to Bucky, whom Cap was able finally to give a military funeral decades after his death when he located Bucky's long-lost sister Rebecca. "Because so much of our work was done in secret, Bucky was never properly honored for his contribution," Cap said. "Something that's bothered me to this day."[19]

Captain America also shows particular concern for minorities who may not have been honored properly because of prejudice and bigotry; in the previous chapter we discussed Cap's relief at hearing that all the astronauts lost in the 1986 Challenger explosion, including women and an African-American man, were honored, as well as his reaction to learning about Isaiah Bradley's mistreatment by the US government.[20] In an emotional story from 1994, Steve Rogers stood alone in the rain beside a priest at a funeral for Clarence "Biz" Duckett, an African-American baseball player who joined the Army when World War II started and endured the same discrimination there that he faced in the segregated baseball leagues. Assigned to laundry detail, he discovered Steve Rogers' secret when he opened the wrong locker in the barracks. Soon thereafter, he suffered a brutal beating by mysterious agents who wanted his secret, until Captain America came to his rescue. While defending Duckett's grave from racists who wanted to desecrate it, Rogers remembered Duckett's reaction to being saved from the thugs by Cap:

> Biz was grateful. He called his rescuer a symbol for America. But his rescuer thought of himself as only a soldier doing his duty. The genuine symbol of America was Biz—his loyalty and bravery. Even if no one could know. That's why I'm here to honor him. Biz never received any medals. There's no funeral with military honors. But that doesn't make him any less of a hero.[21]

While Cap honored all who served, he went out of his way to make sure those who were overlooked—such as Duckett, Bradley, and Bucky, each in his own way—were honored, even if decades after the fact.[22]

The importance to Cap of giving external honors to others is also shown by his habit of saluting military personnel (including his commander-in-chief, the president of the United States). The salute is an outward sign of respect, initiated by the junior person to his or her superior, also signifying the common bond of service and sacrifice for one's country.[23] Saluting is also a way for Captain America to show that he maintains his own integrity and honor even when he disagrees with orders he's given, such as when he salutes the president after he strips Cap of his title.[24] Even though "Captain" America's actual military status is questionable—he himself says on several occasion that he is no longer military personnel—he still adheres to this practice for all of the reasons above.[25]

Personally, I find it most poignant when Captain America salutes a fallen comrade, such as at the funerals of Bucky and Duckett, or one injured in the line of battle, such as Sergeant Bryan Anderson, who lost both legs and an arm in Iraq (but still lifted what remained of his right arm to return Cap's salute).[26] He salutes at military gravesites, such as when he visits Arlington National Cemetery in Virginia (including the John F. Kennedy Memorial Flame) and the Vietnam Veterans Memorial in Washington, DC, soon after he was found in the ice by the Avengers.[27] Cap also extends this sign of respect to fallen comrades outside the military, such as Jeff Mace, the World War II-era hero known as Patriot who served as the second post-war replacement for Captain America (after William Naslund, originally the Spirit of '76).[28] Cap also saluted as the ship carrying the corpse of Drax the Destroyer—an ally who was killed by his daughter, the Avenger named Moondragon—flew into space and exploded, saying "we commend the body of this brave warrior to the vastness of space! Drax—may you rest, at long last, in peace!"[29] Captain America gives salute to honor those who served their causes with honor, regardless of the nature of the cause (as long as it was just) or whom they served, because "any good soldier—no matter your friend or enemy—is truly a brother in arms."[30]

Before we move on to internal honor, we should say a word about the dark side of external honor. While external honor is granted based on adherence to an accepted social code, there is no way to guarantee that this social code is noble, admirable, or ethical according to broader standards. Societies whose honor codes allow and even encourage the subjugation and mistreatment of minorities to preserve the "honor" of the majority provide a particularly heinous example of this. For example, the racists who attempted to desecrate Duckett's grave may have felt they were preserving the honor of the white soldiers buried nearby, but this does not justify their actions, which violate important standards of morality outside their narrow (and narrow-minded) community. This negative aspect of honor societies, which are nothing but a façade to hide the immoral and exploitative practices underneath, can be presumed to account for much of the neglect of the concept of honor in modern scholarship.

This negative side of external honor is made even worse by the steps that people have taken to "reclaim" their honor, including hurting or killing those they hold responsible (correctly or not) for their loss of respect and esteem. Throughout his long years as the Sentinel of Liberty, Captain America has fought plenty of individuals who were devoted to their own code of honor and willing to sacrifice for it—but even more willing to hurt or kill others for it as well. For example, one young man who was driven over the edge by the bombing of the Murrah building in Oklahoma City (which killed his girlfriend) was deemed psychologically unfit for military service, but submitted to an experimental treatment involving cybernetics and drugs to serve the US military as a covert agent—in a Captain America costume, no less. Not aware of his origins, SHIELD called him "the Anti-Cap," and as Agent Ali Morales tells Cap when he objects to the name, "he's you. Only, without the messy scruples or moral center."[31] True to his name, the Anti-Cap serves the American government with no regard to the core American principles the real Cap embodies, and will take any steps necessary to protect what he sees as the nation's interests.

At the conclusion of their long battle, the Anti-Cap asks how the things he's done—such as killing the royal family of Baud Olan, a wealthy (and fictional) Arab country that harbored terrorists—were any different from Cap's killing Nazis during World War II. "The Nazis conquered Europe with a gun," Cap replied. "The Olans conquered the planet with a check book. You don't shoot people for that." Anti-Cap cited the horrendous human rights abuses in Baud Olan: "a woman who is raped, there, is likely to be beaten by her family and thrown out into the street" (which could be described as a honor-driven act).[32] "These are the people you are defending?" Anti-Cap asked, to which Cap answered, "Defending human rights abuses? Never. But imposing American values by murder isn't the answer, either!"[33] It's one thing to believe strongly in a cause, as both Cap and Anti-Cap do, but it is another thing to believe that your cause justifies any and all actions to promote it. Such an "end-justifies-the-means" approach raises your cause to an absolute status, and as we'll see later in this book, there are no absolutes in this world of moral conflict. Killing for "honor"—whatever that may mean to the people who do it—gives honor itself a bad name.[34]

Internal Honor as Integrity

As I hope the last section made clear, Cap never shies away from honoring others for their accomplishments and sacrifices in the name of heroism. But as we saw earlier in the section on humility, he is uncomfortable being honored for what he does. He recognizes the value of the external sense of honor when it comes to other people, but not for himself. As far as he's concerned, he is the only judge of his virtue—and also the strictest one, as we see from the incredible pressure he puts on himself. In terms of his own behavior, Captain America clearly adheres to the internal sense of honor, with little if any role for external honors for himself; rather, he provides himself all the motivation he needs. As philosopher William Lad Sessions puts it, this kind of honor is "intrinsically, sufficiently and effectively motivating."[35]

But we still have to determine what the internal sense of honor itself is. It turns out it's easier to understand what it means to honor someone than what we're honoring them for! For our purposes, let's consider internal honor to be similar to *integrity*, another sort of "super-virtue" in that it ties other, more specific virtues together and ensures that a person exercises them consistently and in line with his or her moral character. (Since the internal sense of honor is the one I'm linking more closely with Captain America, I'll just say "honor" from now on, unless I have to distinguish it from the external sense of honor.) Sociologist and philosopher Peter Olsthoorn gives three examples of honor related to integrity:

1) The West Point credo "duty, honor, country" and the West Point Honor code (a cadet will not lie, cheat, or steal, nor tolerate those who do): Olsthoorn writes that "honor at West Point is synonymous with integrity; the cadet adheres to the code because he accepts it, not because he is concerned about what others might think of him when he breaches it."[36]
2) Richard A. Gabriel's definition, "the ability to recognize moral dilemmas and to have the integrity and strength of character to act upon one's perception."[37]
3) Ted Westhusing's definition, "constancy, harmony, and refinement of the natural virtues of greatness of mind and extended benevolence."[38]

As Olsthoorn writes, "all three definitions see honor as an internally felt duty, not as something with an important external component," which he then goes on in his article to contrast with external honor as motivation.[39]

Of course, asking "what is honor?" and answering "integrity" doesn't answer the question as much as shift it to "OK, then ... what's integrity?" In her cleverly titled paper "Integrity," philosopher Lynne McFall distinguishes between two popular understandings of integrity.[40] The first is integrity as coherence, such as when engineers talk about the integrity of a structure (such as a building or a bridge). A person has integrity in this sense if her principles, values, and beliefs hold together and if she sticks to them. But this conception of integrity seems formal and empty: as McFall points out, a person with a singular focus on experiencing pleasure can have this kind of integrity, but we would be hesitant to use the term to describe her. Integrity seems to require more than mere consistency of principles: those principles need to *mean* something. To have integrity in a more meaningful sense—certainly any sense that matches with honor—it has to mean something ethical. The Red Skull may have integrity in the more limited sense of consistency, but not in the same way we would say that Captain America has integrity.

To get to the bottom of these two meanings, McFall defines integrity in a way that reconciles them: sticking to one's deeply held principles even in the face of temptation.[41] You'll recall from chapter 1 that principles serve to limit the pursuit of outcomes in favor of doing what's right. As the narration in one story read, referring to the concept of heroism young Steve Rogers grew up with,

> When he was a boy, heroes stood for something more than victory; more than triumph at any cost. A hero was a man of moral fiber; a man who would not see one innocent soul sacrificed if there was any alternative ... and, to Captain America, there is always an alternative![42]

Cap wants to defeat the Red Skull, but will not do so "at any cost"—as we have seen, he often criticizes Iron Man for being too quick to compromise his principles. Cap won't sacrifice innocent lives, he won't break his own word, and most important he won't kill—even the Red Skull himself—to beat his oldest foe. By holding to his core principles even when he's tempted to break them (and for good reason), Cap maintains his integrity (and, understood this way, his honor). As we will see later, this picture has gotten murkier of late, but I argue that Cap's integrity still holds even if its nature has evolved.

The Red Skull is certainly consistent in his desire to destroy America, its ideals of liberty and equality, and its living symbol, Captain America.

Furthermore, there is nothing he won't do in pursuit of that goal. In other words, he observes no limiting principles: he'll do whatever it takes to get what he wants. If the Skull has integrity, it's in the simplistic sense that an animal or small child has integrity, since there is only one guiding idea to "integrate," such as getting food or shelter. The Skull wants to destroy America, pure and simple, and will do whatever it takes to achieve that goal. In contrast, Cap wants to protect America just as strongly as the Red Skull wants to destroy it, *but* there are lines he will not cross, actions he will not take, in order to do it. Cap must integrate his goals with his principles consistently over time; to the extent he is successful, he has integrity in the more meaningful sense.

This doesn't mean that everyone has to agree with Cap's goals or his principles—you can say a person has integrity even if you disagree with him or her. But, as McFall writes, "when we grant integrity to a person ... we must at least recognize [his or her principles] as ones a reasonable person might take to be of great importance and ones that a reasonable person might be tempted to sacrifice to some lesser yet still recognizable goods."[43] So even if the Red Skull did recognize principles that limited his tyrannical goals—as more "honorable" villains like Magneto and Doctor Doom do— we still might not regard him as having integrity because we do not recognize his motivating principles and goals as ones that a reasonable—or reasonably *ethical*—person would pursue. Most of us, however, would agree that Captain America's principles (and virtues) do make him eligible for integrity, even if we may not agree with his precise interpretation of them or how he acts in observance of them in every case. (This brand of reasonable moral disagreement will come up in our later discussion of judgment and political disagreement as well.)

We can easily take the requirements of integrity too far, however. For example, integrity doesn't mean people can never change their minds or the way they integrate their goals and principles over time. Just think about politicians who "flip-flop" on big issues such as civil rights, abortion, or torture, who are often accused of lacking integrity. Consider two politicians who do this: one who changed her mind over the course of twenty years in public service, and another who expressed contrasting views two months ago before declaring his candidacy. We would be more likely to doubt the second politician's integrity, given the abrupt nature of his "epiphany" on certain issues that "coincidentally" mean a lot to certain voting blocs, and more willing to credit the first politician's change in opinion to adapting flexible mindset that adapts to new experiences. Integrity doesn't mean a person can't change, but we are more understanding of a change in the nature of a person's integrity if it seems organic and reasonable rather than self-serving and opportunistic.

If this sounds familiar, it's because we used similar language when we discussed character and its consistency over time back in chapter 2. Character is closely related to integrity, since it can be understood as the way a person integrates her goals and principles, as well as how well she lives up to that particular combination. When politicians flip-flop, we often say they lack character—they have no consistent beliefs and positions that we can identify them with over time—and we would say the same about anybody who compromises his or her principles in pursuit of goals. By the same token, a fictional character only has true "character" to the extent he or she is written consistently, with few "mistakes" on the part of creators that would make us doubt their integrity, in both the weak sense of coherence as well as the stronger moral sense of adhering to principles.

Principle and Compromise

In one of their earliest adventures together, Iron Man told Captain America, "I applaud your devotion to your principles."[44] Ironically, however, Iron Man and Cap clashed over the importance and proper role of principles in decision-making throughout their time together in the Avengers, not just during the Civil War but many times before and after.[45] The way in which Captain America most clearly shows his integrity is the way he incorporates his principles into his character. We see this not just in how he follows his principles despite great cost and risk to himself, but also when his judgment forces him to violate them, which he does only with tremendous regret.

First and foremost among Captain America's core principles is the protection of life. As the back cover to an issue of *Avengers* read:

> Always considered a living legend, Captain America has long been seen as the cornerstone of the Avengers. His strict moral code has guided the Avengers throughout their many incarnations, and could be considered the foundation of the Avengers' code of honor. First and foremost in this code of honor is the time-tested commandment, "Avengers do not kill."[46]

While most heroes usually find ways to beat the bad guys and save the day without killing, the Avengers are often involved in situations that can be compared to war, and in such cases Cap often has his hands full enforcing this code.

For example, during the Galactic Storm event, a war between two alien races, the Kree and the Shi'ar, Cap struggled to keep his fellow Avengers from resorting to extreme force against their enemies. For example, he was upset that Sersi threatened to destroy a Shi'ar vessel and its crew; when Hank Pym later dismissed any ethical concerns about their behavior in the conflict, Cap warned him of the slippery slope to which such a line of thinking could lead.[47] Later, Cap ordered the Black Knight not to kill, saying "the day I countenance a move like that is the day I leave the Avengers!"[48] Despite these efforts, Cap failed to stop Iron Man from leading an "execution squad" to kill the Supreme Intelligence (the leader of the Kree).[49] Afterwards, Steve and Tony had a heated ethical debate back home at the Laughing Horse Bar, during which they argued over principles and consequences. Tony nailed it when he said that Steve doesn't believe the ends justify the means—especially when they violate principles that Steve holds dear, and principles he believes the Avengers should hold to well.[50]

Years later, Captain America became aware of the Illuminati, a secret team made up of the smartest heroes in the Marvel Universe—including Iron Man, of course—who joined together to anticipate and manipulate large-scale events (like the Civil War).[51] As Hawkeye told Spider-Man about Cap's likely reaction to this discovery, "it flies in the face of everything he holds dear," especially since Steve Rogers was head of world security at the time he found out—a position from which he defended Iron Man after he failed during his tenure in the position (including letting Norman Osborn take over).[52] In this particular adventure, the Illuminati lost the Infinity Gems, a set of multicolored stones that are incredibly powerful individually but of nearly infinite power when joined together. After getting them back from the person who had stolen them, Cap and Iron Man argued over why the Illuminati had gathered and hidden the Gems in the first place. "Yes, we took the damn Infinity Gems," said Iron Man,

> and we did so because we thought they were safe with us. It was arrogance and it was ego. And it was absolutely right. For all this time. So, though you may think it's your job to judge me and the others for what we did here ... I think it's nothing. Nothing compared to the things we've had to do to keep the world safe. Nothing.

Rogers simply replied, "Maybe I just don't see the world the same way you do."[53]

While this episode with the Illuminati and the Infinity Gems did not involve the direct loss of life, Captain America was still concerned that Tony and the rest of them had neglected the related principle of preventing catastrophic risk when taking on the responsibility of hiding and protecting the Gems. The situation was far more drastic and immediate when, more recently, the Illuminati—including Captain America, who joined after the previous episode—became aware of a series of "incursions," Earths from other dimensions threatening to collide with their own. A mysterious woman named the Black Swan used alien technology to destroy the last alternate Earth, but when Reed Richards started to explain how to use it themselves, Cap was quick to interrupt:

> Let me stop this conversation right here. We are going to handle this exactly like we normally would. We will prepare, gather intelligence, and when the next episode occurs, use that information to figure out a way to win. Because that's what we do.[54]

Reed argued that there wasn't time to look for "nonexistent" answers before the next incursion, and Tony urged that they keep all options on the table, to which Cap responded, "Anthony … what the hell is wrong with you?" He cautioned against succumbing to "necessary evil" too quickly and the slippery slope that such thinking can lead to (as he did during the Galactic Storm), and then proposed using the Infinity Gems to stop the other Earths.[55]

At the next sign of an incursion, Captain America himself wielded the Infinity Gauntlet containing the Gems, and with his incredible willpower behind them he managed to repel the other Earth. But they lost the Gems themselves, leaving the Illuminati with no way to combat the next incursion. Before they reconvened, Cap told his longtime friend and ally the Black Panther,

> the way things are going in there … where the discussion is headed … exploring all avenues … keeping our options open … they're going to do it. They are going to talk themselves into compromising what we're supposed to believe in for expediency. Just because we're desperate, and just because it's easy. It's wrong. I'm not going to just sit there and watch it happen. I can't.[56]

Later, in front of the whole group, Cap argued that they should adhere to their principle of protecting life, urging them not to stop looking for an alternative solution before resorting to destroying another world.

At the end of the argument, Cap says,

> I know you people. You're going to build a machine or some kind of weapon
> without thinking if you should—just because you might need it. And then
> the debate will turn from should we build this, to under what doomsday
> scenarios is it acceptable to use the thing? And then slowly, one by one, you'll
> convince yourselves. We're doing this for the right reasons. There's no other
> choice. It's the lesser of two evils. Isn't that right, brother?[57]

The last part was targeted at Tony Stark, who then apologized to Steve and
promised to make "it" right before he signaled to Doctor Strange to erase
Cap's memories of the entire episode—an event of which, while I write this,
we have yet to see the ramifications. (But I don't think it will be pretty.)

Of course, Captain America lives up to the principle of protecting life in
his own heroic career, not simply when interacting with (and lecturing to)
Iron Man and other superheroes. Cap refuses to kill even his greatest
enemies, such as when the Red Skull made him relive a hellish apocalyptic
vision of the future over and over again, a future that could be prevented only
if Cap ended the Skull's life. Sharon implored Cap to take this necessary step,
but Cap refused, saying "taking a life is always the last resort. I won't accept
that there's not another way."[58] In another story, when the artificial intelligence Machinesmith tricked Cap into killing him, Cap immediately
regretted it, thinking, "I'll never stop believing that life is something most
sacred, something to be sacrificed only for that greatest of causes … liberty!"[59] And when he *is* forced to take a life, such as when he had to shoot a
terrorist ULTIMATUM agent to stop him from firing a rifle into a packed
cathedral, Cap tortured himself about it afterwards, promising to "avenge
him—and my honor!"[60] Even in cases such as this, when Cap has to take
one life to save many more, he still wishes he could have found another
solution or planned better; even if he has no choice in the situation as it
was, he blames himself "for not preventing such a situation from arising."[61]
(We'll talk about this incident much more when we discuss judgment and
compromise later.)

Another one of Captain America's core principles is the idea of "fair play,"
which is often considered an important component of honor. An honorable
warrior observes certain rules of engagement in combat, such as the code of
chivalry among medieval knights, the code of *bushido* among the samurai
of Japan, and the ideals formalized in the Geneva conventions in the
modern day.[62] In sports as well, an honorable athlete observes not only the

official rules of the game but the unofficial rules of sportsmanship too.[63] We also expect political candidates to engage in fair debate by staying on topic and not lowering themselves to personal attacks. Fair play is a form of respect, demanding that people acknowledge each other's moral equality and mutual observance of the rules that govern their interactions. It has many purposes, such as ensuring that the "winner" in a given situation will prevail due to skill and merit rather than deception or trickery, and trying to avoid excessive damage or loss of life (especially in political debate!).

Over the years, Captain America has shown an extraordinary dedication to playing fair, including observing rules of engagement, showing mercy to prisoners, and keeping his word. Often it's "the little things," such as when he called Namor the Sub-Mariner, then fighting against Cap during the epic recent battle between the Avengers and the X-Men, to talk. When Namor showed up, he said, "I'm happy to see this was not a trap," to which Cap replied, "I would never do that to you."[64] Other times it's more significant: in World War II, Cap adhered closely to the official rules of engagement and Geneva conventions when dealing with enemy soldiers who surrendered and were taken as prisoners of war. As he reminds his German counterpart, the Geneva conventions depend on reciprocity, each side promising to treat the other side's soldiers with humanity, but it has to go both ways.[65] Obviously, Cap demands the same fair play from his colleagues as from his enemies: for example, he stopped Iron Man from killing the Molecule Man, citing the latter's rights and the importance of due process, and he also stopped a Skrull from killing a prisoner because the Avengers promised mercy to those who surrender.[66] He even looked askance at Hawkeye when he rigged a bet to defeat the Grandmaster, and later warned Thor during an Avengers baseball game, "watch Hawkeye—he cheats."[67] No deviation from fair play is too small to escape the notice of Captain America!

Perhaps we can see Captain America's dedication to fair play even more clearly by looking at how deeply he regrets violating it. For example, as he says, "I hate using something as underhanded as" hidden gas bombs, and also "feels strange sneaking away from any kind of fight" as opposed to retreating openly.[68] During a battle against a yacht full of female supervillains, Cap was forced to come to aid of the mercenary Paladin: "customarily I don't attack from behind—but with her fingers around Paladin's throat—the customary rules of engagement may be bent a bit!"[69] When fighting Flag-Smasher and his fanatical group ULTIMATUM, who demanded Cap's surrender at risk of hostages' lives, Cap infiltrated them in disguise, thinking "I'm not particularly proud of having to use these terrorists' guerrilla tactics—but 110 lives are at stake! With so little time left before the deadline, I can't waste any time fighting fair!"[70] This shows that honorable conduct is important, but has to bow to the greater principle of protecting lives. Nonetheless, Cap's regret is palpable: "I can't believe Flag-Smasher's pushed me this far! Every second that goes by I'm forced to compromise my ideas of fighting fair!"

More generally, we see in Cap's struggles with fair play that, as with all moral ideals, there are no absolutes, and compromises sometimes have to be made. For instance, after breaking into ULTIMATUM's secret base, Cap threatened to break a guard's hand to get him to talk, but the guard didn't buy it, saying "We've all been briefed on you, Captain America! You are far too honorable to torture for information! You do not frighten me!" After knocking the guard out, Cap thought to himself:

These terrorists play by different rules than the average criminal I face. How am I supposed to get information out of people who'd sooner throw their life away than betray their cockamamie cause? This joker had me pegged all right. I'm not willing to stoop to their level in order to win. My code of ethics won't permit me.

Yet, we've seen that sometimes he does engage in behavior that he's not proud of. His next thought after subduing the guard was, "if I'm going to pull this caper off, I'm going to have to rely on subterfuge and surprise"—after which he donned the guard's uniform as a disguise. Cap wasn't comfortable with this, but he recognized that the alternative was allowing ULTIMATUM to carry out their threats of killing over a hundred people. Perhaps if he had more time to think of an alternate plan, he could have found a way to defeat the terrorists without resorting to spy tactics that he found dishonorable. But time was running out, and Cap had to make a decision between the lesser of two evils, a concept he abhors but a reality he nonetheless must face—especially when he was forced to kill the ULTIMATUM gunman to stop him from massacring the hostages in the cathedral.

While he cannot adhere to fair play at all times, Captain America shows great sophistication in his decision-making regarding when he must compromise it—and also when he turns the concept on its head. For example, when the Champion challenged the combined membership of the Avengers and the Squadron Supreme (a group of superheroes from another dimension) to stop him before he could detonate a gigantic bomb, he warned them that any attempt to contact anyone else would trigger the device. The heroes failed to stop the Champion, but Firestar (a rookie Avenger) found a way to get a message to Giant-Man, who defused the device before the Champion could set it off. The Champion was outraged (understandably), and accused the Avengers of cheating, but as Cap told him, "We never agreed to your conditions, Champion—we simply did what you forced us to do. We played your deranged game—but we played by our rules, not yours."[71] Rules of engagement and fair play in general are based on reciprocity *and* prior consent; as the Champion found out, you can't force someone to play your game and expect them to adhere to your rules out of the goodness of their hearts!

As you might expect, Captain America's sense of fair play was never tested more than it was during the Civil War, such as when SHIELD tried to capture Captain America after he refused to back registration. He defeated a squadron of SHIELD agents, but as he raised his shield to defeat the final one, the agent removed his helmet, revealing the face of Dum Dum Dugan, one of Nick Fury's Howling Commandos alongside whom Cap fought in World War II. "They sent a friend," Cap thought to himself. "Three thousand agents of SHIELD on active duty, and they sent a friend. Dirty pool. I'll remember that."[72] Next, Cap used Dugan's communicator to call into SHIELD, faking Dugan's voice to report that Cap was killed, throwing SHIELD off his scent for a while. "Should take them ten minutes to figure it out. Five more to figure out which way I went. Hopefully, ten more minutes deciding if this entire trick is beneath me." He returned "dirty pool" with same, but still regretted it: "They should have left me in the ice. I'd be a hero."[73]

What's more, both Captain America and Iron Man resorted to "subterfuge and surprise" in their efforts to get the drop on the other. For example, Iron Man faked a news report of a chemical plant disaster (at a facility owned by Tony Stark) to lure Cap's team into an ambush. When Cap agreed to talk and shook hands with Iron Man, he planted an electron scrambler on Tony's armor which disabled it and started the fight anew.[74] Nonetheless, when Iron Man later invited Cap to meet in the ruins of the original Avenger Mansion to talk for real, Tony said he was worried Cap might think it was a trap (again), but Cap said "No. You wouldn't. Not here."[75] Near the end of the conflict, Tony once more summoned Cap to a "conventional military parley" to ask him if he had anything to do with the attack on Tony's best friend Happy Hogan. Cap promised no one on his side had anything to do with it, and "if they did, I'd put a bow on him and hand-deliver him to your penthouse," a sign of honor in itself (disciplining one's own personnel for improper actions against the enemy).[76] But before they could talk anymore, several members of Cap's team came to his "rescue," upsetting Cap, who adhered to basic rules of engagement better than his team did.

All this talk of compromise—and there is more to come later—may be unexpected in a book about Captain America. Recall Cap's speech to Iron Man after his surrender at the end of Civil War, in which he said, "We maintained the principles we swore to defend and protect. You sold your principles. … You know compromise."[77] One thing would seem clear from the last fifty years of comics: Captain America doesn't compromise. We saw at the start of this chapter that Spider-Man regards Cap as the one hero who would never betray his convictions. When Cap accepted the surrendered German soldier as a prisoner of war, one of his troops accused Cap of compromising the mission, to which Cap replied, "better than compromising my principles."[78] When a US cabinet secretary told Nick Fury that Cap compromised a mission by taking responsibility on national TV for inadvertently killing a terrorist, Fury responded, "Compromise? First time I've heard any kind of damn fool accuse Cap of that."[79] Even when many Americans wanted Cap to run for president, he explained that politics necessarily involves compromise, whereas his job is to represent and fight for the ideal (the American dream).[80] This shows that, while Cap chooses to be a symbol of principle, he also acknowledges that compromise is necessary in some circumstances and in some positions—just not his, at least as much as he can avoid it.

In an ideal world, no one would have to compromise his or her principles in any circumstance, but unfortunately we do not live in an ideal world. Neither does Captain America, whom Iron Man (of course) has accused of being "an idealist in a world that is far from ideal."[81] As we'll see when we discuss judgment, when Cap does find himself in a position where he feels he has to compromise his principles, it doesn't mean his core principles have changed—instead, he balances several of them to arrive at a solution that favors the more important principle in the given situation and compromises the less important ones. This makes for fascinating storytelling, especially in terms of a character such as Captain America who will go to great lengths not to compromise *any* principles. But at times he does have to, and during the first episode with the Illuminati and the Infinity Gems, Iron Man identifies why this bothers Cap so much:

> I think you're more mad at you than you are at me. We've made hard choices in our lives. This life that we've chosen—this life—it comes with insane

choices that we have to make every day. Compromises that we have to make every day. And I don't think you like some of yours.[82]

In fact, after the Avengers recovered the Infinity Gems, Cap joined the Illuminati in safeguarding them—after Iron Man claimed to have destroyed them—becoming complicit in their deception of the rest of the heroes.[83]

We'll look at Cap's compromises in more detail in the next chapter when we discuss judgment, which is necessary to settle conflicts of principles. For now, it is enough to realize that, even though Cap has to compromise on occasion, the fact that he struggles so hard with it shows that it runs counter to every fiber of his being. Cap's strong sense of honor is demonstrated by how he stands by his principles and resists compromising them, and that he does this to maintain his own character and moral code. Whether you call it honor or integrity, this kind of internal cohesion of character is something we can all strive towards with our own goals, beliefs, and principles.

Duty and Sacrifice (Again)

Principles, like virtues, are abstract ideals that can guide action in a general way but can be difficult to put into practice. For this reason, Captain America often thinks of principles in the form of duties, both in general terms ("doing my duty") and specific terms (such as duties to do certain things for certain people at certain times). One way to think about duty is as a way to *operationalize* principles and put them in terms of action or inaction ("thou shalt" or "thou shalt not"). Furthermore, duty is closely related to responsibility, which itself is based on basic principles such as honesty and loyalty. To Cap, following duty is just another way of maintaining principles, doing the right thing, and being true to himself, all of which come back to integrity and honor.

Perhaps Captain America's greatest duty is to serve his country as the sentinel of liberty and the living embodiment of its ideals. In the story mentioned earlier in this chapter in which Cap considered running for president of the United States, he remembered one of his schoolteachers, Mrs. Crosley, and her lessons on duty. Mrs. Crosley explained to her class that the freedoms Americans enjoy come with responsibilities: "It's the duty of each one of you to see that the land stays free ... to see that justice is extended to all! ... I have faith that you will come to the aid of your country when duty calls. I pray that you do the right thing … the brave thing." Cap then thought to himself, "We all have our duties to fulfill. I knew that when I first put on this uniform—and it's never been truer than it is today!"[84] Later he made a speech to the country about compromise and politics, and explained that his duty is to protect the American dream without compromise (as much as he can). His duty is not simply to serve at all but rather to serve in the best way he can—just as, he remembers, Mrs. Crosley served in the best way she could, as a teacher who inspired her students.

People such as Captain America who emphasize duty often describe it as a "calling," not a choice they deliberated over and weighed the costs and benefits of before making. When a reporter for *Stars and Stripes* (a newspaper that reports on the US military) interviewed Cap en route to an early Avengers mission, he asked him why Cap continued to fight after giving more than his fair share to his country. Cap answered, simply, "I don't see that I have a choice." After the mission, Cap spoke for all the Avengers when he told a TV reporter that "facing death is part of our job, ma'am. … We do this for the simplest of reasons … because it's the right thing to do."[85] More recently, when on a mission with Quentin Quire, a young X-Man with an attitude reminiscent of Hawkeye in his early years, Cap explained why he joined Project Rebirth: "I'd just had my fill of the injustices I'd seen. People wielding powers that I knew they shouldn't have. What I did—the path that was laid out before me—it wasn't the best or the smartest choice, no. It was simply the only one."[86]

Steve Rogers recently faced this "choice" again after his former sidekick Bucky Barnes apparently died during his time as Captain America. The long passage from his conversation with Sharon Carter that I quoted in the previous chapter contained phrases such as "I never wanted to be Captain America," "I did what my country asked of me," and "I just wanted to serve," all expressions of dutifulness and sacrifice.[87] After setting up a fake Cap to fail on the job in order to nudge Rogers in the right direction, Nick Fury asked him,

> So what's the deal? Have you really changed, Rogers? 'Cause I don't think you have. I mean, you may be good at being me for a while … but you don't have the constitution for it long-term. Your president's calling on you. The Steve Rogers I know wouldn't be able to turn his back on that. Not for long.[88]

Nick knew his old friend far too well to imagine he'd ever be able to resist the call to duty—and he was right. (He usually is!)

It wasn't Steve Rogers' duty simply to answer his president's call, however, for he'd refused his government's orders before—his true duty went far deeper than that. Around the same time as Nick Fury played his little game, Private Wally Young, a vet whom Cap and Bucky saved during World War II, told Rogers over a game of chess that "people are scared now … more than they've been since we were kids. So it strikes me that this is exactly the time we could use a Captain America. Someone who'll rise above the noise and politics … and let them know there's someone on their side."[89] As Rogers said at the end of an earlier episode when he had abandoned the Captain America identity, only to see his untrained and inexperienced replacement get hurt, "there has to be somebody who'll fight for the dream, against any foe … somebody who'll do the job I started right! And God knows I can't let anybody else run the risk that job entails for me!"[90] Ultimately, Cap's duty is to the American people, to protect the American dream and make it the American reality for all.

Of course, Captain America's duty often involves sacrifice, as we discussed in the previous chapter. Like many heroes, both in the real world as well as fiction, Cap risks his life out of duty, but he goes farther in the sense that he often gives up having a life outside of being a superhero. Cap made numerous attempts to reclaim a private life for Steve Rogers, including his first attempt at early retirement after Sharon Carter turned down his wedding proposal (out of her own sense of duty to SHIELD), which prompted the thought, "I've sacrificed everything—in the name of duty! But I'll do it no longer! The next battle I fight—as Captain America— will be—my last!"[91] This "retirement" lasted all of one issue; he faked his own death not long after, this time to convince the world Steve Rogers was dead and protect those close to him, but he came back as Cap two issues later.[92]

As the narration in a later issue read, "there are two sides to Steve Rogers: his personal life … and his duty. His duty always takes precedence!"[93] Also, recall the line quoted in the previous chapter from a yet later episode: "the conflict between my duty to the nation and the semblance of normal life got to be too great. I finally had to drop the trappings of normalcy, and give myself fully to my mission."[94] Even his periodic attempts to become a professional artist, his passion since he was a boy, have to bow to his duty to his country: in the same issue in which he thought to himself, "I've learned that Steve Rogers can take the mask off when he wants to," and landed a job with an ad agency, he heard a report of supervillain activity on the radio and had to abandon his assignment to don the red-white-and-blues, realizing that "my duty to my country comes first, no matter what the cost!"[95] Of course, Steve Rogers also had a responsibility to his employer once he had a job—a responsibility he did not dismiss but rather saw as secondary to his responsibility as a superhero.

No sacrifice Captain America makes for the sake of duty is more poignant than love. Again, it is common for superheroes to forgo romantic relationships out of fear of putting people they care about in harm's way, but no one takes this more seriously than Captain America. Even though Sharon Carter was actually first to reject a life with Cap for the sake of duty, Cap "returned the favor" in spades for years to come. Just several issues after Steve's proposal and his (momentary) retirement, Cap and Sharon were reunited. Falling into each other's arms, Cap asked, "then—what of us? Can we even dare to hope that there still may be a life for us together?" Sharon started to answer, "We each have our duty—," but Cap interjected, "Why is duty such a jealous master? Can it never share the heart with love?"[96] Later, when Sharon tried to get Cap to quit, he responded with the groovy line, "this is my bag ... I've got to stay in it!"[97] Sharon then challenged Cap's bravery: "You haven't got the courage to choose between your uniform—and our happiness!" Cap replied, this time in the language of principle rather than duty, "it isn't a matter of courage! The issue is dedication! Is it wrong to stick to a principle? My dedication to what I do is as strong as my love for you!"[98] To Cap, the question was one of self-interest versus duty, and for him that answer is a simple one: it will be duty every time.

Sharon Carter appeared to die not long after that, another death of someone close to him that Cap carried with him until he discovered many years later that she was alive.[99] As Cap admitted to her then, they've "been the most on-again, off-again couple ever," though it has been more "on" since then, especially since Steve seems to have reconciled himself to being Captain America (as we described earlier).[100] While Sharon was "dead" (actually on a secret SHIELD mission), Steve was involved in a few significant relationships, most notably with glass-blower-turned-lawyer Bernie Rosenthal, a neighbor in Steve Rogers' building. But even while he got to know Bernie, Steve's past continued to haunt him; as a narration box under a despondent Steve Rogers read, "since Sharon's death, he's been understandably reticent about matters of the heart."[101] This reticence stopped him from opening up to Bernie (and later love interests as well).[102] When Bernie proposed to Steve (after she learned about his dual identity), she mocked his fear of the horrible risk he would be imposing on her:

> You can stop right there! I know the whole routine! Don't you think I read comic books when I was a kid? "Oh darling," the hero would sigh, "I cannot marry you for fear of what my arch-enemy, Hairless Harry, might do to you if he found out!" I didn't buy it then, and I don't buy it now! It's bull![103]

She argued that every marriage involves risk and then shamed him into taking this one: "Why don't you do what you do best: Be a hero. Marry me."[104]

Steve accepted, but our lovely couple would not live "happily ever after." Steve had worries even before the proposal, and not merely about Bernie's safety. He thought to himself, "She grounds me. Just being with her makes me believe Steve Rogers can exist without Captain America. And perhaps that's what's really scaring me."[105] As much as he lamented the fact that he could not live separate lives, to some extent he was afraid of what doing so would mean for him in both of his identities and roles, even if only because being Steve Rogers for once would be new and unexplored territory. Ironically, Bernie was the one to break off the engagement and the relationship, enrolling in law school in Wisconsin for fear of getting too wrapped up in Cap's life. In the end, it turned out that she feared losing her own sense of self in Captain America just as much as Steve did![106]

His relationship with Bernie wasn't the last one to be doomed because of his overwhelming sense of duty and issues with his identity. Connie Ferrari, another lawyer, couldn't deal with his secrecy and the fact that Steve's "job as Captain America is what comes first."[107] During their break-up, she asked him one question before declaring their relationship over for good: "When you think of yourself, your daily life, who you are and what you do … do you picture yourself as Steve Rogers or Captain America?"[108] You can guess the answer, and it won't surprise you to know that it spelled the end of that relationship.

Our story isn't over, though! His last words with Connie, together with an earlier chat with Sam Wilson (otherwise known as the Falcon) while on a fishing trip, resulted in an epiphany for Steve. He rushed to find Sharon Carter (remember her?) and told her:

> I was wrong. Trying to be two people when I'm only one. It's almost like I tried to maintain two lives to such a degree—that I thought Cap needed one relationship while Steve Rogers needed another. I couldn't be more stupid.[109]

In the next issue, he submitted to a SHIELD truth serum to reveal to her that "it's not like there's two of me. There's just ... me. Powerful as this symbol is ... it's a uniform. Beneath it—I'm still the same man."[110]

Captain America and Sharon kissed but decided not to resume their relationship—and later in the same issue Cap received a call about a long-lost unexploded nuclear device in New Jersey.[111] (We got it all here in Jersey, folks.) Nick Fury tried to tell him that a bomb squad would handle it, but Cap claimed it was his duty: "why put those men at risk when I can just do it myself?" When he arrived at the town—purchased by the US government and then blocked by environmental groups from further development—he discovered it was full of ex-Nazis in Red Skull masks who overwhelmed Cap (who, even as they ganged up on him, said "please, I don't want to hurt you!"). After he was bound, the false Skulls told Cap of their plans to detonate the device, killing themselves and Cap, and leaving only his shield in the debris to let Americans know that their champion failed them. Cap got loose and hurled the device into the air where it exploded, killing everybody in the area—and neither Cap's body nor his shield were found.[112] For the time being, Captain America was presumed dead, having sacrificed his life out of duty, maintaining his integrity to the end, and demonstrating true honor.

Even though we have discussed honor, integrity, principle, and duty separately, it's hard to separate them completely; when you get to the bottom of it, they're simply different ways to describe the "right thing to do." The honorable person does what is right, and by doing so that person maintains his or her moral integrity (or character) through balancing the various principles and duties that apply in a given situation. Finding this balance, however, is not simple—definitely not "black-and-white"—and requires *judgment*, the topic of our next chapter.

Notes

1 *Daredevil*, vol. 1, #233 (1986).
2 *Avengers*, vol. 3, #63 (2003). For more on these two scenes (including artwork) and their connection to Cicero's writings on public speaking, see my 2011 blog post "'A voice that could command a god': Captain America and the Stoics" at *The Comics Professor* (www.comicsprofessor.com/2011/04/a-voice-that-could-command-a-god-captain-america-and-the-stoics.html).
3 *Iron Man*, vol. 1, #172 (1983).

4   Note that the passage also highlights that Cap's righteousness "stops short of self-righteousness," suggesting that Cap strikes the golden mean with that particular characteristic. (Nice.)
5   *Siege* #4 (2010).
6   *Amazing Spider-Man* #537 (2006).
7   *X-Men vs. Avengers* #4 (1987). (Not to be confused with the more recent *Avengers Vs. X-Men* event, of course.)
8   For a similar experience when writing about honor, see Kwame Anthony Appiah's preface to his book *The Honor Code: How Moral Revolutions Happen* (New York, NY: W.W. Norton, 2010).
9   *Thor*, vol. 1, #390 (1988).
10 Aristotle, *Nicomachean Ethics*, translated by Terence Irwin (Indianapolis, IN: Hackett, 1985), 1123b1.
11 Paul Robinson, "Magnanimity and Integrity as Military Virtues," *Journal of Military Ethics* 6 (2007): 259–269, at 261.
12 Aristotle, *Nicomachean Ethics*, 1123b30.
13 C.H. Cooley, *Human Nature and the Social Order* (New York, NY: Charles Scribner, 1922), p. 184 (quoted in Peter Olsthoorn, "Honor as a Motive for Making Sacrifices," *Journal of Military Ethics* 4 (2005): 183–197, at 185.)
14 *Avengers*, vol. 1, #26 (1966).
15 *Steve Rogers, Super-Soldier* #3 (2010).
16 *Captain America: Sentinel of Liberty* #7 (1999), "An Ending."
17 *Captain America*, vol. 7, #4 (2013); the death of Steve's mother is shown in *Captain America: Sentinel of Liberty* #7 (1999), "An Ending," during which she tells him, "your life is always going to a difficult one, but don't let that harden your heart. A hard life can be a good life, as long as you always do what you can to help others. Never forget that."
18 For example, in *Captain America*, vol. 3, #42 (2001), he said how proud he was to fight alongside Russian soldiers, and in *Captain America*, vol. 3, #50 (2002), "Keep in Mind," he traveled to Paris to visit the graves of French soldiers alongside whom he fought. In *Captain America: Theater of War: A Brother in Arms* (2009) he paid tribute to his fellow US soldiers as well as the captured German medic who helped patch up wounded American soldiers after being captured. Finally, in *Captain America*, vol. 5, #3 (2005), he told Sharon how upset he gets when people doubt the bravery of the French, who "never gave up fighting." This stands in stark contrast to the Ultimate Universe version of Captain America, who famously pointed to the "A" on his forehead and asked, "You think this letter on my head stands for France?" (*Ultimates*, vol. 1, #12, 2003), which many fans suspect led Ed Brubaker to write the line praising the French forces mentioned above.
19 *Captain America*, vol. 3, #48 (2001). This, of course, was before Cap realized that Bucky was kept alive as the Winter Soldier by the Russians.

20   *Captain America: Man Out of Time* #3 (2011); *Truth: Red, White & Black* #6–7 (2003).
21   *Captain America Annual*, vol. 1, #13 (1994), "Symbols."
22   As it happens, I'm writing this section on Memorial Day, and a story was published today about a female World War II pilot, Marie Michell, who is only now receiving military honors ("Female WWII Pilot Gets Posthumous Honors," Associated Press, May 28, 2013, www.armytimes.com/article/20130528/NEWS/305280014/Female-WWII-pilot-gets-posthumous-honors).
23   For more on the salute as a part of military decorum and its basis in Stoic thought, see Nancy Sherman, *Stoic Warriors: The Ancient Philosophy Behind the Military Mind* (Oxford: Oxford University Press, 2005), p. 48.
24   *Captain America*, vol. 1, #450 (1996). He did salute to Sharon Carter a few issues later (*Captain America*, vol. 1, #454, 1996), though more to signal that their relationship at that point was one of respect rather than love.
25   In *Captain America*, vol. 1, #450 (1996), after he left the president, Cap told a general, "even though I'm 'Captain,' I'm not a soldier, really—I serve the American dream, not the military or government." Again, in *Captain America*, vol. 4, #4 (2002), a lieutenant saluted him, and after returning the salute Cap said, "I'm not an officer," to which the lieutenant responded, "we know who you are, sir." Even if Steve Rogers does not officially hold the rank of captain, he seems to have earned the respect that comes with it; for example, see the incident cited at the beginning of this chapter from *Avengers*, vol. 3, #63 (2003).
26   *Captain America: Theater of War: To Soldier On* (2009).
27   *Avengers: Earth's Mightiest Heroes*, vol. 1, #3 (2005); see also *Captain America: Man Out of Time* #4 (2011) for a similar trip of observance and remembrance.
28   Mace died in *Captain America*, vol. 1, #285 (1983); for more on Mace, see the *Captain America: Patriot* (2011) trade paperback collecting the 2010 miniseries written by Karl Kesel and illustrated by Mitch Breitweiser. Also, Bucky and the new Patriot (Elijah Bradley) discuss Mace's legacy in *Young Avengers Presents* #1 (2008), from which we'll draw in chapter 6 when we discuss the nature of patriotism.
29   *Avengers*, vol. 1, #220 (1982). Drax has since gotten better, and is currently a member of the Guardians of the Galaxy (in the comics and the movie).
30   *Captain America Theater of War: A Brother in Arms* (2009).
31   *Captain America and the Falcon* #3 (2004).
32   For more on honor-driven acts against women for losing their virginity—voluntarily or not—see Appiah, *The Honor Code*, chapter 4.
33   *Captain America and the Falcon* #14 (2005).
34   For more on the dark side of honor (and related defenses of positive honor), see William Lad Sessions, *Honor for Us: A Philosophical Analysis, Interpretation and Defense* (New York, NY: Bloomsbury, 2010), chapter 11.

35 Sessions, *Honor for Us*, pp. 33–34.

36 Olsthoorn, "Honor as a Motive for Making Sacrifices," p. 184.

37 Richard A. Gabriel, *To Serve with Honor: A Treatise on Military Ethics and the Way of the Soldier* (Westport, CT: Greenwood Press, 1982), p. 157.

38 Ted Westhusing, "A Beguiling Military Virtue: Honor," *Journal of Military Ethics* 2 (2003): 195–212, at 195.

39 Olsthoorn, "Honor as a Motive for Making Sacrifices," p. 184.

40 Lynne McFall, "Integrity," *Ethics* 98 (1987): 5–20. For other perspectives on integrity, see Damian Cox, Marguerite La Caze, and Michael Levine, "Integrity," *Stanford Encyclopedia of Philosophy* (http://plato.stanford.edu/entries/integrity/).

41 McFall, "Integrity," p. 9.

42 *Captain America*, vol. 1, #268 (1982). There is subtext to this bit of narration: earlier in the issue, Steve Rogers and Bernie Rosenthal (whom we'll meet later in the chapter) saw the 1981 film *Raiders of the Lost Ark*, and Steve found Indiana Jones lacking in heroism and "essentially amoral."

43 McFall, "Integrity," p. 11.

44 *Captain America: Sentinel of Liberty* #6 (1999), "Iron Will."

45 As Iron Man said after one argument about how far he was willing to go to reclaim his stolen technology (during the "Armor Wars"), "I promise you this Steve, when I have finished what I have to do, I'll look you up and we'll have a long talk about ethics" (*Captain America*, vol. 1, #341, 1988). That they have, time and time again!

46 *Avengers*, vol. 1, #366 (1993).

47 *Avengers*, vol. 1, #345 (1992).

48 *Avengers*, vol. 1, #346 (1992).

49 *Avengers*, vol. 1, #347 (1992).

50 *Captain America*, vol. 1, #401 (1992).

51 For more on the Illuminati, see *New Avengers: Illuminati*, vol. 1, #1 (2006) and the 2008 trade paperback *New Avengers: Illuminati*, collecting *New Avengers: Illuminati*, vol. 2, #1–5 (2007–2008), written by Brian Michael Bendis and Brian Reed and illustrated by Jim Cheung and Mark Morales (with several other inkers). (Steve Rogers and the rest of the Avengers discover the existence of the Illuminati at the end of *Avengers*, vol. 4, #8, 2011.)

52 *Avengers*, vol. 4, #9 (2011).

53 *Avengers*, vol. 4, #10 (2011). Cap actually addressed the arrogance of the super-hero years earlier when he thought to himself, "in our job, arrogance is occasionally hard to define. Some would call us arrogant to think we can make a difference in the world … but I've always believed that the line is defined in just how we go about making that difference" (*Iron Man/Captain America Annual 1998*).

54 *New Avengers*, vol. 3, #2 (2013).

55 Ibid.
56 *New Avengers*, vol. 3, #3 (2013). Unfortunately, he starts with the line, "I know I'm locked into seeing things as black and white … that's just who I am." It's one thing for others in the Marvel Universe (and ours) to describe Cap this way but another thing entirely for Cap to say this himself—a characterization with which I disagree, having argued throughout this book that Cap's thinking cannot and should not be characterized as black-and-white, especially by him.
57 Ibid. See the discussion of tragic dilemmas in the next chapter for more on the threat the Illuminati faced here.
58 *Captain America*, vol. 3, #17 (1999). (This "Red Skull" was revealed later to be Korvac, a time-traveling, all-powerful, would-be benevolent dictator.)
59 *Captain America*, vol. 1, #249 (1980).
60 *Captain America*, vol. 1, #321 (1986). As we mentioned when we discussed mistakes and interpretation in chapter 2, Cap claimed in *Captain America*, vol. 1, #322 (1986) that he had "never taken another person's life. Until three hours ago," echoing what he told the Punisher (a gun-happy vigilante) in *Captain America*, vol. 1, #241 (1980): "I've never willingly taken a life and I never will." In the real world, a firestorm erupted in the letters columns (because there was no Internet then—imagine that) about Cap's combat experience and the improbability that he never killed during the war. This also triggered writer Ed Brubaker's comments on the issue (see the end of chapter 2), as well as a snide comment from Wolverine in *Avengers: Endless Wartime* (2013) when Cap said the two were nothing alike: "Not a killer, you mean? That's what you're trying to say? You were in World War Two. Don't tell me you never killed nobody." (Wolverine's the best at what he does, but apparently that doesn't include proper grammar!)
61 *Captain America*, vol. 1, #322 (1986). Cap also refuses to let a foe die if he can prevent it: for example, as he saved the Green Skull (an eco-terrorist playing off a familiar villainous name), he thought to himself, "after three days fighting through his Amazonian eco-fortress—I've got a strong urge to leave him—but that's not the right thing. Today the right thing is a hard pledge" (*Captain America*, vol. 7, #1, 2013).
62 Rules of engagement and other means of reducing the human costs of war are one aspect of *just war theory* (in addition to the question of just war itself). For the seminal modern work in the area, see political philosopher Michael Walzer's *Just and Unjust Wars: A Moral Argument with Historical Illustrations*, 4th ed. (New York, NY: Basic Books, 1977/2006). For an explanation based on Stoicism of why rules of engagement sometimes fail to constrain behavior—using the example of the atrocities performed in Abu Ghraib prison—see Sherman, *Stoic Warriors*, pp. 172–178.
63 On honor in war and sport, see Sessions, *Honor for Us*, chapters 6 and 7.
64 *New Avengers*, vol. 2, #29 (2012). Comics fans know that Namor doesn't respect or like many people, but Cap is one of the few. Monica Rambeau (then going

by the name Captain Marvel) was amazed to see that Cap could calm down the hotheaded Sub-Mariner (*Avengers*, vol. 1, #268, 1986), and the rest of the Avengers were shocked when Namor threw a tirade in a meeting—only to stop when Cap entered the room. "Excuse me, Captain," he said, stepping aside from Cap's chair (*Avengers*, vol. 3, #59, 2002). According to Namor, Captain America is "worthy" (*Avengers*, vol. 1, #310, 1989). 'Nuff said!

65 *Captain America: Theater of War: A Brother in Arms* (2009).

66 *Avengers*, vol. 1, #216 (1982) (Iron Man); *Avengers*, vol. 1, #260 (1985) (Skrull).

67 *Avengers Annual*, vol. 1, #16 (1987). This may explain why Hawkeye is afraid to bluff in poker when playing against Cap: "It would take a braver man than this archer to bluff the living legend of World War II" (*Marvel Two-in-One* #75, 1981).

68 *Captain America*, vol. 1, #251 (1980); *Captain America*, vol. 1, #413 (1993).

69 *Captain America*, vol. 1, #390 (1991).

70 All of the quotes in the next two paragraphs are from *Captain America*, vol. 1, #321 (1986).

71 *Avengers/Squadron Supreme Annual 1998*.

72 *New Avengers*, vol. 1, #21 (2006).

73 Ibid.

74 *Civil War* #3 (2006).

75 *Iron Man/Captain America: Casualties of War* (2007).

76 *Iron Man*, vol. 4, #14 (2007).

77 *Civil War: The Confession* (2007).

78 *Captain America Theater of War: A Brother in Arms* (2009).

79 *Captain America*, vol. 4, #4 (2002). (The terrorist died from a kill-switch seconds before Cap "killed" him, but that didn't change the fact that Cap intended to take someone's life.)

80 *Captain America*, vol. 1, #250 (1980); we'll talk more about the conflict between principle and politics in chapter 6.

81 *Captain America*, vol. 1, #401 (1992).

82 *Avengers*, vol. 4, #10 (2011).

83 *Avengers*, vol. 4, #12 (2011).

84 *Captain America*, vol. 1, #250 (1980).

85 *Avengers: Earth's Mightiest Heroes*, vol. 1, #4 (2005). In *Captain America*, vol. 6, #19 (2012), Cap echoed this sentiment as he sat by the hospital bedside of William Burnside, the Captain America of the 1950s, and recounted his life: "I hadn't wanted to wear the flag and carry that burden ... I just wanted to do the right thing." But contrast this with *Mythos – Captain America* (2008), in which Steve Rogers met for his regular dinner with the Blue Spaders, his World War II squadron—even though only one remained—and said, "my brothers fought, not because it was their duty, but because it was right." While we tend to think of duty and right as the same things, perhaps Rogers meant that the Blue Spaders transcended their sense of obligation; it was still there, but they didn't need it to motivate them. But this is splitting hairs, I think.

86   *A+X* #4 (2013), "Captain America + Quentin Quire."
87   *Captain America*, vol. 5, #616 (2011), "Must There Be a Captain America?"
88   *Captain America*, vol. 5, #619 (2011). (The set-up appeared in *Captain America*, vol. 5, #615.1, 2011.)
89   *Captain America*, vol. 5, #616 (2011), "Must There Be a Captain America?"
90   *Captain America*, vol. 1, #183 (1975).
91   *Tales of Suspense*, vol. 1, #95 (1967), "A Time to Die—A Time to Live!" Did I mention Steve didn't even know Sharon's name at the time? He proposed to "Agent 13."
92   He seemed to die in *Captain America*, vol. 1, #111, followed by a tribute issue in *Captain America*, vol. 1, #112, and his shocking reappearance in *Captain America*, vol. 1, #113 (all from 1969). They just didn't know how to milk a high-profile comics death back then.
93   *Captain America*, vol. 1, #183 (1975).
94   *Captain America*, vol. 1, #325 (1987).
95   *Captain America*, vol. 1, #244 (1980). In a touching tale in *Avenging Spider-Man* #5 (2012), Peter Parker discovered some of Steve's old drawings and tried to inspire him to draw again—successfully.
96   *Captain America*, vol. 1, #100 (1968).
97   *Captain America*, vol. 1, #204 (1976).
98   *Captain America*, vol. 1, #206 (1977).
99   Sharon seemed to die in *Captain America*, vol. 1, #233 (1979), and Cap was shown footage that seemed to confirm her death in *Captain America*, vol. 1, #237 (1979). She didn't resurface until *Captain America*, vol. 1, #445 (1995).
100 *Captain America*, vol. 3, #50 (2002), "To the Core." For the most part Cap and Sharon were together from *Captain America*, vol. 5, #16 (2006)—except when Cap was "dead," of course—to Sharon's heroic death in *Captain America*, vol. 7, #10 (2013). They even served on Avengers teams together, most notably the first iteration of the Secret Avengers (*Secret Avengers*, vol. 1, #1–21, 2010–2012).
101 *Marvel Team-Up*, vol. 1, #128 (1983).
102 See *Captain America*, vol. 1, #270 (1982) for a poignant scene in which Bernie struggled with loving a man who she isn't sure loves her back (though, by the end of the issue, there is no doubt regarding Steve's feelings).
103 *Captain America*, vol. 1, #294 (1984).
104 Ibid. Sharon said a very similar thing upon *her* proposal in *Captain America*, vol. 7, #1 (2013), to which Steve thought, "She's right. I'm disappearing into the uniform. But marriage … might not be so bad."
105 *Captain America*, vol. 1, #286 (1983).
106 *Captain America*, vol. 1, #316–317 (1986). Bernie was not seen again until *Captain America*, vol. 1, #600 (2009) in a story titled "In Memorium" and written by her creator, Roger Stern, in which she described being at the courthouse the day Cap was "killed." After Steve returned from the "dead" and

Bucky was arrested when his past as the Winter Soldier is made public, Steve asked Bernie to defend Bucky in court (*Captain America*, vol. 5, #612, 2011, "The Trial of Captain America Part 2").

107 *Captain America*, vol. 3, #49 (2002).

108 Ibid.

109 Ibid.

110 *Captain America*, vol. 3, #50 (2002), "To the Core."

111 *Captain America*, vol. 3, #50 (2002), "Relics."

112 It seems that no explanation was given for his disappearance; according to *Captain America: Official Index to the Marvel Universe* (2011), "Cap shows up injured but alive" in *Avengers*, vol. 3, #45 (2001). In that issue, however, when General McGinty met Cap bandaged in a wheelchair, McGinty referred to him and his squad being injured in Siberia (where they spent the previous issue in battle).

5

Judgment

As we've seen in the last two chapters, virtues such as courage, humility, and even honor are important to have but too simplistic to practice without more guidance. It is never enough to say "be brave" or "act honorably," because these noble-sounding phrases don't tell anybody what *to do*. Furthermore, as we've seen, real-world situations are messy, bringing various virtues, principles, or duties into conflict with each other in ways that change with the specific circumstances a person finds himself or herself in. In other words, it is easy to say "be virtuous" or "do the right thing," but much more difficult to put that into action.

To help with that, a person—even a super-soldier like Cap—needs a special kind of virtue known as executive virtue, which helps a person put his or her virtuous character traits into action (or "execute" them). We have already discussed one executive virtue, perseverance, in chapter 3. Now we'll look at another executive virtue that Captain America exemplifies: the *judgment* he needs to arrive at the best action in a difficult situation. As Cap thought to himself during one of these situations, "[I] wonder if anyone realizes how hard it is figuring out what the right thing is … not to mention doing it!"[1] Despite his humility, Captain America exemplifies both sound judgment and unshakeable determination, which are often misunderstood as representing "black-and-white" ethics or stubbornness—but as we'll see, nothing could be farther from the truth.

The Virtues of Captain America: Modern-Day Lessons on Character from a World War II Superhero, First Edition. Mark D. White.

Making the Hard Decisions

Contrary to common belief, it's very easy to find examples of Captain America struggling with difficult decisions. "Cap may have trouble deciding how to do it," the Falcon once thought to himself as he watched his partner come to a decision and then swear to carry it out, "but he always knows what he wants to do!"[2] Another time, Cap thought to himself when considering retirement, "Never before have I had such a rough time making a clear decision."[3] And in front of the Avengers, when the entire universe seemed to disappear outside their headquarters, Cap admitted, "I don't want to sound like a quitter, but I have no idea how to deal with this!"[4] Statements such as these may come as a surprise because we assume that it would be easy for Cap to make decisions. After all, he has a strong sense of right and wrong based on the virtues and principles that are an essential part of his character. It would seem to follow that, in any given situation, he would just do the honorable thing, or the courageous thing, or the humble thing, depending on what the circumstances called for. But we know things are rarely that simple; the number of times we saw the word "compromise" in the previous chapter should make this obvious!

One choice that every superhero faces at one time or another is the one between saving lives and apprehending the villain, who often puts people in danger precisely to help him or her get away. (Villains may be evil but they're not stupid.) This basic crimefighting problem only gets more complicated when the lines between hero, villain, and victim become blurred. For example, sometimes the people that Cap needs to save are villains themselves, but he refuses to let anyone die "merely" to catch the bad guys. After freeing several members of the Serpent Society, Cap discovered they were poisoned by Madame Viper, so he had to decide whether to find the antidote or pursue Viper. "Once again forced to choose between saving lives or apprehending felons!" he thought before he asked where to find the antidote, having decided that saving the lives he could was more important.[5] And sometimes the "villain" to be apprehended is a friend, such as when Iron Man went rogue and Cap had decide whether to pursue him. "Where do my priorities lie?" he asked himself. "Would it be worthwhile to forgo all my other responsibilities in order to bring to justice one renegade Avenger on a misguided quest?"[6]

Cases like these are where judgment becomes essential. *Judgment* involves balancing the various virtues, duties, or principles at play in any situation—or, as the narration to one Cap story said, "principles, tempered by understanding, honed by reality."[7] The possibility of conflicting principles or moral rules on both sides of an issue makes ethical decision-making difficult and judgment essential. As Cap explained when resigning his superhero identity rather than serve as an agent of the US government (as required by a contractual agreement dating back to World War II), "My commitment to the ideals of this country is greater than my commitment to a 40-year-old document. I'm sorry, but that's the way it must be."[8]

Moral conflicts can be more mundane, also, such as when Steve Rogers failed to finish illustrating an advertising campaign because his duties as Cap pulled him away. "I try to be responsible in all aspects of my life," he told Bernie,

> but there come times when there are conflicting demands, and I can't do two things at once. Then I have to decide where my greater responsibility lies. Weighing human lives against a mere advertisement, the choice seems pretty clear. Still, I hate to let anyone down about anything.[9]

Even though Cap judged his duty to protect and save lives to be more important than his duty to keep a promise to his boss, both responsibilities were important to him. Just because he chose to act according to the first duty doesn't mean he rejected the other—he simply made a choice regarding which of two conflicting obligations was more important. As a man whose character is based on virtues, principles, and duties, none of which point clearly to one action in many circumstances, Cap faces numerous conflicts in his day-to-day life, few of which are simple to resolve.

How does Cap exercise judgment in these cases? Is there a higher principle or rule that can help him—and us—settle conflicts between more basic principles and rules? Even if there were, eventually that "metaprinciple" would come into conflict with another one, which would require ... well, you get the idea. As Immanuel Kant wrote when emphasizing the need for judgment to put the various duties implied by his moral theory into practice:

> although the understanding is certainly capable of being instructed and equipped through rules, the power of judgment is a special talent that cannot be taught but only practiced. Thus this is also what is specific to so-called mother-wit, the lack of which cannot be made good by any school.[10]

If we could simply apply simple rules of ethics to a moral problem like we apply the rules of arithmetic to a math problem, we wouldn't need judgment. But life is rarely this easy. Rules are sometimes too abstract to apply to real-life decisions, and there is often no rule to help solve conflicts of rules.

That's why we need judges in the law and referees in sports, two areas in which there seem to be countless rules, often written in very precise, legalistic language, but which still leave room for disagreement about the final outcome. The First Amendment to the US Constitution guarantees the right to free speech, but what counts as speech? Even if we could agree on that, the Constitution also guarantees freedom of religion, and what happens if one person's speech interferes with another person's exercise of his or her religion? Likewise, the rules of the National Football League specify many penalties, as well as what happens when there are offsetting penalties against both teams, but there will still be tough cases in which the rules alone cannot help a referee decide if pass interference or illegal contact occurred during a particular play. No matter how precisely rules are specified, at some point judgment will inevitably become necessary. So imagine what it's like for Cap and other superheroes, who have no guidebook of rules to follow as they go about their business, fighting supervillains and saving the world. Perhaps the Superhuman Registration Act contained some procedures and guidelines to help heroes make tough choices, but judgment would have been necessary nonetheless—even for lawyers like Jennifer Walters (She-Hulk) and Matt Murdock (Daredevil)!

We still haven't answered the question of how we're supposed to use judgment if there are no principles or rules to guide it—if it's nothing but intuition or "mother-wit." For this, we can borrow from legal philosopher Ronald Dworkin and his theory of judicial decision-making.[11] We met Dworkin in chapter 2 when we discussed how fictional characters should be written consistently over time by different creators, much as judges should make decisions consistent with past law, history, and tradition. In doing this, Dworkin wrote that judges decide cases based on principle, the fundamental ethical concepts that support a legal system, as opposed to policy, which is the proper domain of a democratically elected legislature. (We'll talk about this more in the next chapter.) But at the same time, he recognized that principles often conflict in specific cases, such as ones involving our First Amendment guarantees of freedom of speech and of religion, and to determine which principle (or right) is more important, we need to use judgment.

When the straightforward application of legal rules doesn't provide a clear answer, making it a "hard case" (in the technical legalese), Dworkin argued that a responsible and dutiful judge must balance all the principles that apply to the case in order find the "right answer." The right answer is the decision that is consistent with the history and philosophy of the legal system built up over years of written law and legal precedents. This is the part of his thought that applies to the consistent depiction of fictional characters: both are based on preserving integrity, either of a fictional character or a legal system. Balancing all the principles relevant to a particular case is a Herculean task, to be sure, and Dworkin realized this—not for nothing did he name his hypothetical ideal judge Hercules! Nonetheless, even human judges can do their best to find the right answer, the one they feel maintains the integrity of the legal system and contributes to the "seamless web" of the law (comprised of all of the written laws and judicial decisions over time).

This is what counts as legal judgment in Dworkin's terms. But what does that have to do with Cap, or *us* for that matter? For starters, Cap adheres to many of the same principles that US judges use. For instance, when Rick Jones came upon Cap reading the Avengers charter, Cap said,

> Been a while since I looked at it … "we dedicate ourselves to the establishment, growth and preservation of peace, liberty, equality and justice under law." Those words carry a lot of weight … I've based my entire adult life on the ideals found in these kinds of important documents. The Declaration of Independence … the U.S. Constitution … now this.[12]

Of course, the legal and political principles upon which the United States of America was founded have a particular importance to Captain America (as we'll see in the next chapter), but so do basic human virtues such as courage and integrity, which are important to everyone, as well as principles such as fair play and preserving life. And even though you and I don't have to deal with the entire body of legal texts and precedents like judges do, we deal with ethical principles, duties, and virtues that, just like similar concepts in the law, are general and often in conflict. Just like judges as Dworkin describes them, we can use our own judgment to find the "right answer" to each moral dilemma, the decision that is consistent with our own principles and maintains the integrity of our own moral character.

While this idea of judgment can be applied to any school of ethics, it has special relevance to virtue ethics because of its focus on integrity of character, the person you think you are and the person you strive to be. Whether we're real (like you and me) or fictional (like Cap and a handsome version of me), our decisions and actions help define our characters, which in turn influence our decisions and actions, in an ongoing cycle of reinforcement and gradual development.[13] Every judgment we make comes from who we are and contributes to who we become, so to maintain our integrity we should make decisions consistent with the type of person we aspire to be. When people say they have to be able to look at themselves in the mirror at the end of the day, this is what they mean. Do I recognize myself in this decision? Is this the decision I would like myself to make? That's an important part of the process of judgment we have to engage in when making a tough ethical decision.

Of course, a person might not always be 100 percent confident in the judgments he or she makes, and Cap is no exception. This is different from saying judgment itself is difficult, which we discussed at the beginning of the chapter; now we're talking about having doubts about a decision after you made it and acted on it. You might be thinking, "but we spent so much time talking about his determination and conviction in chapter 3—now you're saying Cap has doubts?" Yes I am, and the two statements are not mutually inconsistent, as we discussed before. When Cap makes a judgment call, he stands by his decision and carries it out. At the same time, he acknowledges that his decision may have been mistaken, such as when he let a drunken husband who threatened his family with a gun go free (which we discuss more below), or when he broke up a drug deal only to find out he ruined months of undercover work on the part of the police.[14] This reflects his humility, but nonetheless, he can't let that stand in the way of acting or else he would never do anything, always worried that he made the wrong choice.

Furthermore, no one realizes Cap should have doubts more than Cap himself! As we saw on chapter 3, when Steve Rogers, commercial artist, worked for Marvel Comics and was assigned to the *Captain America* title, he told his editor that he had some problems with the script he was assigned to draw. "Well, I realize I'm no expert," he said (wink, wink), "but in a few cases, it seems to me that the writer might have lost sight of Cap's basic character. I think Cap should occasionally have doubts about what he does."[15] Rogers recognized that it's in Cap's—which is to say *his*—basic character to doubt himself. After all, he always pushes himself to be the best he can be, which necessarily involves examining past decisions in order to make better ones in the future.

Whose Right Answer?

This process of judgment leaves room for legitimate moral disagreement, a crucial aspect of a prospering civil society that we'll discuss later in this book. Two judges presiding over the same case may recognize the same principles at play, but nonetheless weigh them differently when arriving at their final decisions. Each judge has a unique understanding of our long legal and political history, which leads him or her to make a decision consistent with the way that judge sees the "seamless web." In the same way, people can disagree on a moral or political issue even if they acknowledge the same principles relevant to it. As Cap recognized about people and moral disagreement, "I think of the conflicts which arise because of their different versions of right and wrong."[16] More specifically, each person forms an opinion based on a balancing of the various relevant principles in a way that preserves the core aspects of his or her character, the personal values that run deeper than any ethical system of rules or formulas.

As the quote in the last paragraph suggests, Captain America certainly recognizes this problem of conflicting judgments and differences of opinion. In an early Avengers adventure, the team was confronted with multiple crises: Black Panther wanted to tackle organized crime families targeting schoolchildren, the Vision wanted to help Red Wolf address injustice against his fellow Native Americans, while Iron Man and Thor wanted to tackle the villainous group the Zodiac. Thor asserted "Aye! Howe'er just may be the Red Wolf's cause—it doth pale beside the menace of Zodiac!" but Cap asked him, "Who's to make that judgment, Thor? You? Iron Man? Or must each man weigh them both, in his own heart?"[17] At the time Cap was very concerned about the unity of the team, but in general he was right: each man (and woman) must indeed weigh all the principles at play in a situation for himself or herself and stand by the decision he or she makes. "I spoke of union before, T'Challa!" he told Black Panther and the rest of the team. "But now, I know there is something more important! And that something is—conviction!"[18] And so the Avengers went their separate ways, each following the dictates of his or her judgment—but not without some dramatic language, of course, such as Iron Man's concern that "we may have witnessed the beginning of the end of the Avengers!"[19]

If you've been reading this book from the beginning, you'll no doubt have noticed that Captain America and Iron Man have had "occasional" disagreements in their time together as Avengers. Certainly, both believe in the same basic principles of heroism, justice, and fairness, but they disagree on how to balance them, which in turn leads to different actions in pursuit of them. At times this has threatened their friendship (such as during the Civil War), while other times it ends with mutual understanding, as they recognize their differences but acknowledge what they share in common as well (such as their discussion following the Galactic Storm incident).[20] Whichever hero you happen to side with, both Cap and Iron Man maintain their integrity by adhering to the principles in which they believe and combining them in a way that is consistent with their individual characters.

Of course, Iron Man isn't the only person to disagree with Cap on matters of judgment; such ideological conflicts are almost as common in Cap's stories as physical ones! Sometimes they're blunt about it, such as when a Navy admiral told Cap, "you did what you thought was right, Cap. You were wrong, of course."[21] But in the best cases, the characters discuss why and what it means to disagree. For example, when Cap comes upon Nomad (Jack Monroe, the "Bucky" of the 1950s who later took up Steve Rogers' temporary identity) beating the voluminous Slug on a flaming yacht, he urged Nomad to help him get the villain into a lifeboat before the yacht exploded. Nomad argued that the Slug deserved to die and that there were other people on the yacht more worthy of being saved. After Nomad ran off, Cap thought to himself, "Nomad's decision angers me. But ... I guess I have to respect him for it. If there is more than one life at stake here—it is our responsibility to see to as many as possible."[22] Why did Cap disagree with Nomad, then, and stay with the Slug? Presumably because, while there may have been other people on the ship who needed saving, there was definitely one at Cap's feet—and an unconscious one at that (whereas the others may have gotten off the ship already). Both Nomad and Cap shared the principle of preserving life but set different priorities on which lives to save first and why.

A more serious challenge to Cap's judgment came from the Anti-Cap, the imitation Captain America we met in the previous chapter who broke loose from his Navy superiors to pursue his own idea of American interests with little regard for human lives. He shared the real Captain America's love for the United States but, unlike Cap, the Anti-Cap had little regard for the core values upon which it was founded. Rather than life and liberty, the Anti-Cap believed in "security first ... stridently, and preemptively—seek the enemy, engage the enemy, kill the enemy ... I admire your ideals, Captain. I really do. But they really don't work in this war."[23] During their first battle, the Anti-Cap questioned Cap's judgment regarding acting in opposition to the US government (a topic we'll explore further later in this book):

> How many times have you placed principle over orders? The ideal of America over the government of America? Or are you the only one who gets to do that? Do we get to defy our government in defense of our freedom only if we do it in a way you agree with? Where exactly is that line, Captain—and who gets to draw it? [24]

Both men were distrustful of politicians but had starkly different views of how to protect America in light of that, as well as their roles in doing so. As the Anti-Cap said to Cap, "you are a product of America's hope. I am the sum of America's fear."[25] Unlike Iron Man or the other Avengers, who share Cap's principles even if they disagree on how to balance them in particular situations, the Anti-Cap embraces a different set of principles, embodying a more isolationist, "us-versus-them" version of American power. As we'll see in the next chapter, Captain America has a more cosmopolitan vision of American ideals, believing that the founding principles of America should be applied to people around the world, not just in the United States itself.

Nonetheless, we can learn something from Anti-Cap's question: Cap uses his judgment to decide when American principles are more important than the American government, so why can't Anti-Cap do the same? This misses a critical point about judgment: we each make decisions that are consistent with our own moral characters and that we can defend to ourselves and others, but that doesn't mean everyone has to agree with them. Even if Cap agreed with Anti-Cap's perspective on protecting Americans, he may not agree with the way he balances it with other ideals—and there's no reason he should, since his method of balancing, based on his unique character, will differ. It's not that Cap denied Anti-Cap's right to make his own judgments, but simply that Cap disagreed with the judgments Anti-Cap made! As we've seen, Cap disagrees with a *lot* of people about how to be a hero, even those with core principles closer to his own (like Iron Man). But the Anti-Cap went too far and endangered lives, and at that point the two men had more than a simple difference of opinion: Cap regarded the Anti-Cap as dangerous and felt he had to stop him. However, remember that after defeating him, Cap refused to hand Anti-Cap over to the corrupt authorities who threatened to kill him as a failed experiment, showing Cap's unwavering dedication to protecting life—even if it meant he would likely face this enemy again (which he did).

Tragic Dilemmas and How to Avoid Them

While many decisions require judgment to translate general virtues into action or to reconcile conflicting principles to choose the more important one, there is a special category of situations that superheroes all too often find themselves in—if only because they make for the most compelling stories! Such choices are what philosophers call *tragic dilemmas*, moral conflicts from which, as we say, "it is impossible to emerge with clean hands." The simplest example of this is having to choose which of two people to save, as in the novel and movie *Sophie's Choice*, a choice often used by philosophers as the seminal tragic dilemma.[26] I don't think Captain America was in that story—I'll check on that—but writers have placed him in plenty of similar situations. For example, during a World War II-era adventure with Nick Fury and his Howling Commandos, the Red Skull captured Bucky and demanded that Cap hand over the Eye of Agamatto, an all-powerful mystical amulet, in exchange for Bucky's life. Cap knew that giving the Nazis such a powerful weapon was out of the question, but to refuse the Skull meant sacrificing his young partner, a tragic dilemma to be sure.[27] In general, most of the examples we've seen in which Cap had to compromise one principle to follow another can be seen as tragic dilemmas (albeit some more tragic than others), because some compromise is inevitable.

The nature of these choices explains why we often see Captain America struggling with them, both as he makes his decision and then when he has to live with the consequences afterwards. And more often than in "ordinary" moral conflicts, tragic dilemmas inevitably lead to regret. By definition, people who face tragic dilemmas must choose the lesser of two evils, and while they may be confident that they made the right decision, they still regret being forced to make the decision at all. Cap's decision to oppose the Superhuman Registration Act can be considered the result of a tragic dilemma: once the law was passed he couldn't support it out of principle, but to oppose it meant denying the will of the American people as expressed through their elected officials, as well as fighting many of his friends and colleagues in the superhero community. Either choice would have been made with regret: the only question is which choice would be less regrettable.

Captain America's regret over the Civil War was clear when journalists Ben Urich and Sally Floyd visited him in custody for an interview after his surrender. Urich asked him how much serious thought he put into the fight, or if it was simply a matter of pride. "Pride was never involved. I believe what I did was right," Cap answered. As he continued,

> If you know me at all, you'll know I'm a simple man at heart. I believe in the fundamental freedoms accorded us by our Constitution, Ben. I believe we have a right to bear arms, a right to defend and a right to choose. I have sworn an oath to defend America from external forces, and from within. If that means standing against my own government, rejecting a bogus law passed by my own superiors, then I suppose that's what it means. I now realize that while my intentions were correct and honorable, I could as easily have come to the table as Tony Stark or Reed Richards. I saw the possibility of a registration act as a basic violation of our rights as Americans. For that, I wish to apologize to the country I love.[28]

As I read him, he didn't apologize for his stance but the extent to which he pursued it; recall that his surrender came after civilians pointed out the carnage the heroes were creating in their wake.[29] Urich then asked Cap why he hadn't come to that conclusion sooner, to which Cap replied, "People only come to a conclusion after they examine all aspects of a problem, Ben. That's what happened here."[30] This highlights the evolving nature of judgment as more information becomes available or as circumstances change. (This evolution occurs over longer periods of time as well, as we'll see later in this chapter.) Cap regretted some of the choices he made in resisting registration and fighting his fellow heroes, even though he stood behind the basic principles that motivated those choices.

In a complex situation such as the Civil War, Captain America has many options available to him, but in other cases there are only two, such as in the tragic dilemma Cap faced in the case of the ULTIMATUM agent we mentioned in the previous chapter. Cap had infiltrated ULTIMATUM's secret base in disguise and soon discovered four of their agents in a cathedral full of innocent civilians. Cap disabled three of the agents but the last one started firing an automatic weapon into the crowd, so Cap shot him dead with the rifle he was carrying as part of his disguise. As the narration read, "it would take five seconds to reach the terrorist—and wrench the gun from his hands ... In that time scores of innocents would die. There's only one way to reach him faster"—which was to shoot him.[31]

This was as close to the seminal tragic dilemma as Captain America could likely face: kill a murderer or allow him to keep murdering innocent people. Most people would agree that Cap had no other choice: he did the only thing he could have done to save as many lives as he could.[32] But we know Cap better than that. He proceeded to torture himself over this event for several years (at least several years of comics), especially the next time he encountered ULTIMATUM, when he thought to himself, "the last time I fought this group of terrorists—I was forced to take one of their lives! The memory of that still churns me up!"[33] Immediately after the original incident, he justified his actions to himself:

> Every second I delayed might cost another life. I had no time to reach him, no weapon to throw at him. So I shot him with the gun that went with my disguise. ... Under the circumstances perhaps I had no choice. It was one life—his—against the many hostages he could have killed.[34]

But nonetheless, he ruminated that "killing is the ultimate violation of individual rights—the ultimate denial of freedom. ... I have never taken another person's life. Until three hours ago."[35]

It didn't help that Cap's status as a private citizen—at the time he was neither military nor SHIELD, according to SHIELD agent Jasper Sitwell—turned the killing into an international incident. Captain America took to the airwaves to explain his actions (and to express willingness to stand trial in Switzerland if necessary):

> It's true, I did take the life of that terrorist. I profoundly regret having done so, but at the time I could see no other way to save numerous lives without taking one myself. My attitude towards killing remains unchanged. I believe killing is morally wrong, and that my actions should not be condoned or sanctioned by anyone. ... What I ask of you is that you understand that I do not take lightly what I did, nor do I advocate murder as the solution to any problem. I also ask that you forgive me for letting you down.[36]

Nonetheless, the events of that day continued to gnaw at him, and his televised speech failed to convince the American people that he was the same Cap they thought they knew. In the next issue he burst into a warehouse, expecting to find smuggled high-tech weaponry, and instead finds a few young men playing soldier with submachine guns that were actually water pistols. When Cap ordered them to drop their weapons, one of them said to another, "Do what he says, Robbie—that's Captain America. He kills people!"[37] Then they justified their war games to Cap, saying they were just learning to fight and kill the enemy like Cap does. As he listened, Cap thought to himself, "how many times must I be reminded of my darkest hour? ... How long is that one incident going to haunt me? How long will the public throw that single indiscretion in my face?"[38] While Cap regretted what he did, he also resented other people for not accepting his explanation and plea for forgiveness—"or worse, they applaud it and want me to go around killing those whose views they disagree with!"[39]

Cap clearly understood that he had no other choice in the situation with ULTIMATUM, but his regret speaks to something deeper: having been in that difficult situation at all. As he thought to himself after justifying his actions, "still, I curse myself for not planning better—for not preventing such a situation from arising."[40] Ideally, Cap would prefer not to end up in situations in which he had to compromise his principles—he would rather avoid tragic dilemmas in the first place! For this reason, Cap often refuses to accept the options provided to him, as we saw in the previous chapter when we discussed the Illuminati's recent argument over how to deal with the global threat from other Earths.[41] He felt that once the others built a world-destroying machine to use "as a last resort," they would grow more and more comfortable with the idea of using it, until they had convinced themselves that using it was "the only option." Cap prefers never to accept an option as the only one if there are unacceptable costs to using it—especially the destruction of an entire planet.

Cap faced a more personal version of this when he learned that his old World War II sidekick Bucky Barnes, long thought dead, had in fact survived, was completely unaware of his original identity, and had been operating as the covert Soviet assassin the Winter Soldier.[42] Sharon Carter told Cap that the Winter Soldier was not the Bucky he knew, and tried to prepare Cap for the eventuality that he might have to take Bucky down. As Cap prepared to face his old comrade-in-arms, he thought about all of the people the Winter Solider had killed, but also realized that Bucky couldn't be blamed because he wasn't in control of his actions. Remembering a mission from 1944 in which he and Bucky faced US troops transformed into zombies by the Nazis, he thought to himself, "I know what Bucky would do in this situation. I know what he'd want ... he'd want me to do whatever it took to stop him. ... I can't believe I'm thinking that Sharon might be right. That I might have to—no. There has to be another way out."[43] As always, Cap refused to acknowledge the limited options that define a tragic dilemma.

In fact, you could say that this is the superhero's job, dismissing the "tragic" dilemma and finding a way out of the problem that involves neither "necessary evil." As Cap told the Illuminati: "I will not tolerate—I will not allow—any talk of the necessity of necessary evil. I have spent my life on that line and every time I've seen someone cross it, death and horror and shame was what followed. So I refuse to entertain it ... especially when we don't have to."[44] Cap said a similar thing after the mutant Avenger the Scarlet Witch lost control over her reality-warping powers, destroying Avengers Mansion and killing several Avengers, including Hawkeye and the Vision.[45] After the dust had settled and the Avengers had regrouped, they met with the X-Men to decide what to do about her. Wolverine and Emma Frost argued that the only option was to kill her before she wreaked more havoc, but Cap maintained that "there is always a way." Wolverine countered with "not always," but Cap stood firm: "Always!"[46]

I'd have to agree with Wolverine that there isn't always a way out of a tragic dilemma, and I suspect Captain America knows this too. But in his heart Cap has to believe there's a way out, if only to make sure he never stops looking for it while there's still a chance, *any* chance, to avoid a morally unacceptable decision.[47] Like he told the Illuminati, once you start to accept a compromise, you start to rationalize it as having been the obvious and only answer all along. But as long as you refuse to accept any compromise, you never stop looking for a better way out—and sometimes you might even find it. As Iron Man thought to himself during one Avengers battle (at the side of the ever-lovin' blue-eyed Thing), "Captain America seems to thrive on accomplishing the impossible!"[48] But actually, he doesn't do the impossible—he just keeps trying after everyone else has given up.

"Black-and-White" or Red, White, and Blue? When Judgment Evolves

As I've mentioned several times throughout this book, one of the most common misunderstandings about Captain America is that he engages in "black-and-white" ethical thinking, easily identifying the right and the wrong in any situation and quickly arriving at a solution that he resolutely follows through to the end. But it's hardly that simple, and Cap himself realizes this, though his awareness of it has changed. Long ago, he would say things such as "the world has moved on without me! Right and wrong aren't black and white anymore! Everything is grey and hazy!"[49] But another comment Cap made not long thereafter reveals that his impressions of the past are much more sophisticated than that.

After Cap and Nomad broke up a domestic disturbance in which a drunk husband held a gun on his family, the wife pled with Cap not to turn her husband in, citing his frustration at not being able to find work and looking for solace in a bottle. After telling the wife that she or her husband can call him at Avengers Mansion anytime, Cap and Nomad left without turning the husband into the police. Nomad told Cap that "things sure seem to be more complex than they were in the 50s ... back then, we would've taken the guy in, sob story or no!" Cap replied, "the world's not really more complex, Jack. We've just stopped looking at things in black and white terms."[50] When the husband went on a shooting spree later the next day, however, Cap wondered if Jack's old-fashioned black-and-white thinking would have prevented it. But in the end he decided that acting with compassion was the better choice, and that he would do the same thing again—a difficult and controversial judgment call, about which Cap nonetheless had doubts, asking himself, "where do the answers lie, Cap? Where?"[51]

As the years went by, Captain America would further revise his thinking about the "good ol' days" when right and wrong were easy to tell apart. In a dark 2002 storyline that took place in the jungles of Colombia, a young sergeant argued with Cap about duty, fear, and perseverance. "Take a look around, Captain!" Sgt. Solo said. "We don't live in a black-and-white movie anymore! It might've been easy to do the right thing back in your times, but this is a different world! A hard one!" Cap replied, "You are mistaken, Sergeant Solo. It's never been easy. Always choices, always pressures. The world has always been hard."[52] Writer Roger Stern confirmed this in his own way in his introduction to the trade paperback of his classic run on *Captain America* with penciller John Byrne. After researching the period in which Steve Rogers grew up, Stern wrote,

> I soon rediscovered why Cap was able to function so easily in today's world ... he had grown up in an era of economic upheaval and government corruption, in a time when political and religious demagogues used the airwaves to increase their personal power and wealth. When Cap came out of suspended animation and rejoined the world after his decades-long sleep, things hadn't really changed that much.[53]

In another interview years later, Stern wrote that "Steve is a patriot and an idealist, but he's no starry-eyed fool. As he grew up, he saw corruption, bigotry, and hypocrisy first hand—none of that is new or unique."[54] In the end, it's not that times were simpler "back in the day," implying that Cap's ethics are out-of-date now. The truth is that things haven't changed much at all, and if Cap's way of seeing the world worked then, we have every reason to believe it will still work now.

Let's not be too quick to ditch the concept of "black-and-white" thinking altogether, however. There are some aspects of Cap's ethics, aspects I've taken great pains to emphasize and promote in these pages, which can justifiably be called "black-and-white": namely the basic virtues and principles that Captain America holds dear and which make up his character. In one story, a Navy admiral ridiculed Captain America's "moral absolutes," which Cap later discussed with *Daily Bugle* editor-in-chief Robbie Robertson, saying "Admiral Westbrook called me a 'horrible' liberal because I believe in moral absolutes. Good and evil. Right and wrong. An uncomplicated man in a complex world." Robertson's reply was very wise:

> And Pepsi used to cost a nickel. Steve—when we stop caring, we sin. When we stop feeling—we're dead. Somewhere between the two extremes are these little lines we draw so we can occasionally sleep at night. Don't stop caring. Don't stop feeling. But draw the lines. Just do what you do, Steve. In your own way and in your own time and for your own reasons.

Cap appreciated that boost, and when he proclaimed, "Robbie—there *are* moral absolutes," Robertson agreed, "you betcha. Never doubt that."[55]

In other words, Captain America's basic principles may be black-and-white, picking out right from wrong and good from evil. But these principles alone do not determine his actions, for there are often several right or good things to do in any situation, and many times these options have aspects or consequences that are wrong or bad. Cap needs to use judgment to decide which principle, duty, or virtue is the one he should pursue in any given situation—and this judgment is hardly black and white, not in the 1940s and not now.

Of course, "black-and-white" is not the only way people criticize Captain America's moral code; many choose to play the "old man Steve" angle as well. Many people have told Captain America that his "quaint Pearl Harbor values" (as the Anti-Cap called them) don't work today.[56] The Red Skull—who normally has such nice things to say about Cap—regularly taunted him, saying things such as "Can't you see? You're an anachronism! You belong in the dead past! The world has no more use for idealism!"[57] Madame Hydra, after capturing Cap and other Avengers, told him, "you don't belong here. You never did. This is why your ways don't work. You're a round peg in a square hole."[58] And sometimes even his fellow heroes say these things also. As they abandoned the anti-registration fight during the Civil War, Nighthawk (a former member of the Defenders) told Stature (a Young

Avenger) that Cap's "just another old man afraid of the future."[59] Rogue, an X-Man who joined Cap's "unity squad" of Avengers, called him an "antique with a God complex" who puts "his prehistoric morality ahead of saving the world."[60] Even the Vision, longtime fellow Avenger and usually a voice of calm, calculated reason, told Cap, "you are a man out of time … 1940s solutions will not work for today's problems!"[61]

Of course, the Captain America we know couldn't care less what other people say about his ethics: he knows all too well that he is a "man out of time" and he is a proud idealist.[62] Nonetheless, in some ways, Cap's behavior and the decisions, especially (as written) in the last two decades, suggest that his ethical judgment has been changing in substantial ways, as if in response to these criticisms.[63] For example, while Cap long steadfastly opposed killing, not only refusing to do it himself but also stopping his fellow heroes from crossing that line, more recently he seems to have become more comfortable with other people doing dirty work for him.

In a flashback to one of Cap and Sharon Carter's first cases together—after they had developed feelings for each other but before learning each other's real names[64]—they were pursuing renegade SHIELD Agent 9, whose photographic memory had made him a high-level threat to national security. Sharon received a termination order for Agent 9 addressed to Cap from the president of the United States, but she didn't give it to him immediately. When Cap found it, she told him she was planning to carry it out rather than put him in the position of having to violate his principle of not taking a life:

> You've never hesitated to do whatever your country has asked of you. For as long as anyone can remember, you've been a perfect soldier … but never an assassin. You don't kill—not in cold blood. When I saw that you were suddenly being asked to choose between duty and conscience … I decided to spare you the burden.
>
> I'm a soldier, too … There are times I have to kill. I'm not proud of it … but my job gets dirty. Sometimes, the only way I can keep going … is to know that there's still one man out there who can do the job clean.[65]

When Cap asked if Sharon had no problem killing Agent 9, she said her only problem with it was personal: how it will affect things between them.

At the end of the story, as Agent 9 was about to escape in a teleporter, he taunted Cap: "I'm gone. The controls are locked. The only way to stop me is to blow them—but that would kill me. And that's not what you do … is it?"

Not having his shield, Cap picked up a nearby gun and aimed it—only to see Sharon fire into the control panel first, shutting down the teleporter and killing Agent 9. After several moments full of awkward glances and silence, Cap said, "Today, I had to wrestle with two questions. What would I do ... and how do I feel about you. Because of you, I never had to answer the first. The other ..." Instead of finishing his thought, Cap and Sharon embraced in a kiss, clearly signaling that Cap accepted what Sharon did as part of her job. As the story returned to the present day (in 1998), Sharon had become the new director of SHIELD, which Cap questioned, reminding her of her problems with the agency in the past. "SHIELD's been involved in some dirty ops in its time," she said. "That time is over. I'll order my soldiers to do their jobs ... but move heaven and earth ... to do them clean."[66]

While Sharon worked to clean up SHIELD, more recent stories have revealed that Cap's policy of accommodating "dirty pool" on the part of his colleagues goes back to his World War II days, especially when it comes to his sidekick Bucky Barnes. According to the traditional origin story, told time and time again, James "Bucky" Barnes was the mascot of Camp Lehigh who stumbled upon Steve Rogers as he changed into his red-white-and-blues and then became his sidekick. But in modern versions, presumably to give him a background more consistent with his time as the Winter Soldier, Bucky was portrayed as having been training for covert operations long before he met Cap, and was partnered with Cap in part to preserve the Sentinel of Liberty's squeaky clean image.

After one early World War II adventure in Wakanda, Nick Fury testified to the military brass that Cap is "a superb fighting man. Brave, inventive, inspiring." However, "I think he might be better served with a partner. One that will conduct black ops without hesitation. That way his image can remain unsullied while ... the 'necessary' things get done."[67] The army must have taken Fury's advice, because in 1941 General Phillips drove Steve Rogers to see Bucky in training, telling Rogers that "just like Captain America has symbolic value, an American teenager fighting alongside him ... that's a powerful symbol too ... And if he gets his hands a little dirtier than most soldiers when no one's looking ... well, that'll be our secret, right?"[68]

In the modern day, Cap told Fury about a mission in Russia in 1942, in which Cap and the Russian troops stayed hidden outside a Nazi camp "while our advance scout cleared the way"—by which he meant that Bucky snuck into the camp and killed their guards. According to Cap, that was "the real secret of what Bucky was":

The official story said he was a symbol to counter the rise of the Hitler Youth … and there was some truth to that. But like all things in war, there was a darker truth underneath. Bucky did the things I couldn't. I was the icon, I wore the flag … but while I gave speeches to troops in the trenches … he was doing what he'd been trained to do … and he was highly trained.[69]

Sometimes Bucky even kept his orders secret from Cap. In another wartime story (featuring Wolverine as well), Bucky pulled Fury aside to talk, which aggravated Cap. "I don't like to be kept in the dark, Bucky—I've told you this before," he said, to which Bucky replied, "There are some aspects of some missions that you just can't be privy to—that comes from the top." When he realized Bucky had been ordered to kill a top Nazi agent (Baron von Strucker), Cap asked him, "you don't have a problem with that?" Bucky answered, simply, "I don't question my orders, Captain," and in the next issue Bucky did kill von Strucker (although he turned out to be a robot).[70]

Speaking of Wolverine, Cap has also become more tolerant of killing among the Avengers. Traditionally he would become outraged at his fellow heroes' willingness to kill, such as during the Galactic Storm episode that we discussed in the previous chapter. Afterwards, however, as he prepared to teach his seminar on superhuman ethics, he thought to himself,

seems like my style of professional behavior is out of fashion, at odds with this increasingly violent society. Maybe guys like … Wolverine are the answer to the kinds of threats America faces today. Maybe bad attitudes and lax moral codes are the only way to make headway. The values I've striven for my entire career seem so … untenable in this present clime.[71]

Not long after, during a fight with the Kree, one of them told Cap, "your team impresses me, Captain. I had not expected such tenacity … such savagery from them," to which Cap replied, "maybe that's because, over the years, the stakes have gotten higher … our enemies more vicious, more evil! Maybe—just maybe—it is time for a new type of Avenger!"[72]

And it would seem that Cap meant it. For example, after Warbird killed the self-styled "Master of the World" during a war with Kang, one of the Avengers' greatest foes, she submitted to court-martial (again).[73] Whereas Cap was quick so convict Hank Pym for shooting an enemy in the back nonfatally—as we saw in chapter 3—he was more understanding later with Warbird's deadly action. Based on the "extraordinary and unusual" circumstances, the level of the threat posed by the Master, and the lack of viable alternatives, Cap announced that the members of the court-martial "find that the Avengers interdiction against the use of lethal force was suspended—that the death of the Master, while regrettable, was justifiable—and that no punishment or censure is merited."[74] In a later adventure, Cap recruited a mysterious hero known as Ronin (on the recommendation of Daredevil) to infiltrate the Japanese underworld to find an escaped supervillain, the Silver Samurai. He explained the mission to Ronin, ending with "if you do have to fight your way out ... please ... if at all possible ... no killing."[75] The request sounds like the old Cap, but the "if at all possible" certainly does not.

But perhaps Cap gave up the ship when he allowed Wolverine, a super-hero well known for his willingness to kill, into the Avengers. After Wolverine helped a new version of the team in a mission in the Savage Land, Iron Man asked him to join—and then Cap asked Iron Man for a word.[76] Tony explained that, just as Cap was the missing ingredient that completed the original Avengers, Wolverine is the same for the latest line-up. Cap replied, simply, "Tony, he's a murderer." "He's a Samurai warrior," Tony said, and referencing recent disastrous events around the Avengers, continued, "we can't afford not to have him. We're going to need someone to go to that place that we can't. And you know exactly what I mean." It seems that Wolverine was going to be to the (New) Avengers what Bucky was to Cap during World War II: plausible deniability. All Cap could say in response was, "I wish that wasn't true."[77]

To Captain America's credit, he has been uneasy with Wolverine being an Avenger ever since. During the team's recent battle with the X-Men (another group with which Wolverine claims kitchen privileges), Cap and a team of Avengers were flying in a Quinjet in pursuit of Hope Summers, a young mutant who they assumed was the target for the cosmic Phoenix Force headed to Earth. Wolverine, who had experienced firsthand the destruction the Phoenix left in its path and had already lost fellow X-Man Jean Grey to it years ago, told Cap, "I'm willin' to do what it takes because I've seen what the Phoenix does! I've seen it destroy people I love! You think you can lock Hope up somewhere it can't get to her, but you're wrong, Cap." Cap told him, "I won't let you just kill that girl!", and they fought until Giant-Man snuck up on Wolverine, pummeled him in the back, and kicked him out of the Quinjet. After landing in the Antarctic snow below, Wolverine called Cap a "blind old-fashioned fool."[78] Cap upheld the Avengers' code against killing that day, but he clearly compromised his principle of fair play to do it!

As I write this, it seems that Captain America may have had his fill of Wolverine's killing. After he found out about assassinations ("a secret murder spree," in Cap's words) carried out by Wolverine's black ops team X-Force that led to new attacks on the Earth, Cap grabbed Wolverine and yelled, "I made you an Avenger!" The Wasp stood by Cap, saying "I'm sorry, I won't compromise my ethics for another minute. I won't serve with him. He's a killer and never should have been an Avenger." After other Avengers chimed in over Wolverine's actions, Cap laid down the law: "Allowing Wolverine membership was a mistake, and not one I plan to continue making."[79] Time will tell if he stands by this, as well as if his opinion has truly changed since agreeing with Iron Man that the Avengers needs someone like Wolverine to do what the rest of them won't.

But perhaps Cap shouldn't be too judgmental of Wolverine and his X-Force team, seeing that he ran a shadow ops team of his own for several years. After Steve Rogers came back from the "dead" and led the other heroes in their defeat of Norman Osborn during the Siege on Asgard, "The Heroic Age" began in the Marvel Universe, including new line-ups of the two main Avengers teams (in the titles *Avengers* and *New Avengers*). A third Avengers team also helped usher in the Heroic Age: the Secret Avengers, a team that enabled Steve Rogers, Super-Soldier, to use "stealth tactics and preemptive intervention ... [to] go where we're needed and perform surgical strikes," befitting his role of the "new Nick Fury."[80] As he told his teammate Sharon Carter (who by then had left SHIELD), "it's actually a lot like how the Invaders worked, back in the war ... with everything that's happened, it's nice to be out of the spotlight but still doing good work."[81]

But you can hardly imagine the Captain America that fought alongside the Invaders in World War II endorsing—much less using—the tactics that Steve Rogers used with the Secret Avengers. For example, in a story similar to the Wikileaks controversy—and published two years before Edward Snowden revealed the NSA's surveillance activities—a nameless whistleblower in a USAgent costume found and released a list of the Secret Avengers' underworld contacts. As Cap updated his team on the situation, the Beast—genius X-Man and former Avenger—was shocked to find names of people he fought on the list. Cap defended his actions, saying:

Everyone on this list provided us with information that saved lives. Some did it for the right reasons, some did it to evade imprisonment, some just did it for profit. Pretty soon I'm sure the entire world will be having a conversation about this program's moral legitimacy and effectiveness. Good. When that time comes, I'll answer for it.[82]

Cap assured his team he would take responsibility, but that still leaves his judgment in doubt. If readers didn't know better, they would be more likely to think Iron Man was behind the plan, which resembles his dealings with the underworld during the Civil War.[83] Furthermore, when Cap expressed his intention to save the people on the list from the consequences of being outed, Beast and War Machine assured him that it's impossible to save all of the 419 people on the list. Cap simply said, "Of course we can't. We're not going to. We're going to extract one of them," specifically the one person Cap believed gave him intel for "noble" reasons—an understandable judgment call, to be sure, but not a particularly ambitious one!

But wait—it gets worse. After the team captured a member of the villainous Shadow Council and tied him to a chair with a single light shining on him, he asked Cap, "Am I supposed to be scared or something? I mean, I know who you are … Captain America isn't going to torture a captive." Rogers agreed, saying "that may be true …," and then Sharon and the Black Widow come in the light.

BLACK WIDOW: But my friend Agent 13 and me …?
SHARON CARTER: We've got no such qualms.
STEVE ROGERS: And I'm not Captain America anymore. So tell me what I want to know, or I set these women loose on you …
SHADOW COUNCIL MEMBER: You won't.
STEVE ROGERS: I will. I just won't be sure I can trust the intel.[84]

The scene is left ambiguous regarding the outcome, so we can give Cap the benefit of the doubt and assume he didn't go through with it. But even the mere threat of torture can be considered a form of psychological torture, and Cap used the "good cop/bad cop" routine to convince his enemy that the threat was real even if he didn't believe Cap would do it himself. (Even if he's "not Captain America anymore.")

In time, however, Cap made good on similar threats. On the basis of intel suggesting a double agent of the Shadow Council was working in the US government, Rogers, Black Widow, and Moon Knight broke into the command room of the Office of National Emergency building in Houston, where they found three people. Rogers demanded to know which one was the traitor (although he seemed to know). When none of them answered, he turned around while saying, "Okay, then. I don't believe in torture. It's ugly, dishonorable and unreliable. So I'm going to let my colleagues do it."[85]

He used the same line as before, but this time he followed through. Or, rather, his teammates did: Moon Knight pinned one person's hand to his desk with a sharp blade while Black Widow shot another in the leg. After Moon Knight threatened to cut his man's face off, the third person confessed to being the Shadow Council spy. Note what this implies: the two people brutalized by Cap's teammates were innocent, and Moon Knight and Black Widow used them as pawns to get the third to talk.

This is not the Cap we know. Or is it?

Hitting the Threshold

What can explain this "evolution" in Captain America's thinking? For decades, he showed nearly unswerving devotion to fair play and the sanctity of life, but as I detailed above, recently he's begun excusing and even justifying torture and killing. When Sharon Carter first noticed that Cap was seriously injuring those he fought, perhaps not killing his enemies but not trying as hard to save them, she said, "Look, Steve, I know it's different now. I know it's a new world. I'm on the front lines in it, just like you are. But the man I knew didn't hit that hard unless he had to."[86] During a Secret Avengers mission, the Black Widow tells Steve Rogers, "you're acting more like Nick Fury every day," referring to his newfound skill at strategically keeping secrets, even from his teammates.[87] And when Sharon made an argument for registering and training new superheroes at the beginning of the Civil War, Cap responded with "It's not the 1940s anymore, Sharon, and it's not that easy."[88] Has the world truly changed that much, or is it Cap who's changed—or both?

Looking at Captain America within his ongoing storyline, we can ask if his new behavior and judgment reflect a change in his character or merely the same character reacting to different circumstances (or a combination of the two). If we do think his essential character has changed, was it a reasonable change in response to the "new world" (within the broader storyline), or an abrupt one brought on by the increasing violence and brutality in modern comics (outside the story itself and in response to the changing comics marketplace)?

If we think of Captain America's character as made up of his various character traits and dispositions (according to virtue ethics) or the principles and duties he believes in (according to deontology), we can ask if any of his recent behavior signals a change in any of these core aspects of who

Captain America is. For instance, while he's still extremely hesitant to take a life himself, he is more willing—maybe "less uncomfortable" would be more accurate—to let people die and even to let his colleagues kill. He's also more willing to engage in deceptive and sneaky tactics that he once rejected, even to the point of endorsing torture, which can be considered to be the most egregious violation of basic concepts of dignity and humane treatment. Do these new attitudes and actions imply that Captain America has changed his core virtues or principles?

It would be all too easy to say "yes," wouldn't it? Of course, this might be the correct answer, but it might also be the easy way out. When you see a friend do something you would never expect her to do, you don't automatically say, "wow, she's changed!" First you try to find out if there's some reason she acted that way, any unusual circumstances that led her—within her established character—to act the way she did. Only if you can't find a reason do you start to think you might not have known your friend as well as you thought, or that she has changed since you first got to know each other—especially if the strange behavior continues. This is also why social scientists, in trying explain changes in large-scale behavioral patterns (such as shifts in political orientation or consumer behavior) are very hesitant to say that people "simply must have changed." While this may be true, they first want to rule out all other more precise reasons (such as changes in demography or income) that offer more satisfying explanations of the new behavior they see.

So it may be true that Captain America is truly a changed man, less devoted to the principles he swore to defend and more willing to compromise them in pursuit of the mission at hand. But let's explore the other possibility, that it's not Captain America who has changed, but the world around him, which has led to a different pattern of behavior on his part. How could this be the case? Remember that virtues and principles merely provide simple guidelines, such as "be courageous" and "don't kill." These basic moral concepts don't lead directly to specific action; a person needs to use judgment to take his or her virtues or principles and apply them in a particular context and circumstances. If these circumstances change enough, it could alter the way a person balances the various principles at play in a particular situation, resulting in a different judgment and action.

Take a simple example from the law: after Captain America accidentally interfered in an undercover police operation infiltrating a drug ring, as mentioned above, he thought to himself, "I'm not sure I approve of subsidizing small criminals just to get at bigger ones."[89] This sentiment applies just as well to plea bargaining, a punishment negotiated between a prosecutor and a criminal defendant in lieu of a trial, and another practice on which Cap has made his opinion clear. When a detective told Cap that a criminal (Blockbuster) he had just captured would receive a plea bargain in exchange for the name of his boss, Cap said, "but that means that Blockbuster could come away with a light, or even a suspended, sentence! And in view of what he's done—that strikes me as being a criminal act in itself!"[90]

We don't have to go that far to recognize that in an important sense, plea bargaining is by definition unjust. If the suspect is guilty, he or she receives a lesser punishment than is deserved, and if the suspect is innocent, receiving any punishment at all is more than what is deserved.[91] So the principle that lawbreakers should be punished in proportion to their crimes—a central tenet of *retributive justice*—is violated by plea bargaining. But there are reasons that prosecutors make plea bargain offers: to get information on a more serious offender, or simply (if sadly) to save on time and money that could be devoted to prosecuting more serious offenders. These reasons may sound like expediency and the plea bargains like trade-offs, but these trade-offs are made in the interest of the same principle of retributive justice—to punish wrongdoers—within a system of limited resources. As the detective who told Cap about the plea bargain said, "nobody ever said the justice system was perfect. We do what we can."[92] It would be great if the criminal system could catch, prosecute, and punish every lawbreaker, but it can't: the criminal justice system would absorb all of the government's resources, leaving little for other services such as national defense and education.[93] Judgment calls have to be made, and one principle is necessarily compromised for the sake of a more important one. If you could only catch one criminal, which would you rather catch: the guppy or the shark? That's the choice prosecutors often have to make, and if they cannot prosecute both, then they face a tragic dilemma: they have to sacrifice justice in terms of one suspect or the other.

This is not to say that prosecutors will pursue plea bargains in every case, but only those in which the circumstances justify it: when the costs, in terms of justice foregone, are low enough and the benefits, in terms of the justice achieved, are high enough. The police won't cut a deal with one drug dealer just to get information on another drug dealer—they want the dealer's source. And they won't cut a deal to get the source if there's an alternative that avoids a plea bargain and allows them to nail the source at the same time. Prosecutors and police don't want to cut deals with people they've been following for months if not years, but they might have to if an even bigger catch comes out of it. They bite the bullet, so to speak, compromising justice in a smaller way to increase it in a larger way.[94]

In the same way, circumstances in the "new world" of today may have led Captain America to change his judgment about how he balances the various principles he's concerned with. Perhaps in the past, Cap felt he could do his job—promoting the American dream and its ideals of freedom, justice, and equality—without violating his personal principles of protecting lives and adhering to fair play. Most of the villains he faced then were not existential threats to humanity—the closest was the Red Skull, who was obsessed with destroying the ideals to which Cap is devoted and tried time and time again to turn America into a new Nazi regime. Yet, Cap always managed to stop the Skull and all the others without having to compromise his integrity.

But as people keep telling him—and as he apparently realizes, based on what he said to Sharon Carter—it's not the 1940s anymore. Instead of supervillains with crazy schemes for riches or world conquest, today the primary threats to freedom come from "normal" human beings armed with weapons of mass destruction, whether explosive, biological, or technological. One person now has the potential to do more harm than entire armies could have done several hundred years ago, with much less chance of being detected beforehand (or, in the case of a suicide attack, no fear of being caught afterwards). Even the traditional comic-book supervillains have gotten more ambitious in their plans and more brutal in their tactics, as Cap noted; their schemes often threaten the entire human race and they're willing to sacrifice anything to achieve it. Whatever the source of the threat, the stakes in terms of lives are tremendously higher and information has become the most valuable resource—both reasons that have been used to justify the use of killing and torture, not just by nation-states in the real world but also by superheroes, including Captain America.[95] Perhaps in the past Cap could do his job without violating his core principles, but now the costs of maintaining those personal principles may be too high in the face of the competing principles of saving millions of lives and protecting the American dream for all.[96]

How do we know when these costs are too high? We could try to calculate the value of the various principles at hand and compare them, but it is very difficult to quantify the value of a life, much less ideal concepts such as justice.[97] In the end, a person faced with such a decision must use his or her judgment to balance the principles at hand just as he or she does with more personal principles, making the decision that best maintains his or her moral integrity. That may seem like a dodge, but I've maintained throughout this book that in real-world ethics there are no formulas or rules that can spit out simple answers. And as always, reasonable people may disagree over the precise costs and benefits of a choice, as well as how much cost, in terms of violating one principle, is enough to justify compromising another one.[98]

For example, consider when Captain America stood firm against the Illuminati as Earths from other dimensions were threatening to destroy their own.[99] This is clearly a global threat, but Cap would not consider the option of destroying the other Earths pre-emptively. Even though the stakes were as high as they could be, the solution favored by the rest of the Illuminati involved imposing the same cost on the other Earths. This wasn't a case of killing one person to save billions—which would still be somewhat controversial, especially if the one person is as innocent as the billions.[100] This is a case of killing billions to save billions, in which the stakes and the costs are both enormous but roughly equivalent. Furthermore, Cap's not one to save "his own" at the expense of others. He wants to protect all life, and will not consider the option of destroying one world to save another—even his own—without making sure every other possible option is considered, discovered, or developed first.

The other Illuminati did not share his judgment, of course. They had all hoped the Infinity Gems would be able to repel every encroaching Earth, but the powerful stones were lost after Cap successfully drove back the first incursion. After that, the other members were willing to consider more drastic measures in order to save their Earth and their loved ones in an act of global self-defense, which is generally considered to be excusable in both law and morality. As we saw in the previous chapter, Cap accused his friends of choosing the easy option out of expediency, but he needn't have been so cynical; as Reed Richards pointed out, "you're acting like the decisions we're facing aren't difficult for us as well. It's, well, quite insulting."[101] The other Illuminati shared the same concerns and principles as Cap, but they simply balanced them differently than he did. To put it a different way, they saw the costs of pre-emptive destruction of the other Earths as acceptable, whereas Cap didn't. Cap warned Richards of losing his integrity: "You will lose yourself in this, Reed. You'll wake up one day and have no idea who is looking back at you in the mirror." Perhaps so, Reed admitted, saying, "You seem surprised that I would be willing to sacrifice myself for my family. Why?"[102] But Reed need not have admitted that he would "sacrifice himself" (meaning his integrity): as a hero, he would only have done what he thought was right, and regretted only that he was forced to make the choice at all. In a tragic dilemma such as this, that's all one can do—and by doing so, a person maintains his or her moral integrity.

As we know, at the end of this debate Doctor Strange erased Captain America's memory of the meeting (and, presumably, the incursions themselves), so we will not find out if Cap would have changed his mind as time ran out and a choice had to be made. (As of this writing, the storyline continues and Cap's mindwipe has not yet been addressed.) In other situations, Cap did make difficult choices and violated his principles of preserving life and dignity when he felt he had to. I believe that we can accommodate these decisions into Cap's character—as odd as it may seem after decades of highly consistent behavior—by recognizing that Cap's judgment adapted to new circumstances while relying on the same virtues and principles by which he has always lived. Those core aspects of his character are the only "black-and-white" part of his moral decision-making; his judgment was never that clear-cut and never that simple. Given the changing scope and breadth of modern threats, Cap may feel that the maximum cost he is willing to bear (or impose on others) for maintaining his principles is more often reached, and his judgment changes in reflection of that—regrettably, to be sure, but with the same resolve and determination he has always shown.

You don't have to agree with his judgment, of course, and you're perfectly entitled to think he's gone too far. I may even think that myself sometimes! I'm arguing merely that Cap's more "accommodating" behavior can be understood within his long-standing character, consistent with his integrity, and reflecting his sense of honor. As Iron Man said to Captain America when he entrusted the leadership of the Avengers to him for the first time, "Idealism and pragmatism. Understanding their coexistence is the key to the Avengers' survival."[103] Applying basic moral virtues and principles to specific circumstances, including all of their context, nuance, and subtlety, is the key to sound judgment, and that's just as important to you and me in the real world as it is to Cap in the comics.

So far, we've spent a lot of time talking about Captain America's character, his virtues and principles, and his judgment. But we haven't talked much about the role that "America" plays in Captain America. What is Cap's relationship to the US government, to America as a political entity, and to American ideals? And, as I've mentioned several times, what does it mean that Cap takes a cosmopolitan approach to American principles? We'll look at all of these questions in the next chapter.

Notes

1 *Captain America*, vol. 1, #331 (1987).
2 *Captain America*, vol. 1, #184 (1975).
3 *Captain America*, vol. 1, #332 (1987).
4 *Avengers*, vol. 1, #315 (1990). Rest assured, before long he was in command. When Spider-Man—who picked the wrong day to help his buddies out—said, "you … you sound almost like you're giving up, Cap!", Cap replied, "Not yet, Web-Slinger! If I've learned nothing else in my years of battle, I've learned the absolute truth of one saying: while there's life, there's hope!"
5 *Captain America*, vol. 1, #342 (1988).
6 *Captain America*, vol. 1, #341 (1988).
7 *Captain America*, vol. 1, #184 (1975).
8 *Captain America*, vol. 1, #332 (1987).
9 *Captain America*, vol. 1, #309 (1985).
10 Immanuel Kant, *Critique of Pure Reason*, trans. Paul Guyer and Allen W. Wood (Cambridge: Cambridge University Press, 1998), A133/B172. (Most modern editions of this *Critique*, the first of three Kant would write in his "Critical period," are combinations of the 1781 and 1787 editions, signified by A and B, respectively. This quote appeared in both editions, hence the dual page numbering. Unfortunately, it has nothing to do with alternate universes or evil twins—that we know of.)
11 For the essential details, see Ronald Dworkin, *Taking Rights Seriously* (Cambridge, MA: Harvard University Press, 1977), especially chapters 2–4. For the expanded version, see his *Law's Empire* (Cambridge, MA: Harvard University Press, 1986), or Stephen Guest's *Ronald Dworkin*, 3rd ed. (Stanford, CA: Stanford University Press, 2013).
12 *Avengers: Earth's Mightiest Heroes*, vol. 1, #8 (2005).
13 For an influential account of this, see Christine Korsgaard, *Self-Constitution* (Oxford: Oxford University Press, 2009).
14 *Captain America*, vol. 1, #284 (1983); *Captain America*, vol. 1, #325 (1987).
15 *Captain America*, vol. 1, #314 (1986).
16 *Captain America*, vol. 1, #198 (1976).
17 *Avengers*, vol. 1, #80 (1970). Now you know why Thor saying "pain in the ass" recently (as described in chapter 2) seemed so out of place. (Verily!)
18 Ibid.
19 *Avengers*, vol. 1, #81 (1970).
20 See *Iron Man/Captain America: Casualties of War* (2007) and *Captain America*, vol. 1, #401 (1992), respectively; see also *Iron Man/Captain America Annual 1998*, which we will discuss in the final chapter.
21 *Captain America and the Falcon #9* (2005).
22 *Captain America*, vol. 1, #325 (1987).

23 *Captain America and the Falcon* #4 (2004).
24 Ibid.
25 Ibid.
26 William Styron, *Sophie's Choice* (New York: Random House, 1979); the film adaptation was released in 1982.
27 *Captain America/Nick Fury: The Otherworld War* (2001).
28 *Civil War: Front Line* #11 (2007), "Embedded Part 11."
29 *Civil War* #7 (2007).
30 *Civil War: Front Line* #11 (2007), "Embedded Part 11."
31 *Captain America*, vol. 1, #321 (1986).
32 This can also be described in terms of a *trolley problem*, a thought experiment devised by philosopher Philippa Foot and popularized by another philosopher, Judith Jarvis Thomson. (See Thomson's essay "The Trolley Problem," reprinted in her book *Rights, Restitution & Risk*, ed. William Parent, Cambridge: Harvard University Press, 1986, pp. 94–116.) In the classic version, you are standing next to a railroad switch, and you see a runaway trolley car carrying five passengers rushing towards you. If they continue down the same track, they'll hit an obstruction and crash, killing all five. If you pull the switch, the car will be diverted onto the other track, saving the five passengers, but killing a person whose foot is stuck in the track. Do you pull the switch, saving the five passengers but killing the one on the track, or do you do nothing, allowing the five passengers to die but not actively killing the one on the track? This classic thought experiment invokes issues of harming versus permitting harm, the right versus the good, and responsibility. Cap's case is complicated by the fact that the one person (the ULTIMATUM agent) who Cap considers killing is the same person who put the "passengers" (the people in the cathedral) in danger. For a situation similar to this, see my chapter "Why Doesn't Batman Kill the Joker?" in Mark D. White and Robert Arp (eds.), *Batman and Philosophy: The Dark Knight of the Soul* (Hoboken, NJ: John Wiley & Sons, 2008), pp. 5–16.
33 *Captain America*, vol. 1, #349 (1989).
34 *Captain America*, vol. 1, #322 (1986).
35 Ibid. Again, this was the comment that started the controversy over Cap's experiences in the war, mentioned near the end of chapter 2 and in note 60 in chapter 4.
36 *Captain America*, vol. 1, #323 (1986).
37 *Captain America*, vol. 1, #324 (1986).
38 Ibid.
39 Ibid.
40 *Captain America*, vol. 1, #322 (1986).
41 *New Avengers*, vol. 3, #2–3 (2013).

42 This story was told in the 2006 trade paperbacks *Captain America: Winter Soldier, Vols. 1* and *2* (collecting *Captain America*, vol. 5, #1–9 and #11–14, 2005–2006), written by Ed Brubaker working with several artists, and was adapted for the 2014 film *Captain America: The Winter Soldier*.

43 *Captain America*, vol. 5, #12 (2005).

44 *New Avengers*, vol. 3, #2 (2013).

45 See the 2005 trade paperback *Avengers Disassembled*, collecting *Avengers*, vol. 3, #500–503 (2004) and *Avengers Finale* (2005), written by Brian Michael Bendis and illustrated by David Finch, Danny Miki, and a legion of guest artists (contributing to issue #503 and *Avengers Finale*).

46 *House of M* #1 (August 2005); Cap and Wolverine had a similar argument in *Avengers: The Children's Crusade* #3 (2011) when the Avengers discovered where the Scarlet Witch was. Actually, Wolverine and Captain America's uneasy friendship goes back to World War II. During one of their recent team-ups, Wolverine said to Cap, "You're as set in your ways as you were 50 years ago!" Cap's response? "I was in suspended animation—what's your excuse?" (*Wolverine/Captain America* #2, 2004).

47 Recall the narration quoted in the previous chapter: "A hero was a man of moral fiber; a man who would not see one innocent soul sacrificed if there was any alternative … and, to Captain America, there is always an alternative!" (*Captain America*, vol. 1, #268, 1982).

48 *Marvel Two-in-One* #75 (1981).

49 *Captain America*, vol. 1, #232 (1979).

50 *Captain America*, vol. 1, #284 (1983).

51 Ibid.

52 *Captain America: Dead Men Running* #3 (2002).

53 Roger Stern, "Remembering Cap," in *Captain America: War & Remembrance* (2011).

54 *Marvel Spotlight*, vol. 3, #18 (2007), "Remembering 'Remembrance': Stern & Byrne Take Their Turn with America's Fighting Legend."

55 *Captain America and the Falcon* #14 (2005).

56 Ibid.

57 *Captain America*, vol. 1, #101 (1968).

58 *Avengers*, vol. 4, #22 (2012).

59 *Civil War* #4 (2006).

60 *Uncanny Avengers* #10 (2013).

61 *Captain America*, vol. 1, #250 (1980).

62 While in his Nomad identity, Cap refused to accept money for what he did (as Luke Cage and his Heroes for Hire do), and thought to himself, "so … that makes me an idealist. After all these years, I still just want to do something for people!" (*Captain America*, vol. 1, #183, 1975).

63 I will not speculate on what role the tragedy of September 11, 2001, played in this shift, though an argument can easily be made for such an influence. However, as we'll see, signs of changing behavior don't appear until well after that date, and volume 4 of *Captain America*, which focused on the aftermath of the disaster most closely, did not display any shift from his core principles, especially the one regarding killing. (For example, see his reaction to thinking he had killed a terrorist in *Captain America*, vol. 4, #3, 2002.)

64 No clue if he'd proposed to her yet, as mentioned in note 91 in chapter 4 (*Tales of Suspense*, vol. 1, #95, 1967, "A Time to Die—A Time to Live!").

65 *Captain America: Sentinel of Liberty* #1 (1998).

66 Ibid.

67 *Captain America/Black Panther: Flags of Our Fathers* #4 (2010). This Black Panther was Azzuri, the father of T'Chaka and grandfather of T'Challa and his sister Shuri, all of whom carried the mantle of the Black Panther.

68 *Captain America*, vol. 5, #12 (2005).

69 *Captain America*, vol. 5, #5 (2005).

70 *Wolverine Origins* #18 (2007), a story in which Wolverine remembers realizing how alike he and Bucky were, especially in their attitudes towards killing. For another story of Wolverine and Cap meeting during World War II (unfortunately absent any deep philosophical discussion between them), see *Uncanny X-Men*, vol. 1, #268 (1990).

71 *Captain America*, vol. 1, #401 (1992).

72 *Avengers*, vol. 1, #366 (1993), "The First Rule!"

73 She killed the Master in *Avengers*, vol. 3, #48, confessed in *Avengers*, vol. 3, #54, and was put on trial in *Avengers*, vol. 3, #55 (all from 2002). (Her first court-martial was in *Avengers*, vol. 3, #7, 1998, and was discussed in chapter 3.)

74 *Avengers*, vol. 3, #55 (2002). Note that justification is a higher standard than excuse: as usually understood in both the law and morality, a justified act is the right thing to do given the circumstances, whereas an excused act is wrong but the circumstances surrounding it relieve the person of any responsibility for it (such as in cases of temporary insanity). For more on this distinction and its limitations, see Kent Greenawalt, "The Perplexing Borders of Justification and Excuse," *Columbia Law Review* 84 (1984): 1897–1927.

75 *New Avengers*, vol. 1, #11 (2005).

76 As we discussed in chapter 3 in the context of perseverance, this was the mission in which Cap and the rest of the Avengers were hung naked—if you're one to remember such a minor narrative detail.

77 *New Avengers*, vol. 1, #6 (2005).

78 *Avengers vs. X-Men* #3 (2012).

79 *Uncanny Avengers* #9 (2013). In the next issue, Cap explained to the Wasp that he had been trapped in Arnim Zola's dimension for over a decade (while only a half-hour passed in the "real" world), where he experienced terrible loss. (See

the discussion of perseverance in chapter 3 for more.) "What happened there," he said, "it led to my outburst against [Wolverine]. I'm afraid personal issues colored my judgment," which serves as yet another example of his tendency to rush to judgment as well as his willingness to reconsider it (*Uncanny Avengers* #10, 2013).

80 *Secret Avengers*, vol. 1, #1 (2010).

81 Ibid.

82 *Secret Avengers*, vol. 1, #12.1 (2011). He did, in a way, when he apprehended the fake USAgent at the end of the issue—we'll discuss their conversation in the next chapter when we talk about Captain America's relationship to the US government and its policies.

83 See *Civil War: War Crimes* (2007), in which Cap too plays an interesting—and not exactly noble—role.

84 *Secret Avengers*, vol. 1, #7 (2011).

85 *Secret Avengers*, vol. 1, #21 (2012).

86 *Captain America*, vol. 5, #1 (2005).

87 *Secret Avengers*, vol. 1, #7 (2011).

88 *Captain America*, vol. 5, #22 (2006). Funny, I thought it's *never* been easy …

89 *Captain America*, vol. 1, #325 (1987).

90 *Captain America*, vol. 1, #258 (1981).

91 For more on this, see Kenneth Kipnis, "Criminal Justice and the Negotiated Plea," *Ethics* 86 (1976): 93–106.

92 *Captain America*, vol. 1, #258 (1981).

93 Don't believe me? See my chapter "Retributivism in a World of Scarcity," in *Theoretical Foundations of Law and Economics*, edited by Mark D. White (Cambridge: Cambridge University Press, 2009), pp. 253–271.

94 An open question is how to—or whether to even try to—quantify the justice gained and lost in situations like this. Michael Cahill argues for quantifying them in "Retributive Justice in the Real World," *Washington University Law Review* 85 (2007): 815–870; I argue against it in "*Pro Tanto* Retributivism: Judgment and the Balance of Principles in Criminal Justice," in *Retributivism: Essays on Theory and Policy*, edited by Mark D. White (Oxford: Oxford University Press, 2011), pp. 129–145.

95 This assumes that torture results in reliable information, which is widely contested. Even Cap recognizes this: after all, he did tell the Shadow Council agent he threatened with torture that he can't "be sure he can trust the intel" (*Secret Avengers*, vol. 1, #7, 2011). But he may have gone through with it anyway—we'll never know.

96 As Hercules told the Falcon regarding Cap's actions in *Civil War: War Crimes* (2007), "'Tis war, friend Samuel. And at the end of the day, thy Captain is but a soldier. As such, he doth recognize that sometimes in war, hard decisions must be made to achieve thy goal. And should that cost thee a piece of thy soul? So be it."

97   Of course, in fields like the economics of health care, accident law, and insurance, the monetary value of a life is routinely calculated: for a concise overview of such methods, see Ike Brannon, "What Is a Life Worth?", *Regulation* 27(4) (2004): 60–63 (available at www.cato.org/sites/cato.org/files/serials/files/regulation/2004/12/v27n4-8.pdf).

98   For an influential discussion of these trade-offs in the context of torture, see Michael S. Moore, "Torture and the Balance of Evils," in his book *Placing Blame: A Theory of the Criminal Law* (Oxford: Oxford University Press, 1997), pp. 669–736. Moore suggests a *threshold deontology* in which rules such as "do not torture" are to be followed until the costs reach a "threshold" level; for a criticism of this theory, see Larry Alexander, "Deontology at the Threshold," *University of San Diego Law Review* 37 (2000): 893–912, as well as my book chapter "*Pro Tanto* Retributivism" (which argues for the method of judgment outlined above).

99   *New Avengers*, vol. 3, #2–3 (2013).

100 This would be like the trolley problem from note 32 above—except we're gonna need a bigger trolley.

101 *New Avengers*, vol. 3, #3 (2013).

102 Ibid.

103 *Avengers: Earth's Mightiest Heroes*, vol. 1, #8 (2005).

6

Principle and Politics

So far in this book, we have discussed the time-tested personal virtues and character traits that make Captain America a great role model and moral exemplar. In this chapter, we're going to shift our focus to the "America" part of his name and explore the more political aspects of his life and character. We'll look at patriotism in general and how to characterize Captain America's brand of it; Cap's uneasy relationship with politics and the United States government; and how Cap puts principles above politics, even if it means defying his own government and giving up the shield and the title. By the time you finish this chapter, I hope to have shown that Captain America's relationship to America is more nuanced than is often portrayed outside of comics, where he is sometimes painted as a simplistic, flag-waving "America first" puppet in the service of American interests. Instead, I will explain that Cap's devotion to his country is based on the principles and ideals upon which it was founded, not its policies at any point in time, and he regularly holds his government accountable to those same standards, which he interprets as inclusive and cosmopolitan, applying to the world outside America as well as everybody within it.[1]

Patriotism: The Captain and America

I'm sure I don't have to present pages of dialogue and narration from the comics describing how Captain America represents the ideals, hopes, and dreams of his country and the people he protects. (If I did, this book could

The Virtues of Captain America: Modern-Day Lessons on Character from a World War II Superhero, First Edition. Mark D. White.

easily be twice as long!) Instead, I'll let his fellow Avengers tell you, courtesy of "testimonials" many of them gave over the years (and shown in issues of *Avengers* during the war with the Midgard Serpent), intended to be read in sequence:

> HAWKEYE: Captain America doesn't just wear the flag.
>
> LUKE CAGE: It's like … he is the flag.
>
> MARIA HILL: He doesn't just protect the nation or the ideals that make America what it is supposed to be. I think he has this—this empathetic relationship to the country as a whole.
>
> IRON MAN: If the country is prosperous, he seems prosperous. If the country is sad … he's pretty sad.
>
> WASP: If the country is angry … holy lord does he get angry.
>
> HAWKEYE: He literally transforms into—into the sentinel of whatever we need him to be at the time we really need it. … In his DNA … in the space between his molecules … he is America.[2]

And to provide the perspective of one person without superpowers or fancy tights, we'll give the last word to lawyer (and former love interest) Connie Ferrari, who said, "when we're at the brink, when America faces the ultimate test, Cap is there to fight for America."[3]

Of course, this portrayal of Captain America as "the living symbol of the American dream" ultimately comes from the writers (that phrase in particular courtesy of Roger Stern).[4] In an interview, Steve Englehart described Steve Rogers' upbringing: "He's a product of Roosevelt's rebuilding of the country's spirit, enhanced by World War II patriot spirit; he believes deeply in the ideal of America, the things they taught us all in school about why this is the greatest country on Earth. Which is why, when the actual America falls short of that, his first reaction is to try to set things right."[5] As writer Rick Remender described him in his first issue of Cap's book:

> Steve Rogers is a patriotic soldier, directed by a personal ethical compass, belief in the American dream and faith in his fellow man. … He is fighting for the safety of humanity, freedom, liberty and justice for all. He believes a perfect world without war or strife is a possibility worth fighting for. He will no doubt spend his entire life protecting people from the endless sea of chaos that surrounds the Marvel Universe.[6]

Remender's description of Captain America raises an interesting question: what does Cap's patriotism mean, and how consistent is it with "fighting for the safety of humanity, freedom, liberty and justice for all," assuming "all" means people around the world? When Sharon Carter calls Cap "patriotism personified," what exactly does this mean?[7]

In today's global world, patriotism is a controversial topic among philosophers (indeed, most academics), among whom nationalism is often suspect and more cosmopolitan attitudes are favored. Captain America, always with his finger on the pulse of academia, understood this well as he thought to himself, "Throughout the world, the image of Captain America has become a symbol—a living embodiment of all that democracy stands for! But now—there are those who scorn love of flag—love of country! Those to whom patriotism is just a square, outmoded word!"[8] To its critics, patriotism merely reflects favoritism and an "us-versus-them" mentality, whereas philosophers often favor universal values that emphasize the shared humanity of people across national borders.[9]

But Alasdair MacIntyre, one of the philosophers responsible for the revival of virtue ethics in the 1980s, published a famous lecture in 1984 titled "Is Patriotism a Virtue?" in which he suggested a way to conceive of patriotism in a positive way.[10] MacIntyre argued that there is no universal morality but instead a moral code specific to each community. In order for people within each community to live good, flourishing lives, they must have a patriotic feeling towards the community which provided them their moral values and which therefore makes up an important part of each member's identity. MacIntyre's conception of patriotism has been criticized, however, especially concerning its contrast with more cosmopolitan ideals. Other philosophers, such as Marcia Baron and Stephen Nathanson, provide defenses of patriotism that avoid this criticism—and we'll see that Nathanson's version of patriotism, in particular, describes Cap's own patriotism fairly well.[11]

The most important thing to understand about Captain America's patriotism is that it is based on the ideals and principles upon which the United States of America was founded, concepts that Cap regards as timeless.[12] As the narration to one issue of *Captain America* read:

Captain America is a patriot, one of a dying breed in these days of cynicism and lack of confidence. He's a man who's sworn to serve with unwavering loyalty ... a hero who has risked his life more than once to defend the shores of this nation he calls home. To him, the principles and ideals of personal freedom on which America was founded will never become old hat or out of fashion. Perhaps that is what makes him special. Perhaps that is what makes him Captain America![13]

When a reporter asked Cap (presumably referring to his costume), "don't you think your brand of rather ostentatious flag-waving has had its day?", Cap answered, "as long as there's an American dream for our people to reach for ... I'll do my best to embody that dream—to stand as a symbol of hope— and better tomorrows. In my opinion, that's what this country is about."[14]

In the Marvel Universe (as well as the real world), many people connect Captain America's patriotism with his "old-fashioned" ethics. For example, a member of Hydra, a villainous organization that began as the research arm of the Third Reich, told Cap that "you are a pawn ... of ideals that not even your fellow countrymen follow! After your countless victories, what was your reward? Hollow praise and ephemeral glory—both of which are freely given and promptly forgotten by a fickle populace!"[15] Flag-Smasher, who was opposed to nationalism of any kind, accused Cap of self-righteousness, moral smugness, and being "a relic of outmoded values."[16] Even his good friend Nick Fury wrote in a report to SHIELD that Cap's "patriotism is skewed and out of date."[17] (Gee, with friends like these ....)

But Cap doesn't buy it; he believes the ideals that he represents are as true and valuable today as they were during World War II or the American Revolution. When Super-Patriot—John Walker, another fanatical pretender who later replaced Steve Rogers as Captain America before adopting the name USAgent—first fought Cap, he told him, "your concept of America and her ideals is as dated and obsolete as you are! You're out of step with America—you don't know what makes the country and the people tick anymore!" Cap responded as you would expect: "America's ideals are timeless ... liberty, justice, and the pursuit of happiness never go out of style!"[18] Like the personal principles and ideals we described earlier, these American ideals don't change, but the way the country applies them in changing circumstances does. Furthermore, each of us, including Captain America, has to judge for himself or herself how well the country does that, especially in new and controversial situations. (More on this soon!)

Cosmopolitanism

Another aspect of Captain America's patriotism is that he believes that American ideals apply to everyone—not just all Americans, but all people around the world. This cosmopolitan patriotism of Cap's was even written into one retelling of his origin, explaining that after receiving the super-soldier serum and the Vita-Ray treatment, he became "a symbol of America's move away from isolationism."[19]

Let's start by looking at how Cap values the diversity of cultures within America and how this is consistent with patriotism. After Cap first fought the anti-nationalist Flag-Smasher, he defended his version of nationalism that incorporates an appreciation of multiculturalism:

> There is nothing harmful about having a sense of national identity or ethnic heritage. America is made up of a multitude of different ethnic groups, each of which has had its own part to contribute to American culture. Be proud of your heritage, but never let that pride make you forget that beneath it all, we are all human beings and have the same wants and needs and deserve the same respect and dignity.[20]

Here, Cap acknowledged the contribution made by the numerous cultures and ethnicities that make up the United States, but at the same time he emphasized that at our core we are all the same: human beings deserving of equal dignity and respect.

But Captain America's attitude of inclusiveness and universal respect does not stop at our national borders; as we can see from the comics, his cosmopolitan application of American ideals has been clear for years. In a story from the early 1980s, after discovering that a renegade American intelligence organization was plotting an attack on the Soviet Union in order to leave the United States the last remaining superpower, Cap fought back, saying, "I represent the American dream! A dream that has precious little to do with borders, boundaries, and the kind of blind hatred your ilk espouses!"[21] He expects the same from his allies as well. In another adventure, when Namor the Sub-Mariner—Prince of Atlantis and a fellow hero from World War II—refused to help fight the Red Skull's latest plans to destroy America, Cap replied, "I have never understood how you can be so selective in your self-righteousness! Some see injustice—and stop it wherever it is found!"[22]

In this way, Captain America's love of country resembles philosopher Stephen Nathanson's "moderate patriotism," which balances devotion to one's country with ethical demands to care for all. Arguing against an exclusionary interpretation of patriotism or a "my country, right or wrong" type of jingoism, Nathanson writes that

> we can hold that patriotism is a virtue so long as the actions it encourages are not themselves immoral. So long as devotion and loyalty to one's country do not lead to immoral actions, then patriotism can be quite laudable. When concern for their own country blinds people to the legitimate needs and interests of other nations, then patriotism becomes a vice.[23]

This corresponds to Cap's position that no one should pursue his or her country's interests without regard for the interests or rights of other countries or peoples. For instance, after John Walker had served as Cap's replacement and USAgent, he once again posed as Cap for a covert government mission—one that involved killing innocent people. When the real Captain America learned of this, he was angry especially because "Walker puts American interests above human rights and innocent lives."[24] Every country has its interests and the right to pursue them, of course, but this should always be done with at least minimal consideration and respect of other nations and peoples—and certainly not at the cost of sacrificing the country's own principles, especially those on which the country was founded and of which it serves as an example to the world.

Given his cosmopolitan attitude, it is no surprise that people have questioned Captain America's true loyalties to the United States. Inali Redpath, a SHIELD agent who served with Cap on a mission in the Balkans, argued with him over how far they would go to complete their mission (as Redpath brandished his gun). "So, who's the better American, Steve?" Redpath asked. "The man who does what his government wants, no matter what? Or the man who runs around dressed in a flag and lives a higher ideal than the country whose name he shares?" Cap answered, "the better American is the man who does what his heart tells him is right—for the betterment of all mankind—not just for other Americans."[25] And in the storyline mentioned above, John Walker told Cap "you never understood duty to country ... whatever it takes to keep our shores safe, you do it!" Cap replied, "Captain America represents the ideal, Walker! An ideal for all people! All countries!" After he defeated Walker, he reaffirmed that "To truly honor the country, Walker—you must honor the world."[26]

Of course, this is not to say that Captain America would not fight to defend the United States from wrongful attacks, but only in defense—and he would do the same for other nations that were the victims of aggression. Some of his enemies claim a different type of patriotism and urge a more active stance towards threats, but Cap refuses to see an enemy in every face that doesn't look like his. A perfect counterexample is the Anti-Cap, whom we've discussed in the last two chapters. After the Anti-Cap killed the royal family of a Middle Eastern country that he deemed to be a threat to US security, he told Cap, "You fight evil where you find it, Captain. 'With us or against us.' Fight them over here so we don't have to face them at home." Cap then asked him,

"Them" ...? Who's "them"? The terrorists are surely "them." I suppose the royal family were "them." Problem is, the more you look through eyes like yours ... the more you see "them." Religious leaders—social activists—postal workers—anyone who disagrees with you becomes "them."[27]

As Cap thought to himself years earlier, "Playing insidious games of 'them versus us' doesn't do a blasted bit of good! The years have taught me that we're all 'us'! And the sooner we accept that, the better off America—and the world—will be!"[28]

When Captain America faced Flag-Smasher for a second time and tried to explain his open-minded patriotism, Flag-Smasher asked him a reasonable question: "why alienate the rest of the world with 'America' in your name? Why don't you call yourself Captain Freedom [or] Captain Justice?"[29] The two are interrupted, so Cap doesn't get a chance to answer, but I'll take a shot. While his values, the ideals and principles he's sworn to uphold, are cosmopolitan in nature, they are still American values, deriving from the founding documents of the country (as he explained to Rick Jones while he was rereading the Avengers charter).[30] We can borrow from MacIntyre's theory of patriotism here to point out that Steve Rogers first learned his values from people such as his mother, his teachers, and President Roosevelt (through his weekly radio addresses)—all part of the American community. So to Steve, his values are American values, and he learned to love his country for embodying them (however imperfectly they were put into practice). He does not think of himself as imposing American values on the rest of the world, but rather as being their spokesman, standard-bearer, and symbol.[31]

As Cap tried to get to Flag-Smasher by fighting his ULTIMATUM agents, one of them remarks that Cap is "just one man." Cap replies:

> That's right. I'm just one man. One man who's dedicated his life to the ideals of freedom, justice, and equality. Some folks misunderstand me. They think I represent the American government, its political system, or its official policies. I don't. I represent the American dream—the notion that human beings should have the opportunity to better their lives and attain their noblest aspirations.[32]

One way to think about it is that Cap believes all people deserve a shot at the American dream no matter where they live—not because it's American, but because it represents an ideal of freedom, justice, and equality that Cap believes in.

The American Dream Versus the American Reality

As much as Captain America loves the idea of the American dream, however, he knows the American reality is often an entirely different thing.
When he fought William Burnside, the bigoted Captain America of the
1950s who received only part of the Project Rebirth procedure (which left
him mentally unhinged), Cap told him that "times have changed. America's
in danger from within as well as from without! There's organized crime,
injustice, and fascism," although Burnside saw evil only in the name of
communism.[33] Cap knew, however, that the problems that plagued America
in the current day were not new. As writer Roger Stern put it, "Steve is a
patriot and an idealist, but he's no starry-eyed fool. As he grew up, he saw
corruption, bigotry, and hypocrisy first hand—none of that [today] is new
or unique."[34]

Captain America's love for his country never prevented him from
pointing out its problems, although sometimes he failed to notice them
while battling the Red Skull or saving the Earth with the Avengers. But he
was reminded of them during a speech at a high school, when a student
shouted him down, yelling "We've all had enough of your bull about the
American dream, flag-waver! Let's talk about the American reality—about
unequal distribution of wealth—about poverty, frustration, and death! Or
are you afraid of the truth?!" He then pulled a gun and began shooting at
Cap, who easily subdued him. Afterwards, the student read the confusion
on Cap's face and told him:

> You wanna know why, man? Because you're the symbol of everything that
> stinks in this country! Yeah—you're the shining example who says, "you can
> be what I am if you only try!" It's the American success sickness: strive to be
> something—scramble to the top of the heap. But you know that only one in
> ten thousand is gonna make it! So what about the rest of us? What about the
> failures?[35]

He then spit on Cap, but Cap stopped the principal from slapping him.
Throughout the rest of the issue Cap thought about what the student had
said—especially when a costumed "Everyman" took his words and actions
to the next level, killing several police officers to drum up publicity for his
message. As Cap rushed to the scene, he cursed Everyman's methods but at
the same time admitted to himself, "It took time for me to become aware of

the huge gap between the American dream and the American reality—and perhaps there were times I could have worked even harder to bridge it!"[36]

After Cap apprehended Everyman at the end of the issue, several kids whom Cap befriended earlier cheered him, but he wouldn't join in: "I'm afraid I'm not as exultant about this as you are, boys! There's such a mood of renewed patriotism sweeping this land that it's easy to forget the dark underbelly of the American dream. But this whole day has been one grim reminder." However, the others said that Cap inspired them to find a better way to address their problems. Maggie, a member of Everyman's gang whom he then used as a hostage during his fight with Cap, said:

> Everyman, and all of us who followed him, made a choice. We chose despair over hope—we chose to lash out against people instead of working with them ... That just keeps the darkness alive. It swallowed Everyman tonight. But I'm not gonna let it swallow me. So maybe I won't be rich or famous— maybe I won't live the great American success story. So what? Those things aren't America. People are America. Ordinary people willing to help one another up out of the despair—who are willing to share a little love along the way![37]

Cap liked what he heard, adding, "perhaps if we try—each in his own way— to bring those words to life, this American dream of ours will become reality."[38]

Again, Cap is not naïve enough to think this will happen today, tomorrow, or even in his lifetime, and he knows that he can't solve all of America's problems himself—it's a task everybody has to work towards by working together. Nonetheless, he recognizes his own role in this, which demands more than merely protecting the world from supervillains and alien marauders, as he declared during this speech following the "Capmania" (during which a Skrull impersonated Cap and abused his identity):

> In the past, I've said I stand for the American dream ... the American way. But those terms are becoming harder to define with each passing day. This country doesn't know what it is anymore. We're all wondering what our role will be in the dawning of a new millennium ... so let me lay down my role, once and for all. Captain America is not here to lead the country. I'm here to serve it. If I'm a captain, I'm a soldier. Not of any military branch ... but of the American people. Years ago, in a simpler time, this suit and this shield

were created as a symbol to help make America the land it's supposed to be ... to help it realize its destiny. Ricocheting from super-villain duel to super-villain duel doesn't always serve that purpose. There's a difference between fighting against evil and fighting for the common good. I'm not always able to choose my battles ... but effective immediately, I'm going to make an effort to choose the battles that matter. Battles against injustice ... against cynicism ... against intolerance. I will still serve with the Avengers. I will continue to defend this nation from any and all threats it may face. But as of today, I am not a "super hero." Now and forevermore ... I am a man of the people. Together, you and I will identify and confront America's problems. Together, we will figure out what we are ... and what we can be. Together, we will define the American dream ... and make it an economic reality.[39]

Cap does not fool himself into thinking that continued improvement will be easy—he is fully aware that it will take constant work, attention, and vigilance, and he stands ready to play his part, inspiring others and serving as a symbol through his actions and words, not just his stars-and-stripes.

This also shows that Captain America is ever hopeful that America's problems can be addressed and that the country is improving. As Cap told Colonel Jimmy Newman in *The Chosen*, "We aren't perfect. A great nation can admit that."[40] During one of the Red Skull's many attempts to "ignite the flame" of America's "cauldron of hate waiting to erupt," Cap assured him that "Americans have moved beyond that"—not entirely of course, but enough that the Red Skull's attempts to destroy America from within would fail.[41] Even in the 1940s, after accepting the costume and shield from General Phillips, Cap said that "this land of ours may have seen some hard times, and maybe it hasn't always lived up to the promise of its founding fathers ... but America at its best has always stood for the rights of man, and against the rule of tyrants!"[42]

As Sharon Carter once thought to herself after Captain America died following the Civil War, "he made it look easy. Even though it never was. And he never stopped fighting for what he believed in ... or for what he believed his country should be."[43] That final phrase was echoed by the Young Avenger named Patriot as he remembered Cap explaining what patriotism meant to him:

It wasn't about blindly supporting your government. It was about knowing what your country could be ... and trying to lead it there through your example. And holding it accountable when it failed. I remember he said: "There's nothing patriotic about corruption or cover-ups ... or defend-ing them. But exposing them, well, that takes a hero."[44]

At the end of the day, Captain America's patriotism means standing by American ideals and principles and holding all Americans accountable for them—even his own government. As we'll see in the next section, he has not been shy about doing this when he felt strongly that he must, reflecting his conviction and determination in following his best judgment. And woe be the president or senator who stands in his way!

"I'm a Hero, Not a Politician!"

So Captain America exclaimed when the Scorpion told him he was expect-ing Spider-Man, not the Sentinel of Liberty (questioning Cap's "jurisdic-tion").[45] Cap has long had an uneasy relationship with politics, in particular the politics of his own government. In one Avengers tale, Cap and the team were called out to Mount Rushmore to investigate a cloud of deadly red dust beginning to spread across the countryside, only to discover that it was a biological agent produced by the United States government. When the Vision said that Cap must be as disgusted as he is "that this plague could spawn from our own country," Cap said, "I may be idealistic but I'm not stupid."[46]

In a more precise statement of his patriotism, Captain America laid out his position on American principles and the American government to Flag-Smasher as he dragged him through the snow after saving his life:

> I'm not a knee-jerk patriot. I don't believe in my country right or wrong. I support America in its concept, its essence, its ideal. Its political system, its foreign and domestic policies, its vast book of laws—I am not America's offi-cial advocate of any of that. What I represent are the principles that America's politics, laws, and policies are based upon ... freedom, justice, equality, opportunity.[47]

This stance is consistent with Cap's devotion, first and foremost, to these American ideals, as well as his moral integrity that demands that he makes judgments and decisions consistent with those principles, whether or not those choices are in line with what the US government tells him to do.

The fact that Captain America puts principle above politics in general will be an increasingly important point as we progress through the rest of this book. As we'll see below, Cap makes a distinction between the principles upon which America was founded and the politics involved with governing the country. Politics demands too much give-and-take, with its logrolling and deal-making, for Cap to be comfortable with—not to mention, on the darker side, the rumors, leaks, and political espionage, for which he has no patience and which offends his sense of honor and fair play (as we discussed in chapter 4).

Cap especially resents when serious issues became material for political pundits or muckrakers. For example, Cap raged at a reporter who asked him during a riot, "What side of the issue do you come down on?", yelling back, "Are you kidding me? I'm anti-riot. Now go home!"[48] On the first anniversary of Cap's death following the Civil War, Thor (who was "dead" himself during that conflict) summoned the spirit of his fallen comrade-in-arms, who bemoaned the politicization of his name and image since his death:

> All my life, I fought to become a symbol. A symbol of all the things that were right about this country. All the things I loved. And now, they're trying to turn that symbol into whatever's most convenient, whatever will best serve the political agenda of one side or another. I can hear them talking nonstop ... the media, the press ... They don't understand. It was never about politics. It was never about me. It was always about the country. But they can't hear that truth above their own voices.[49]

At least a Japanese TV reporter got it right when, informing his audience of Cap's success in stopping a terrorist attack, he said, "all eyes were on Captain America as he saved hundreds of lives ... not in the name of any nation, but rather, in the name of mercy."[50]

Captain America is not comfortable with politics even at its best. One of the many times that public sentiment turned against the Avengers, Iron Man and Black Panther urged Cap to action, and Cap admitted, "I hate this. All my training, my instincts—they all say to just do a good job, and let public reaction take care of itself. This sort of political wrangle ... it's alien territory to me."[51] When this happened again years later—thanks to Norman Osborn, who was trying to reclaim the position he had lost after his failed Siege of Asgard—the president of the United States himself asked Cap to rouse the Avengers and "send the charming ones out to the press." When he asked Cap himself to go on the Sunday morning talk shows to talk up the team, Cap said:

All due respect, sir ... I'm not running for office. I'm not trying to win a popularity contest. I'm trying to protect the world as best I can. I don't want to play a P.R. game against a madman who twists our words and actions to those dumb enough to believe he is anything but a—

He was interrupted by the president saying "Captain, go make nice with the people."[52] To Cap, however, inspiring speeches to the American people are one thing, but political pandering is another entirely, and he is extremely wary of crossing that line.

Furthermore, he refuses to get involved directly in political campaigns, as he told Congressional candidate Andrew Bolt during "Capmania."[53] He later wondered, however, if his neutral stance was truly consistent with his mission to protect America; as he asked Sharon Carter, "shouldn't Cap be doing more about ineffective officials? I stay shy of politics. Is that a mistake? I'm supposed to be a man of the people, all the people ... but if I know there's a good man like Bolt who I'm certain can make this country better ... how can Cap not champion that?"[54] After Bolt clued him into possible corruption in his opponent's campaign, Cap uncovered links between the other candidate and the technological terrorist group AIM. But Bolt convinced him not to go public with it, arguing that absent solid proof, the news would only backfire on Bolt and tarnish Cap's image. Later, Cap thought to himself,

On the one hand, I know all too well that all that's required for evil to triumph ... is for good men to stand by and do nothing. What use is Captain America to anyone if he can't even bring in wrongdoers? On the other hand, this suit I wear has to symbolize more than just the political system. In order to earn their trust, I have to stand for all people. I have to be Everyman in a country that's becoming more diverse and fractured every day.[55]

In the end, Captain America decided not to campaign for Bolt—but Steve Rogers did, taking advantage of the freedoms he enjoys as an "ordinary" citizen (during one of the few periods during which he actually kept his identity secret!).

The idea that Captain America should avoid politics is embraced also by the American public in the Marvel Universe. When Bucky Barnes—then serving as Captain America—was arrested for his previous activities as the Winter Soldier, it was clear that regardless of the outcome of the trial he could no longer be Captain America, and Steve Rogers had to confront the possibility of being Cap himself once again. As we mentioned in chapter 4, Nick Fury gave him a little nudge, setting up a man named David Rickford as "the new Cap" to draw Rogers out and get him back into the fold. After Rogers rescued Rickford from AIM, he ordered him to stop wearing the uniform, which Rickford resisted:

> RICKFORD: That's not ... you don't get to say. You gave it up.
> ROGERS: Captured by AIM and almost turned into a monster on your first day? I do get to say.
> RICKFORD: No, you don't! 'Cause you forgot about all the people counting on you to be their symbol. You're supposed to be the guy who knows right and wrong ... outside the partisan crap that's ruining our country ... We need someone, Cap ... who we can believe.[56]

As if that weren't enough, soon thereafter Steve Rogers played chess with Professor Wally Young, an Army private whom Cap and Bucky saved during World War II. Rogers asked the professor if there needs to be a Captain America, or if he can do just as much good "out of the spotlight." As we saw in chapter 4—but I think it bears repeating—Young answered, "People are scared now ... more than they've been since we were kids. So it strikes me that this is exactly the time we could use a Captain America. Someone who'll rise above the noise and politics ... and let them know there's someone on their side."[57] This shows that the ordinary person on the street in the Marvel Universe values Cap's apolitical stance as much as he does, largely due to the cynicism and suspicion that attaches to politicians and the political process and a desire to have someone represent principle over partisanship.[58]

Principle over Politics

But what exactly does it means to value principles over politics? For this we can turn once again to philosopher Ronald Dworkin: this distinction played a central role in his theory of judicial decision-making, especially regarding how the role of judges differs from that of legislators. As Dworkin wrote,

> I call a "policy" that kind of standard that sets a goal to be reached, generally an improvement in some economic, political, or social feature of the

community... I call a "principle" a standard that is to be observed, not because it will advance or secure an economic, political, or social situation deemed desirable, but because it is a requirement of justice or fairness or some other dimension of morality.[59]

There are two features of this distinction that I want to emphasize. First, just as personal principles sometimes constrain the pursuit of our goals, national principles sometimes constrain a government's pursuit of its policy goals. For instance, a typical democratic government may adopt a goal of increasing college enrollment by offering incentives such as tax breaks for tuition, but they would probably draw the line at forcing people to enroll—that would violate a basic principle (or right) of autonomy and self-determination, especially for adults. Dworkin is famous for claiming that principles or rights can "trump" goals, which is merely an elegant way of saying that the ends do not always justify the means, a familiar idea from the first chapter in this book that can hold on a national level just as much as it can hold on a personal level. (For Captain America, of course, they're one and the same!)

Second, policies or goals are collective, in the sense that they're adopted by society through a process that balances the interests of competing groups—a function usually performed by a legislature. The purpose of a legislative body is to allow representatives of various interest groups to make their cases for policies to benefit their interests. This shouldn't be read as sinister; we're not talking about "special interests" in the modern sense, relatively small groups disproportionately influencing policy through intense lobbying efforts. What I'm describing here is representative democracy at its finest, citizens speaking through their elected representatives in the legislature to push for policies that are in their interests, such as education, health care, or public services. In our world of scarce resources, there is not enough money or time to devote to every goal suggested by the people or their representatives, and a democracy selects which goals to pursue through a political process characterized by bargaining and compromise. When Cap describes the presidency as having to "represent the best interests of an entire nation ... ready to negotiate—to compromise—24 hours a day," it is not a cynical statement, but an accurate picture of the political process doing what it was designed to do.[60]

Principles, on the other hand, derive from the legal and political history of a country and represent the ideals that define its national character.

When Cap read the Avengers charter and told Rick Jones that "I've based my entire adult life on the ideals found in these kinds of important documents. The Declaration of Independence ... the U.S. Constitution ... now this," he was saying he found his own guiding ideals in the same places that judges do (well, except for the Avengers charter!).[61] Unlike policies, principles are not subject to legislative bargaining or even popular vote: they are the essential national ideals that limit the policies that a legislature may choose to pursue or the means they decide to take in pursuit of them. As such, decisions of principle are the proper domain of judges, who are usually insulated from popular opinion and election. By the same token, it is not the role of the judge to determine policy: that belongs to a legislature representing the people and equipped to negotiate the trade-offs necessary to determine the best goals to pursue at a certain time. Judges step in only when the goal itself, or the means chosen to pursue it, violates some moral and legal principle (such as when the Supreme Court of the United States finds an act of Congress to be unconstitutional under the doctrine of judicial review).

We've seen this kind of conflict arise many times between Captain America and Iron Man, with Cap arguing for principle over Tony's "expediency." One particularly relevant case also came up between Cap and the Avengers' federal security liaison Duane Freeman when a group of superpowered beings called the Exemplars threatened to declare war on the Earth unless they were allowed to kill Juggernaut, a foe of the X-Men who betrayed the other Exemplars. (Note: Don't believe for a minute that they're exemplars of anything.) While Cap and Freeman were gathering information on their "guests," Freeman asked Cap if it really made sense to try to stop the Exemplars from killing Juggernaut, considering the risk they posed to the United States and Juggernaut's record of crimes. "It's only Poland, right?" Cap asked (invoking a bit of World War II history that he knew all too well), and then continued:

> If the Exemplars are allowed to come onto American soil and execute someone—anyone, even a criminal—without due process—and with the benign approval of the government—then what happens when they come back? And they will come back—people like them always do. The point isn't whether we like the Juggernaut—it's whether the kind of thing the Exemplars stand for—tyranny, force, and murder—should be opposed.[62]

It's not just the principles that Cap and the United States would be violating by sacrificing the Juggernaut to the Exemplars, but also the consequences of setting such a precedent. In this case, both principle and expediency point towards the same action.

Similar to the way we connected duties to principles earlier, rights are often a way to put principles into more concrete terms (although there is usually a need for further interpretation). Most of the guarantees contained in the Bill of Rights (the first ten amendments to the United States Constitution) serve to put principles of liberty, autonomy, and dignity into more applicable and enforceable terms. As we saw in the last chapter, Cap told Ben Urich after the Civil War, "I believe in the fundamental freedoms accorded us by our Constitution, Ben. I believe we have a right to bear arms, a right to defend and a right to choose. ... I saw the possibility of a registration act as a basic violation of our rights as Americans."[63] In other words, it's not that Cap disagreed with the goal of training heroes and installing a mechanism to hold them accountable—he just disagreed with the way the government (and Iron Man) were going about it, specifically by compromising essential rights.[64]

There are many instances—far too many to mention here—in which Captain America cited basic civil rights to stop what he considered the unjust pursuit of a goal. He often defends the First Amendment guarantee of free speech on behalf of those he disagrees with, including Flag-Smasher, Super-Patriot, and neo-Nazis, as well as protesters who call Avengers fascists and who criticize them for admitting Namor as a member after he led an invasion against Manhattan.[65] He recognizes the due process rights of criminal suspects (such as the Juggernaut), even when those rights may help guilty criminals escape prosecution. Sometimes the circumstances are extreme, such as when Cap tried to stop the Punisher from killing mob bosses in cold blood by shouting "they have rights—just as you do! No man can be denied those rights, or else none of us have any rights!"[66] But other times the circumstances are more ordinary, such as when Cap criticized lawyer Connie Ferrari, who was defending the head of AIM—an attorney-client relationship that was putting a strain on their budding romantic relationship. After Connie defended her actions to Cap, he found evidence to help convict the AIM leader and then apologized to Connie, admitting that she did the right thing by "giving him the very best defense possible. A Constitutional right covering all of us."[67] And when Cap and Sharon Carter came upon what Sharon called a riot, Cap said, "No, Sharon ... it's democracy ... 'The right of the people to peaceably assemble' doesn't say anything about doing it quietly."[68] Even though a riot did develop and people did end up getting hurt, Cap was hesitant to stop it too soon for fear of limiting the people's rights to gather and to speak freely, which he placed above any possible negative consequences from the people exercising them (until the situation became dangerous).

Even if we recognize the important role of rights as the embodiment of principles, we must also realize that few rights are absolute. Ronald Dworkin certainly recognized this: after explaining that rights *could* be absolute, depending on the political system that maintains them, he wrote that "rights may also be less than absolute; one principle might have to yield to another, or even to an urgent policy with which it competes on particular facts."[69] You'll recall both of these possibilities from our discussion of personal judgment, and it's no surprise that they arise in governmental decision-making as well.

After Steve Rogers returned from the "dead" during Norman Osborn's Siege of Asgard and was installed as the new head of global security, he had a little chat with Tony Stark:

> ROGERS: I'm not convinced letting you keep that armor is in the best interests of the country, Iron Man. I haven't made up my mind.
>
> STARK: There will never be an appropriate time to tell me that I can't have what is rightfully mine.
>
> ROGERS: Well, look who's all for civil rights all of a sudden.
>
> STARK: That has nothing to do with anything—
>
> ROGERS: Fine.
>
> STARK: So, what you're saying is these inalienable rights that you were willing to die for—freedom of power, all that ... all of that goes out the window now that you're in charge!
>
> ROGERS: I'm saying that it was you who put this entire country in danger when you let a maniac like Norman Osborn have the keys to your armory![70]

Even the "inalienable rights" in which Captain America believes so strongly may have to bend to some circumstances, such as what he perceived as Iron Man's irresponsibility with power. But this is nothing new to us, dear readers: this is just necessary compromise all over again. Just as Cap has had to compromise some principles in favor of other, more important principles or goals in the past, the same holds for rights—which are simply principles in slightly different clothes.

Captain America in (Principled) Action

Early in his career in the "modern" world, Captain America reflected on his role and purpose during one of his existential crises:

> This is the day of the anti-hero—the age of the rebel—and the dissenter! It isn't hip to defend the establishment! Only to tear it down! And, in a world rife with injustice, greed, and endless war—who's to say the rebels are wrong? But, I've never learned to play by today's new rules! I've spent a lifetime defending the flag—and the law! Perhaps I should have battled less—and questioned more![71]

And before long he *was* questioning, which we see most clearly in three huge storylines: the two times Steve Rogers gave up the Captain America identity to protest his government's actions, as well as the Civil War in which he led the resistance against the Superhuman Registration Act. Each of these incidents shows us a unique aspect of Cap's respect for principle over politics.

Secret Empire/Nomad

In the mid-1970s, Captain America found himself being defamed on television, framed for murder, and declared an unlawful fugitive, all due to the mysterious Secret Empire. During their final battle with Cap in Washington, DC, the Secret Empire's leader ran into the White House. When Cap caught and unmasked him, he turned out to be the president of the United States, who then shot himself in front of Captain America.[72] For Cap, this was the beginning of a significant crisis of faith in his identity and purpose as the symbol of his country. As word spread that he was considering quitting, he received advice from many of his friends and colleagues, but Peggy Carter— his World War II love and Sharon Carter's aunt—hit the nail on the head:

> Politicians come and politicians go—but America is still the greatest country on this grand, green Earth! Sure we've had scandals, but we've exposed them—publicly—and gotten back on the right track! There's nothing wrong with us—at least, no more than at any other point in history![73]

But this did not settle the issue for Cap, who once alone thought to himself, "I always tried to serve my country well—and now I find that the government was serving itself," which he struggled to understand. In his mind, this was the final straw, and once he came to that realization he told his collected friends that he would be Captain America no more![74]

But Steve Rogers (Captain, retired) found the call to heroism too strong (especially after being goaded by his old buddy Hawkeye), and soon he adopted the superhero name Nomad, representing his belief that he was a "man without a country." After an emotional visit to the Lincoln Memorial in Washington, during which he asked himself, "why did our forefathers seem to understand America more clearly than we do now?", Rogers found Roscoe Simons, a fan who adopted the Captain America identity and began working with the Falcon, dead at the hands of the Red Skull.[75] He started to talk things through with the Falcon to help process his disillusionment with the US government: "The people who had custody of the American dream had abused both it and us! There was no way I could keep calling myself 'Captain America,' because the others who acted in America's name were every bit as bad as the Red Skull."[76]

With this last phrase, Rogers had an epiphany, realizing that he had taken the noble patriotism of others who served America for granted and therefore saw threats only from villains outside of the government, not within it. "Oh Lord," he said, "if I wasn't prepared for any and all threats to the American dream, then what was I doing as Captain America? ... I thought I knew who the good guys and the bad guys were! ... I couldn't understand how the good guys could put their faith in a man so bad!" Rogers came to the conclusion that America didn't let him down, but rather he let the country down, in part because he should have "paid more attention to the way the American reality differed from the American dream."[77] Once he realized that American principles and the American dream needed protection more now than ever, and that he couldn't let others sacrifice their lives for the mission he was created for, he decided to become Captain America once again, promising that "whatever the threat—wherever it originates—I won't be blind again!"[78]

As Captain America pursued the Red Skull in the next issue, the narration drew a parallel between personal and national principles and their connection to integrity: "Steve Rogers was Captain America until he saw how America failed its ideals. Then he was Nomad ... until he saw how he failed his ideals."[79] As we discussed earlier, integrity requires maintaining one's principles consistently, and this applies to both persons and countries (as well as other institutions). This was the first significant violation of American principles by its elected leaders that Captain America witnessed (at least as shown in the comics), and Cap's reaction to it was a violation of his principles as well. But as Peggy Carter said, at its best America accounts for and learns from its mistakes, and so would Cap. As he thought to himself near the end of this episode, his battle with the Secret Empire and his time as Nomad led him to "a greater awareness of corruption, deceit, and the madness of power" as well as "a greater awareness of myself, as a man— and as a superhero. ... I've broken away from the blindness of the past, which can only mean a better future for myself—and the country."[80]

The Captain

When Cap next gave up his uniform and shield, it wasn't in response to a secretive government plot, but rather a disagreement over the proper role of Captain America that struck at the heart of his sense of meaning and purpose. When Cap was called before "the Commission, a specially appointed task force operating under the direct command of the president," the Commission's leader Mr. Yates informed him that the identity of Captain America, the costume, and the shield were all property of the US government. Furthermore, he argued that Steve Rogers signed an agreement in 1941 to serve the US government—an agreement which the Commission still regarded as valid, notwithstanding Cap's time on ice or his distinguished service to the country and as an Avenger since. "You fail to make an important distinction," Yates told him. "You are not Captain Avenger, Captain Shield, or Captain Solo—you are Captain America. Your service to those independent agencies, regardless of the nature of your activities, does not constitute an acceptable alternative to fulfillment of your tour of duty to your country."[81]

When Captain America balked at the Commission's demand that he resume his "position as America's super-soldier," Yates replies, "What reason could you possibly have to disobey a presidential mandate? Have you not pledged yourself to the service of your country? We are America, Rogers. We are your commanding officers. It had not even crossed our minds that you would have any difficulty obeying our directive!" We don't have to read any further to know what Cap's response to that would be: no person or committee, elected or appointed, "is" America. To Cap, America is a nation of people gathered under an ideal and pursuing a dream, and that dream is what Captain America serves and protects for the American people. "Those men are not my country," Rogers thought to himself after returning home. "They are only bureaucrats of the country's current administration. They represent the country's political system—while I represent those intangibles upon which our nation was founded ... liberty, justice, dignity, the pursuit of happiness." He worried that returning to official duty would compromise his ability to be a symbol of those principles, a symbol that "transcends mere politics."

When he returned to the Commission to hand over his costume and shield, he made the following statement:

> In all good conscience I cannot accept your conditions of employment. Captain America was created to be a mere soldier, but I have made him far more than that. To return to being a mere soldier would be a betrayal of all I've striven for, for the better part of my career. To serve the country your way, I would have to give up my personal freedom ... and place myself in a position where I might have to compromise my ideals to obey your orders. I cannot represent the American government; the president does that. I must represent the American people. I represent the American dream, the freedom to strive to become all that you dream of being. Being Captain America has been my American dream. To become what you want me to be, I would have to compromise that dream ... abandon what I have come to stand for. My commitment to the ideals of this country is greater than my commitment to a 40-year-old document. I am sorry, but that's the way it must be.[82]

We'll have reason to return to this speech later in this chapter (so free feel to dog-ear the page, or the electronic equivalent). For now, note that Cap takes a type of moral ownership over the identity of Captain America, claiming that he changed it over the years, integrating his own values into what the name Captain America means. He doesn't argue that this grants him legal rights to the name, but simply that he cannot call himself Captain America while following orders that might conflict with his own principles. In other words, to maintain his integrity as Captain America, he had to give up being Captain America rather than let the US government control his actions.

But the Commission found another person to serve as Captain America: John Walker, the former Super-Patriot. Alongside one of Super-Patriot's old sidekicks, Lemar Hoskins—operating under the name Battle Star—Walker started training to be the new Cap.[83] Because of his unstable temperament, however, Walker started brutalizing and sometimes killing his enemies, especially after a militant group called the Watchdogs killed his parents.[84] And as before, Steve Rogers could not stay inactive for long, but neither would he violate the Commission's order or "declare war on appointed officials of my nation's government," which he worried would only further weaken the American people's faith in their elected leaders.[85] He rejected the name Nomad (which at the time was being used by Jack Monroe, the "Bucky" from the 1950s) because "I am not a nomad, a man without a country. I have a country—America. And I intend to keep on serving my country and its people, no matter what obstacles politicians throw in my way!"[86] We see from this quote that Cap's previous experience with giving up the Captain America identity reinforced his purpose and his distinction between American values and the American government; this time around, he gave up being Cap in order to serve the American dream *better*, without compromising his principles for politically based government orders.

Now operating as simply "The Captain" (in a red, white, and black variant of his original costume), Cap led his friends on a series of heroic missions that eventually found them back in Washington to confront the Commission. Along the way, Cap found himself on the opposite side of the law (despite his compliance with the Commission's orders): for example, he and his friends caused property damage and interfered with the authorities while helping to stop a casino robbery. Afterwards, he had a discussion with the Falcon that foreshadowed some of his actions years later during the Civil War: "We have broken the law, and whatever the penalty is, we'll abide by it. Still, we caught the criminals, saved four lives, and prevented a robbery. Despite the law, I believe we did the right thing." Falcon pointed out, "by the same token, Cap—just because the Commission has the law on their side, maybe the right thing to do is to oppose them."[87] After all, Cap himself admitted earlier that the Commission "had the legal right to dictate the terms of my being Captain America. The moral and ethical right, no."[88] Cap considered what Falcon said and thought to himself, "Once a person decides to disregard the law, how will he know when he's gone too far?"[89] Clearly, judgment is the key, balancing principles of basic morality and compliance with the law—a key conflict in cases of civil disobedience, which we'll discuss more soon.

Despite his growing doubts regarding the legitimacy of the Commission, Cap decided to turn himself in. After some soul-searching about why he didn't fight harder against the Commission—wondering if he'd gotten tired or if he simply wanted a new kind of challenge—he took advantage of a power outage to escape and ended up fighting Flag-Smasher (of all people) alongside John Walker and Battle Star.[90] Finally, he came face-to-face with the man behind the Commission: not the president, as he thought, but the Red Skull himself, now a perfect double for Steve Rogers (due to clever cloning on the part of Arnim Zola).[91] Skull explained that his latest plot against America was to destroy the name and reputation of Captain America himself, by handpicking the violent Walker to replace Rogers and then having the Watchdogs kill his parents to push him over the edge. During his final battle with Walker, Cap realized that his confidence had suffered ever since Walker almost defeated him when they first met, and this led him to give in to the Commission without a fight. But in the end, it worked out for the best: "I've had to fight the good fight without [my title and uniform]. I've had to swallow my pain and anger and re-create myself as the Captain. I see how that was my way to harden myself! To use adversity to regain my fighting edge!"[92]

After defeating both Walker and the Red Skull—who got away, naturally, to fight again another day—both Captains faced the Commission. Their new leader, Valerie Cooper, asked Rogers to resume the identity of Captain America, admitting that "while it's true that the government owns the name, the uniform, and the shield of Captain America—the majority of us decided it is you, Steve Rogers, who made that name, uniform, and shield mean something!" But Cap turned it down, saying that he learned from this experience that he "can serve my ideals—the ideals of this great country— even without that uniform! I've learned that it's the man that counts, not the clothing!" He stormed out, but Walker caught up with him to say, "Who's kidding who? You may not have come up with the name or stitched the uniform together, but you created the role of Captain America—his code of conduct, his reputation, his legend!" He urged Rogers to take the name back, if only "to prevent them from getting yet another poor slob to try to do the job you do so easily!"[93] Walker's message must have worked, for when we turn the page Steve Rogers is once again wearing the red-white-and-blues, confident that he *is* Captain America. Furthermore, he knows that the name is more than a title: it represents what Steve Rogers made that title mean through his years of service and dedication to the ideals upon which America was founded.

Civil War

Our last significant example of Captain America standing up to the US government out of principle deals not with corrupt government leaders but a law which, by all appearances, was passed legitimately in response to public outcry. This, of course, was the Superhuman Registration Act against which Cap led the resistance during the Civil War. This event has been discussed throughout this book, so we'll be brief here, focusing on the nature of Cap's civil disobedience during this period.

Captain America's issue with registration was similar to the last situation—that it would place himself and other heroes under direct supervision of the US government—and his reaction was much the same as well. As he told SHIELD Director Maria Hill when she first tried to take him into custody, heroes have to stay above politics or Washington starts telling them who the villains are.[94] He added an element of political corruption when he explained to Sharon Carter that "the registration act is another step toward government control. And, while I love my country, I don't trust many politicians. Not when they're having their strings pulled by corporate donors. And not when they're willing to trade freedom for security."[95] This relatively new element of suspicion of politicians was also on his mind when he thought to himself, "they want superheroes to be controlled by the government. They want us to be puppets to a corporate shill structure, like their politicians and everything else on the planet. They don't see that we're all that's left keeping them truly protected and free."[96] This matter aside, the primary issue for Cap remained the freedom of superheroes to operate freely and legally while protecting their identities and private lives as well as voluntarily remaining accountable for their actions.

Cap made his civil disobedience clear to Ben Urich in his post-surrender interview when he said: "I have sworn an oath to defend America from external forces, and from within. If that means standing against my own government, rejecting a bogus law passed by my own superiors, then I suppose that's what it means."[97] Cap was frozen under water when Dr. Martin Luther King Jr. published his 1963 "Letter from Birmingham Jail," now considered one of the most profound justifications of civil disobedience ever written.[98] In it, Dr. King responded to fellow clergy who objected to the demonstrations that he led in Birmingham and for which he was incarcerated. He addressed the central issues head on:

One may well ask: "How can you advocate breaking some laws and obeying others?" The answer lies in the fact that there are two types of laws: just and unjust. I would be the first to advocate obeying just laws. One has not only a legal but a moral responsibility to obey just laws. Conversely, one has a moral responsibility to disobey unjust laws. I would agree with St. Augustine that "an unjust law is no law at all."

St. Augustine shared Dr. King's belief in *natural law*, the idea that man's law should not conflict with the moral law (or God's law).[99] Captain America also believes that laws and government policies should not conflict with morality, but more precisely that they should not conflict with the fundamental values of America itself.

Dr. King provided an example of such a law, based not on theology or basic morality but upon the idea that "all men were created equal" as enshrined in the Declaration of Independence:

> Let us consider a more concrete example of just and unjust laws. An unjust law is a code that a numerical or power majority group compels a minority group to obey but does not make binding on itself. This is difference made legal. By the same token, a just law is a code that a majority compels a minority to follow and that it is willing to follow itself. This is sameness made legal. Let me give another explanation. A law is unjust if it is inflicted on a minority that, as a result of being denied the right to vote, had no part in enacting or devising the law. Who can say that the legislature of Alabama which set up that state's segregation laws was democratically elected? Throughout Alabama all sorts of devious methods are used to prevent Negroes from becoming registered voters, and there are some counties in which, even though Negroes constitute a majority of the population, not a single Negro is registered. Can any law enacted under such circumstances be considered democratically structured?

He cited no biblical verse or commandment here, nor any "old-fashioned ethics"—just the principles of democracy and representation that America promised its citizens from its founding, but is still struggling to implement.[100]

Even in the face of such an unjust law, however, Dr. King did not advocate anarchy or general lawlessness, but resisting only the unjust law. He wrote that

> One who breaks an unjust law must do so openly, lovingly, and with a willingness to accept the penalty. I submit that an individual who breaks a law that conscience tells him is unjust, and who willingly accepts the penalty of imprisonment in order to arouse the conscience of the community over its injustice, is in reality expressing the highest respect for law.

Of course, Cap did not willingly accept imprisonment to make his point, but rather fought until he decided it was too costly to keep fighting. But he did focus his resistance on the registration act, and regretted any other illegal activity in which he engaged at the time.

Dr. King may have justified civil disobedience and explained how to identify unjust laws, but a question still remains. Lucky for us, the Anti-Cap—who, like many zealots Cap has faced over the years, took civil disobedience too far—once asked Captain America that very question, as we saw before: "How many times have you placed principle over orders? Ideals over government? Are you the only one who gets to do that? Do we get to defy our government in defense of freedom only if you agree with it? Where is that line, and who gets to draw it?"[101] As before, the Anti-Cap's question is misguided: nobody "gets to do that" in the sense of getting away with it. As Dr. King showed through his words and his actions, the law is the law, just or unjust, and true civil obedience means accepting the penalty for breaking the law. That said, any person "gets to do that" when he or she feels that a law is unjust, as long the person can honestly justify that act to himself or herself as the right thing to do according to his or her principles and is willing to accept the consequences of it.

What if other people don't agree? Many didn't agree with Dr. King and the rest of the Americans who demonstrated for civil rights—but if most people had agreed with what they were doing, they wouldn't have had to do it in the first place! In a speech we first saw in chapter 3, Captain America expressed a similar sentiment to Spider-Man when the younger hero wondered how Cap could stand up so confidently against registration when so many people supported it:

Doesn't matter what the press says. Doesn't matter what the politicians or the mobs say. Doesn't matter if the whole country decides that something wrong is something right. This nation was founded on one principle above all else: the requirement that we stand up for what we believe, no matter the odds or the consequences. When the mob and the press and the whole world tell you to move, your job is to plant yourself like a tree beside the river of truth, and tell the whole world—"no, you move."[102]

Consensus is wonderful—and, as we'll see in our final chapter, not as implausible as we tend to think—but as we know, principles are not subject to a popularity test or a vote. At the end of the day, all you have are your beliefs, opinions, and judgment, whether they're popular or not. And if you believe you're right and your cause is just, then you stand by it, as befits a person of conviction and honor.

Having detailed three examples of Captain America defying the United States government, I must note that while Cap is often skeptical or critical of people in charge of the government at specific points in time, or the ways that politics sometimes works (or doesn't work), he is not anti-government in general. After he first encountered Thor as "The Captain" and explained to his friend what had happened, Thor wanted to "journey to Washington—and overthrow these madmen!" But Cap calmed him down, telling him that "even though I wouldn't let the current administration use me for a pawn, I still can't allow you to topple it. … I still believe in and respect the American system of democracy!"[103] When he told the American people that he wouldn't run for president, he said that "the presidency is one of the most important jobs in the world. The holder of that office must represent the best interests of an entire nation. He must be ready to negotiate—to compromise—24 hours a day, to preserve the republic at all costs!"[104] When the Avengers discovered that the red poison gas emanating from Mount Rushmore was developed by the US government, She-Hulk noted that Cap didn't look surprised. "I'm not shocked, Jennifer," he said. "Just disappointed. The system. I believe in it. I believe our government can work. And has. But sometimes it just takes one idiot at the top—hiding somewhere—to make the dominoes fall."[105]

Perhaps the best statement of Captain America's attitude towards the American political system came after he (again with the help of Thor) defeated his old friend Inali Redpath and prevented him from furthering his murderous revolution on behalf of his fellow Native Americans. As Cap thought to himself then,

> This government can be wrong. Our politics can be flawed. We are, after all, a complex system run by human beings. But the country is good and though it's no longer easy—I still feel pride in her. I still love her and will fight to the death to protect her and keep her safe—so others can—as I know they will—make her right again—most of the time.[106]

As James Madison wrote in *The Federalist No. 51*, "If men were angels, no government would be necessary. If angels were to govern men, neither external nor internal controls on government would be necessary."[107] An effective system of government constrains those who work within it from acting in their own self-interest and in violation of their duties and responsibilities. But no system of government is perfect; as Cap said, it's a "complex system, run by human beings," and we have to work continually towards refining that system so those human beings work for the country, not themselves. That, you could say, is part of the American dream that Cap dedicates his life to protecting, and the idea that he urges us all to work together to promote.[108]

How does this affect Captain America's patriotism, though? Despite the advice Cap gave him before he died after the Civil War, the Young Avenger known as Patriot still had doubts about the value of patriotism based on how his fellow African Americans were treated throughout America's history (and how his grandfather, Isaiah Bradley, was treated after the government tried to turn him into another super-soldier). Soon thereafter, he spoke to Bucky, who had yet to take up the Captain America identity himself. Bucky told him, "You have to realize that America is bigger than its politics or its problems. Steve would say, America is an idea. ... I know, just like you, Steve hated a lot of things this country has done. But somehow, he still managed to see the dream. The idea that made this place great to begin with."[109] Politicians come and go, but the American system is based on sound principles of representative democracy and separation of powers, just as the country itself is based on the timeless principles of freedom, equality, and justice. As always, it is these core principles to which Captain America is loyal, and in which he will never lose faith.

In this chapter I hope to have dispelled any illusions that Captain America is a jingoist flag-waver, and explained instead that he embodies an inclusive and cosmopolitan patriotism that balances idealism with clear-eyed pragmatism. Furthermore, he stresses principles over politics, opposing his government when it does not live up to the same standards to which he holds himself, and has even handed over the name and shield in protest—at least until he realized that Captain America had become more than a title but an intrinsic part of who he is.

In the next and final chapter, we'll apply the insights from this chapter to the current division of political opinion that seems ready to crack America in half. Some have tried to restore unity to the American people, to bring the red states and the blue states closer together, but many think we are irreparably split on the important issues of the day. I will argue that this is wrong, and that we can use Captain America's perspective on principle and politics as an example to show us a possible way out of our current American crisis.

Notes

1   Appropriately enough, I began writing this chapter on July 4th!
2   *Avengers*, vol. 4, #16 (2011).

3   *Captain America*, vol. 3, #44 (2001).
4   Roger Stern, "Remembering Cap," in *Captain America: War & Remembrance* (2011).
5   *Marvel Spotlight*, vol. 3, #18, 2007, "Cap in Crisis: Steve Englehart's Captain America."
6   *Captain America*, vol. 7, #1 (2013).
7   *Captain America*, vol. 3, #31 (2000).
8   *Captain America*, vol. 1, #122 (1970).
9   For a survey of philosophical views on patriotism—both for and against—see Igor Primoratz's entry on patriotism in the *Stanford Encyclopedia of Philosophy* (http://plato.stanford.edu/entries/patriotism/), his edited collection *Patriotism* (Amherst, NY: Humanity Books, 2002), and most recently the special issue of *The Journal of Ethics* (vol. 13, no. 4, 2009) that he edited on the topic.
10 Alasdair MacIntyre, *Is Patriotism a Virtue?* (Lawrence, KS: University Press of Kansas, 1984), reprinted in Primoratz, *Patriotism*.
11 Marcia Baron, "Patriotism and 'Liberal' Morality," in David Weissbord (ed.), *Mind, Value, and Culture: Essays in Honor of E.M. Adams* (Atascadero, CA: Ridgeview, 1989), pp. 269–300, and Stephen Nathanson, "In Defense of 'Moderate Patriotism,'" *Ethics* 99 (1989): 535–552, both reprinted in Primoratz, *Patriotism*.
12 It is worth noting, I think, that MacIntyre does not consider patriotism based on national ideals rather than historical loyalties to be patriotism in the purest sense, because non-Americans could be just as devoted to American ideals as Americans are, but it would be odd to call the former "American patriots." (See "Is Patriotism a Virtue?" in Primoratz, *Patriotism*, pp. 43–44.)
13 *Captain America*, vol. 1, #243 (1980).
14 *Captain America*, vol. 1, #261 (1981).
15 *Captain America*, vol. 1, #273 (1982).
16 *Captain America*, vol. 1, #322 (1986).
17 *Secret War* #5 (2005).
18 *Captain America*, vol. 1, #327 (1987). Years later, Sally Floyd made similar accusations to Cap following the Civil War, albeit much more cynically. After asking Cap if he knows what Myspace is (remember, this was 2007) or who won the last *American Idol* competition, she told him, "Your problem is that you're fighting for an ideal—it's all you know how to do. America is no longer about Mom and apple pie … it's about high cholesterol and Paris Hilton and scheming your way to the top" (*Civil War: Front Line* #11, 2007, "Embedded Part 11"). If her point is that Cap must remember the American people behind the American ideals, indeed he has struggled with this problem, at one time thinking, "I've always understood the spirit—the ideals—I've been protecting … but how does a man get a handle on the untold millions of people attached to those ideals?" (*Captain America*, vol. 1, #289, 1984).

19 *Mythos – Captain America* (2008). For a survey of up-to-date thinking about cosmopolitanism, see Gillian Brock, "Contemporary Cosmopolitanism: Some Current Issues," *Philosophy Compass* 8 (2013): 689–698.

20 *Captain America*, vol. 1, #312 (1985). This resembles Nathanson's point that patriotism within a large community (such as a country) involves balancing the moral and cultural systems of subcommunities within it ("In Defense of 'Moderate Patriotism,'" in Primoratz, *Patriotism*, pp. 98–100).

21 *Captain America*, vol. 1, #268 (1982).

22 *Captain America*, vol. 3, #47 (2001).

23 Nathanson, "In Defense of 'Moderate Patriotism,'" in Primoratz, *Patriotism*, p. 90. For an extended discussion of moderate patriotism, see Nathanson's book *Patriotism, Morality, and Peace* (Lanham, MD: Rowman & Littlefield, 1993).

24 *Avengers*, vol. 3, #84 (2004).

25 *Captain America*, vol. 4, #8 (2003).

26 *Avengers*, vol. 3, #84 (2004).

27 *Captain America and the Falcon* #14 (2005).

28 *Captain America*, vol. 1, #267 (1982).

29 *Captain America*, vol. 1, #322 (1986). (In the comics, Flag-Smasher was cut off before he could finish his question.)

30 *Avengers: Earth's Mightiest Heroes*, vol. 1, #8 (2005); see the previous chapter.

31 Geographer Jason Dittmer explores how "nationalist superheroes" such as Captain America represent the concept of the nation-state in his book *Captain America and the Nationalist Superhero: Metaphors, Narratives, and Geopolitics* (Philadelphia, PA: Temple University Press, 2013).

32 *Captain America*, vol. 1, #322 (1986).

33 *Captain America*, vol. 1, #156 (1972); Burnside's history is explained in *Captain America*, vol. 1, #155 (1972), and it was his bedside alongside which Cap reminisced in *Captain America*, vol. 6, #19 (2012) (see note 85 in chapter 4).

34 *Marvel Spotlight*, vol. 3, #18 (2007), "Remembering 'Remembrance': Stern & Byrne Take Their Turn with America's Fighting Legend."

35 *Captain America*, vol. 1, #267 (1982). For an example of kids agreeing with Cap's message of "you can be what I am if you only try," see the end of *Captain America's Bicentennial Battles* (1976), in which kids from a poor neighborhood say things like "things may get tough for me, brother—but that won't stop, if I wanta make it!"

36 *Captain America*, vol. 1, #267 (1982).

37 Ibid. Afterwards, Maggie said, "Sheesh! Will you listen to me—making speeches like a regular … Captain America!"

38 Ibid. This American dream/American reality dichotomy was a regular theme in writer J.M. DeMatteis' run on *Captain America* (which is one of my favorites). In *Captain America*, vol. 1, #284 (1983), for instance, he told Nomad (Jack Monroe) that "One thing you're going to have to learn … fast … is that

the American dream we're both sworn to defend—is oftentimes light years removed from the American reality!"

39 *Captain America*, vol. 3, #7 (1998).
40 *Captain America: The Chosen* #6 (2008).
41 *Captain America*, vol. 3, #46 (2001).
42 *Captain America*, vol. 1, #255 (1981).
43 *Captain America*, vol. 5, #25 (2007).
44 *Young Avengers Presents* #1 (2008).
45 *Marvel Team-Up*, vol. 1, #106 (1981).
46 *Avengers*, vol. 3, #67 (2003).
47 *Captain America*, vol. 1, #322 (1986).
48 *Fear Itself* #1 (2011).
49 *Thor*, vol. 3, #11 (2008).
50 *Captain America*, vol. 3, #1 (1998).
51 *Avengers*, vol. 3, #23 (1999).
52 *Avengers*, vol. 4, #24 (2012).
53 Cap refused to endorse Bolt in *Captain America*, vol. 3, #4 (1998), although his Skrull impersonator did two issues later in *Captain America*, vol. 3, #6 (1998).
54 *Captain America*, vol. 3, #13 (1999).
55 Ibid.; we can safely presume Cap did not mean the Everyman we described above, but rather the general concept of the typical American. Also, the passage about good men allowing evil to occur is often attributed as a line by philosopher and political theorist Edmund Burke, but this is in dispute; for more on this, see http://quoteinvestigator.com/2010/12/04/good-men-do/.
56 *Captain America*, vol. 5, #615.1 (2011).
57 *Captain America*, vol. 5, #616 (2011), "Must There Be a Captain America?"
58 The Mighty Thor, the Odinson and Prince of Asgard, is hardly the "man on the street," but even he wondered if his fellow warrior was cut out for government service, such as his position as head of global security. "Heavy is the crown, dear Captain?" he asked Cap at the time. "As much of a leader and a military man as you are, there is also a side of you that has a more … rebellious streak, I believe is the term. If I may … you are always at your best when you buck the system. And if that is true, how can you be at your best if you are the system yourself?" (*Avengers*, vol. 4, #25, 2012).
59 Ronald Dworkin, *Taking Rights Seriously* (Cambridge, MA: Harvard University Press, 1977), p. 22.
60 *Captain America*, vol. 1, #250 (1980).
61 *Avengers: Earth's Mightiest Heroes*, vol. 1, #8 (2005).
62 *Avengers*, vol. 3, #25 (2000). *That's* why the Exemplars are definitely not … you know … exemplars.
63 *Civil War: Front Line* #11 (2007), "Embedded Part 11."

64 Cap's concern about accountability was shown after he fought William Burnside in *Captain America*, vol. 1, #156 (1972). As the narration read, "In his thoughts, he is once again a gawky youngster named Steve Rogers, wanting so desperately to fight America's enemies that he volunteered to test an unknown serum—and so became the guardian of his country. But no one knew anything about Steve Rogers—least of all himself. There had been no security checks on him, before entrusting him with his power. What if he had had the fatal flaw, that would have driven him to super-patriotism, madness, and mayhem? What if things had been just slightly different?"

65 In order, *Captain America*, vol. 1, #312 (1985), #323 (1986), and #269 (1982), and *Avengers*, vol. 1, #329 (1991) and #270 (1986). Cap did, however, remind Flag-Smasher (in *Captain America*, vol. 1, #312, 1985) that while "everyone has the right to express himself … no one has the right to force others to listen"—an aspect of the guarantee of free speech that is too often forgotten.

66 *Captain America*, vol. 1, #241 (1979).

67 *Captain America*, vol. 3, #41 (2001).

68 *Fear Itself* #1 (2011).

69 Dworkin, *Taking Rights Seriously*, p. 92.

70 *Avengers Prime* #1 (2010).

71 *Captain America*, vol. 1, #122 (1970).

72 An atrociously compressed summary of the events captured in the 2005 trade paperback *Captain America and the Falcon: Secret Empire*, which collected *Captain America*, vol. 1, #168–176 (1973–1974), written by Steve Englehart and Mike Friedrich and illustrated by Sal Buscema, Vincent Colletta, and Frank McLaughlin. This storyline was an homage to the Watergate controversy, and though it was not stated explicitly in the comics, Steve Englehart has made it clear since that he intended for the leader of the Secret Empire to be President Richard Nixon (*Marvel Spotlight*, vol. 3, #18, 2007, "Cap in Crisis: Steve Englehart's Captain America").

73 *Captain America*, vol. 1, #176 (1974).

74 Ibid.

75 For the full-length version of these events, see the 2006 trade paperback *Captain America and the Falcon: Nomad*, which collected *Captain America*, vol. 1, #177–186 (1974–1975), written by Steve Englehart with John Warner and pencilled by Sal Buscema, Frank Robbins, and Herb Trimpe (with various inkers). (The quote regarding Lincoln is from *Captain America*, vol. 1, #181, 1975.)

76 *Captain America*, vol. 1, #183 (1975).

77 I never said J.M. DeMatteis was the *first* one to use this phrase!

78 All the quotes in this paragraph are from *Captain America*, vol. 1, #183 (1975).

79 *Captain America*, vol. 1, #184 (1975). In the same issue, when Cap found the Red Skull, he told him that "you made me remember what was important

about this country, Skull—the dream it was built on, not the deadwood thrown on top." (I guess that was his way of saying "thank you.")

80 *Captain America*, vol. 1, #184 (1975).

81 All quotes in this paragraph and the next are from *Captain America*, vol. 1, #332 (1987).

82 Ibid.

83 Hoskins, who is African American, originally went by the name Bucky (in a larger version of the original's costume) until an older African American man told him that "buck" was a racial epithet in some areas of the country (*Captain America*, vol. 1, #341, 1988).

84 *Captain America*, vol. 1, #345 (1988).

85 *Captain America*, vol. 1, #336 (1987). Before declaring this to himself, he had met Brother Nature, a former park ranger who had discovered corruption in the management of federal woodlands and then resorted to ecoterrorism, which Rogers rejected as a violation of his own principles.

86 *Captain America*, vol. 1, #337 (1988).

87 Ibid.

88 *Captain America*, vol. 1, #336 (1987).

89 *Captain America*, vol. 1, #337 (1988). The Captain confronted Iron Man during this episode while Shellhead was fighting his own "Armor Wars" against the US government; see *Iron Man*, vol. 1, #228, and *Captain America*, vol. 1, #341 (both from 1988).

90 *Captain America*, vol. 1, #349 (1989).

91 *Captain America*, vol. 1, #350 (1989); the first story, "Seeing Red," concludes the story with the battle between Cap and the Skull, while the second, "Resurrection," explains how Skull ended up blue-eyed, blond, and buff.

92 *Captain America*, vol. 1, #350 (1989), "Seeing Red."

93 All the quotes in this paragraph are from *Captain America*, vol. 1, #350 (1989), "Seeing Red."

94 *Civil War* #1 (2006). After all, Cap had more than his share of experience with the Avengers being overseen by the US government or the United Nations and the political interference that followed; for example, the US government once voided the Avengers charter as part of an arms treaty with the Soviet Union! (See *Avengers*, vol. 1, #327, 1990.)

95 *Captain America*, vol. 5, #22 (2006).

96 *New Avengers*, vol. 1, #21 (2006). This focus on money in politics isn't entirely new to Cap; remember his experience with AIM's lobbying a Congressional candidate (*Captain America*, vol. 3, #13, 1999).

97 *Civil War: Front Line* #11 (2007), "Embedded Part 11." As Cap told TV audiences years earlier, "this nation was founded by dissidents—by people who wanted something better! There's nothing sacred about the status quo—and there never will be!" (*Captain America*, vol. 1, #130, 1970).

98   See   www.africa.upenn.edu/Articles_Gen/Letter_Birmingham.html   (all quotes from Dr. King below are from this document). You can also see Cap's reaction to learning about Dr. King—and hearing his "I Have a Dream" speech, also from 1963—in *Captain America: Man Out of Time* #3 (2011).

99   For more on natural law, see John Finnis, "Natural Law Theories," *Stanford Encyclopedia of Philosophy*, at http://plato.stanford.edu/entries/natural-law-theories/.

100   This portion of Dr. King's speech also evokes John Stuart Mill's concept of *tyranny of the majority*, in which the majority of citizens vote to restrict the essential rights of the minority; we'll talk about this in the next chapter.

101   *Captain America and the Falcon* #4 (2004).

102   *Amazing Spider-Man* #537 (2006).

103   *Thor*, vol. 1, #390 (1988).

104   *Captain America*, vol. 1, #250 (1980).

105   *Avengers*, vol. 3, #67 (2003).

106   *Captain America*, vol. 4, #11 (2003).

107   See www.constitution.org/fed/federa51.htm.

108   Captain America took that role on himself when, after the "Red Zone" incident ended, he asked the president to make sure any other chemical weapons operations were shut down, and in turn the president asked Cap to help correct any further mistakes the government might make (*Avengers*, vol. 3, #70, 2003).

109   *Young Avengers Presents* #1 (2008).

7

Can Captain America Help Us Achieve Greater Unity and Civility?

I had two goals in mind when I set out to write this book. First, I wanted to show how Captain America's virtuous and principled ethics, so often mocked for being anachronistic and "black-and-white," are actually timeless and nuanced. If we do live in more complicated times, then a moral code like Captain America's, one that applies time-tested ideals to novel problems, is exactly what we need. At risk of mangling a metaphor, we don't need to reinvent the wheel—we just need to learn how to steer it over new terrain.

Most of this book has been spent on the first goal, but starting with the discussion of judgment in chapter 5, we have been building up gradually to the second one: to show how Captain America's approach to principle and politics can remind us in America what we have in common in this time of divisive acrimony. If we can keep our shared ideals in mind, they can form a common ground from which we can discuss our differences of opinion about how to interpret and implement them. This can only raise the level of political discourse and debate in this country, enabling us to address the problems we face rather than just simply arguing past each other which, in the end, solves nothing.

The "Divided States of America," Then and Now

You can't open a newspaper, turn on the news, or browse the Web for long without reading some commentary arguing that Americans are more politically divided than ever. While there is surely some truth to this, we

The Virtues of Captain America: Modern-Day Lessons on Character from a World War II Superhero, First Edition. Mark D. White.
© 2014 John Wiley & Sons, Inc. Published 2014 by John Wiley & Sons, Inc.

should be careful not to jump to any conclusions. I will argue in this chapter that while we are polarized on narrowly defined issues, we agree on more basic principles, ideals, and goals—which don't get as much attention in the media compared to arguments over how we should pursue them.

The around-the-clock news cycle and widespread access to the Internet from our phones and computers has made us more informed about events at home and around the globe. But the constant barrage of information can also make it seem as though the nation has changed when we may simply know more about what's happening in it. Today, we look back at the era leading up to and during World War II and admire the collective spirit of Americans—for good reason, certainly—but some may be surprised to learn that there was significant dissent even then. This should not be surprising, however, because the country was still reeling from the devastating effects of the Great Depression and seeing yet another global war on the horizon. Also, we've seen that Captain America was struck by the level of mistreatment of women and African Americans compared to the improved (but not perfect) situation in the modern day when he had a chance to travel back to 1945 to search for Bucky.[1] In addition to the ongoing struggle for equality on the part of minorities in the 1940s, there was broader social unrest, including large-scale protests and union strikes trying to bring attention to poverty and unemployment; large demonstrations against becoming involved in the war (which largely subsided after Pearl Harbor was attacked); and criticism of President Franklin Delano Roosevelt's actions in the economic and political realms, such as his New Deal legislation and his attempt to pack the Supreme Court. And that's just the most visible part of social and political conflict; as we saw in chapter 5, thanks to writer Roger Stern, Cap "had grown up in an era of economic upheaval and government corruption, in a time when political and religious demagogues used the airwaves to increase their personal power and wealth."[2] Of course, the reach and diversity of the "airwaves" in the 1930s and 1940s paled compared to today, but people then listened to the radio as much as people today watch TV or surf the Internet, so we discount its impact at our own peril.

Each generation's problems are unique in that they are experienced against the background of new technology, ever-changing demographics, and a shifting culture. Look beneath the surface, however, and you'll find the same issues raised time and time again. In the 1930s and 1940s people protested the effect of the Great Depression on already rising levels of inequality; in recent years we have the Occupy movement. Back then, they had protests against joining the War in Europe; today we have protests against America's involvement in the Middle East. Franklin Delano Roosevelt was accused by his critics of overreaching and extending the reach of government—as has Barack Obama during his two terms as president. The acknowledgment that things were not so great "back then" should not make us feel better about "right now," of course, but it can grant us some perspective and humility.

The divisions within American society have been a theme in Captain America's stories for almost as long as he's been defrosted from the ice. (They probably started with people wanting him to go back under!) In 1966, Cap thought to himself, "This is a new world—a new age! An age of atomic power, space exploration, social upheaval—yet, an age over which the threat of war hangs heavy again!"[3] A few years later, in 1970, Cap thought that "this is the day of the anti-hero—the age of the rebel—and the dissenter! ... And in a world rife with injustice, greed, and endless war—who's to say the rebels are wrong?"[4] The following year, he told his new partner the Falcon that "the world's like a giant powder keg—waiting for the slightest spark of hatred to set it off!"[5] Finally, as he told William Burnside, the bigoted 1950s Captain America, "America's in danger from within as well as without! There's organized crime, injustice, and fascism."[6] And that's all before Cap has his run-in with the Secret Empire that led him to abandon the Captain America identity to become Nomad (as we saw in the previous chapter). This episode not only made him more skeptical of politicians, but also opened his eyes to the influence of propaganda and the media on public opinion, which he was alarmed to find was even more powerful than in his "past life."[7]

As we move closer to the current day, we have seen Captain America dealing with foes like Everyman, Flag-Smasher, Super-Patriot, and the Anti-Cap, all of whom represented various points of view in America (regardless of their questionable methods of "expressing" themselves). Despite his experiences in the 1970s, Cap is still amazed at the power of the media and popular culture during the many times the public grew angry with the Avengers, as well as the "Capmania" period that led to a Skrull invasion.[8] It was around that time (in 1999) that he described America as "a country that's becoming more diverse and fractured every day," referencing the balance the country has long struggled to find between the diversity of races, ethnicities, and cultures that makes America unique and the underlying unity and equality we need to prosper as a nation.[9] Near the end of the Civil War, Cap was even more dramatic (and understandably so), telling Sally Floyd that "we're becoming swaths of red and blue on an election-night map. Welcome to the Divided States of America."[10]

Finally, since the financial collapse of 2007–2008, the focus has been on fear in America as reflected in the *Fear Itself* event, during which Iron Man told Captain America, "people are mad right now, and broke and they've been lied to and ripped off—and when people who're already mad get scared than all hell kinda breaks loose."[11] This point is brought home more directly when cable news blowhard Reed Broxton ranted about Cap on his show, saying that "I'm appreciative of Captain America's good deeds. But what has he done to save us from the rising unemployment rate? Escalating gas prices? The crashing economy?"[12] Cap knows better than to believe that he's responsible for economic policy—and he also knows better than to believe what Broxton says, although he acknowledges his influence over viewers—but he's still concerned about the country, telling SHIELD agent (and former villain and girlfriend) Rachel Leighton: "Rioting in the streets, super heroes fighting each other ... no jobs ... no security ... People aren't just scared anymore. They're angry. The cracks are starting to show ... and I'm not sure if the American people have enough faith to hold the country together."[13] Rachel assured Cap that he could help them, but even the living symbol of the country wondered if he had the strength.[14]

Of course, Captain America doesn't have do it alone; as we saw earlier, he emphasizes that it's every American's responsibility to help make our country a better place.[15] In the real world, of course, we don't have a Steve Rogers, super-soldier and sentinel of liberty, so we *have* to do it ourselves. So where we do start? Here's my idea, inspired by Cap: We should refocus on what we as Americans have in common rather than what divides us— starting with our core American ideals and principles.

The Three Core American Ideals

During one of their many physical and ideological battles, the Red Skull scoffed at the idea of equality for all, calling it a "myth." Captain America asked him:

> A myth, is it? Then America herself is just a myth—as are liberty, and justice—and faith! Myths that free men everywhere, are willing to die for! It's tyranny which is the myth—and bigotry which is an abomination before the eyes of mankind! It's you who are the fool! For, humanity has come of age— and, so long as love, not hatred, fills men's hearts—the day of the tyrant is ended![16]

Over the years, Captain America not only defended justice, equality, and liberty to the Red Skull, but has represented them as the core ideals of the United States of America. I believe that refocusing our attention on these ideals, remembering what we have in common while debating our differences, is the first step towards recovering a sense of national unity and restoring civility to our political life.

Of course, this will not be easy. It may seem that Americans of various political orientations can't agree on anything these days. As Cap said, we're the "Divided States of America," and getting farther apart as we absorb news and commentary that confirms our own beliefs and makes the other side seem even more different from us (if not simply "stupid" and "evil"). But I believe we do agree on something: the basic principles upon which this country was founded. To the extent we disagree about these ideals, we differ regarding how they're interpreted and implemented, not their basic meaning and importance. If we can focus on the core beliefs we share, then we can concentrate our arguments on where we truly differ: how we should understand these principles, balance them against each other, and put them into practice. Political disagreements are all too often cast in terms of "right" and "wrong" or "good" and "evil," whereas they're actually matters of nuanced judgment. Simply appreciating the complexity of the issues involved, and the sincere effort of many Americans to consider them in light of their ideals and principles, may make us more respectful, sympathetic, and maybe even understanding towards each other's points of view.[17]

Justice

Justice is an incredibly difficult concept to define, but for our purposes we can say it's concerned with making sure every person gets what he or she deserves in interactions with other people, in terms of both individuals and society as a whole. Of course, this just shifts the problem to the meaning of *desert*: what does a person deserve in a given situation? In most modern democratic societies, this question is answered by citing the equal dignity of all persons—a version of equality, which we'll discuss next—which implies that every person deserves to be treated with equal consideration and respect. The connection of justice to equality is also captured by the concept of *fairness*, which often works as a substitute for justice.[18]

Our discussion of justice here will be brief, because it harkens back to many concepts we've touched on throughout this book. For instance, justice is often said to be "what's right" as opposed to "what's good"; in other words, justice is normally understood to be a deontological idea of right and wrong rather than a utilitarian one of better and worse. We saw this in Captain America's discomfort with the idea of plea bargaining, which seems to sacrifice justice by offering a lesser sentence to a criminal to further some other goal. While Cap understood the reasoning, he found it unjust.[19] In fact, justice is often contrasted with the law, because law serves as an imperfect mechanism designed by human beings to approximate justice. We see this in the resolution of court cases in which the opinion is regarded as legally correct but the outcome of the case is found to be unjust. (One common trope in fiction, whether comics, novels, movies, or television, is having the hero say something like "I don't serve the law ... I serve justice!"[20]) As we've seen, even Captain America has had occasion to violate the law in the sense of a greater good—which can also be called justice. The civil disobedience of the Reverend Martin Luther King, Jr. can also be understood as defying the law to promote justice—in his particular case, the equal treatment of African Americans.

The deontological nature of justice also explains its close relationship with rights, which are often instituted and enforced to serve the greater cause of justice. For example, the guarantees in the Bill of Rights that we discussed in chapter 6, especially the ones that address civil liberties such as the rights to due process, the right to an attorney, and protection against improper search and seizure, can be understood as helping to ensure that a criminal defendant receives a fair trial by holding the prosecution up to a high standard of proof. Also, the rights that are guaranteed by laws of property and accident (or *tort*) help protect people and their belongings from being abused, stolen, or destroyed by others—including the government—without the appropriate procedure and compensation. Even if someone can prove that by violating your rights they could increase their well-being— perhaps even more than it lowered yours—your rights are there to protect you against this kind of wrongful interference. (This is another example of Ronald Dworkin's position that rights can "trump" welfare, which is true in legal decisions both large and small.)

Insofar as justice is understood as doing the right thing, based on equality and fairness, the basic concept itself seems indisputable. But there is significant disagreement over how justice is to be interpreted and implemented in particular situations. There are different sorts of justice that can come into conflict: for example, seeking justice for the victims of a terrorist attack can seem to be at odds with following the rules of justice that govern a fair trial, which raises further issues of whether terror suspects are owed the same constitutional guarantees accorded to a "normal" criminal defendant, which can be extended into the debate over military tribunals and detention for terror suspects as well as the operation of counterterrorism operations (such as the use of unmanned drones) in the Middle East. (Whew—that would be a great exam question, wouldn't it?) There are many issues packed in there, but all of them hinge on differing and contrasting conceptions of justice that must be sorted out and balanced to arrive at an opinion, policy, or law. All of us agree that the "right thing" must be done, but we disagree on what that is—and we have to find a way to discuss it that focuses on our differences of opinion regarding how to understand and implement justice while at the same time not forgetting that, at its core, we agree on what justice is.

Equality

In the most general terms, justice can be thought of as equality put into action. Treating people as equals in the terms of the law, political involvement, and everyday interactions, is something that everybody can believe in as an essential ideal—just as Captain America does, as we've seen numerous times throughout this book. They often disagree on how to interpret equality and how to implement it, however, especially when it conflicts with other principles (such as liberty).

Of course, it's impossible to deny that some people in America still don't believe in equality for *all*. There are still a number of people who refuse to support the rights of women and African Americans that were the result of years of struggle and were long overdue when they were enacted. Such people believe that they are superior and entitled because of their gender or their race, which stands against the Enlightenment ideals upon which this country was founded (even if several of its important documents betrayed those ideals when they were written). As I write this, even though their fight for substantive equality goes on, women and African Americans have achieved a formal equality that gays and lesbians still struggle for, especially in the areas of discrimination, marriage, and family law, and transsexuals continue to face challenges and battles of their own. In my opinion, the idea that equality under the law should apply to all Americans regardless of ... well, *anything*, is beyond question, and I will treat it as such as we proceed.

If we believe that all Americans deserve to be treated as equal under the law, what disagreements could possibly remain regarding equality? Many, actually, although I'll mention only two, one more practical in nature and the other more theoretical. The first one is the appropriate legal treatment of noncitizens, which comes to a head most often in the case of undocumented aliens or illegal immigrants. While there are people who have negative feelings towards undocumented aliens based purely on racism and bigotry, others who bear no such animus nonetheless believe that undocumented aliens' status as noncitizens, compounded by the fact that they're residing in the country illegally, makes them ineligible for certain legal rights and privileges to which citizens are entitled, such as the right to work, to hold a driver's license, and to vote. According to this view, restricting the rights of undocumented aliens is a matter of justice, based on the idea that like cases must be treated alike and unlike cases must be treated differently.[21] Specifically, undocumented aliens do not have equal legal status with citizens (and legal visitors and residents), and some believe this difference in status disqualifies them for some of the protections that citizens have. (Issues of liberty also intersect here, including the freedom to locate where one chooses and the freedom to find work, which often sets citizen workers against immigrants whether legal or not.) But even those who hold this position regarding status must confront the question of what rights undocumented aliens *are* entitled to simply as human beings—surely they are equal to American citizens in that regard. This opens another can of worms, as does the entire issue of illegal immigration, even for those who agree on the basic idea of equality.

A second area of disagreement with respect to equality can be captured by the title of economist and philosopher Amartya Sen's paper "Equality of What?"[22] Equality can refer to many things, each with its own implication regarding the proper design of law and policy as well as the practice of justice based upon it. For instance, we saw in the first chapter that both utilitarianism and Kantian deontology are based on the equal dignity and moral status of persons, which is the bedrock of modern liberal societies and enshrined in the Declaration of Independence (albeit in anachronistically gendered terms). But moral equality, while of great importance, is far too general to put into practice. For instance, what does it imply about the relationship of the state to the individual? Should the state work to guarantee that all of its citizens have equal opportunity to pursue their goals and dreams? Should citizens be given equal resources with which to pursue them, and if so, does that mean an equal amount of money or a certain amount of essential goods, such as food, clothing, and shelter—not to mention education and health care? Should they receive equal compensation for their efforts even if they exhibit different levels of effort or have unequal levels of talent? How about luck: should the effect of good luck and bad luck be equalized (or distributed) among people?

The answers to all of those questions—or the general question "equality of what?"—would define what kind of *egalitarian* you are.[23] While everyone believes in equality as an abstract ideal, there are many ways to interpret what equality should mean, from the minimal (but essential) equality of moral status to the more ambitious goal of equalizing outcomes, and defenders of each one argue its merits based on more basic ethical principles. Furthermore, when put into practice, each of those varieties of egalitarianism will inevitably conflict with another principle such as justice and liberty. For instance, efforts to reduce the inequality of wealth through redistributive taxation conflict with conceptions of justice and liberty that support strong property rights and flatter tax systems. In such cases, equality is cast as a goal or policy that may be constrained by the principle of liberty (or the right to one's property), but unless property rights are treated as absolute—which they rarely if ever are—some compromise between the two will be reached. We see the different results of these compromises in the United States and Europe: in the United States, the majority is more reluctant to sacrifice property rights (and low taxes) to support a welfare state than many European countries (such as Sweden) are. Once again, the people of both the United States and Sweden believe in the principles of liberty and equality, but they interpret, balance, and implement them differently— as do different political factions and parties within the United States.

In the words of Captain America, "the American dream has to be there for everyone or it works for no one."[24] This is a fine statement, and one we all can agree on, but it still leaves plenty of room to disagree on the specifics, including whether noncitizens count in "everyone" and the broader question of what the American dream means in terms of equality (as well as justice and liberty). But if we can keep in mind what we all agree on, the basic principle of equality, we can focus our disagreements on what we really disagree on—the details.

Liberty

As much as Captain America values justice and equality, his passion truly shows when he is fighting for liberty against the forces of tyranny, whether the Nazis in World War II, the Red Skull into the modern day, or the various intergalactic overlords he faces alongside the Avengers. His righteous indignation at seeing the strong abuse their power over the weak was born in his early days as a scrawny kid on the streets of New York, watching his alcoholic father abuse his mother while at the same time Hitler marched across Europe. Tyranny offends justice and equality by placing some people over others based on nothing but privilege, but it is the threat to human dignity and autonomy that tyranny poses that inspires Captain America to resist it wherever it arises.[25]

After the Supreme Hydra mocked his ideals, Cap told him,

> You're glib—but so was Hitler. Like every other tyrant, your lust for power masks your true motive—fear of a free society! For, with freedom, man has pride, dignity and a sense of destiny! Your fear causes you to arrogantly mock those concepts! You seek to reduce mankind to your own level! But against every despot there has always arisen a champion of liberty! That is why I exist—and why men like me shall always win![26]

In most modern liberal societies, liberty represents the ability to pursue your own idea of the good life, without interference from others, provided you don't wrongfully interfere with anyone else doing the same. The idea that governments should respect the freedom of each person to determine the path of his or her life is called *liberal neutrality*, and, just like justice and equality, it is based on the equal dignity of persons.[27] This is a concept that justice must take into account when determining what legal treatment people deserve when their chosen way of life interferes with the beliefs of others. It's also one that equality must confront, such as when a person's life-choices put him or her in need of more resources, which must be taken from others who made different choices that may be judged by some to be "better" or more responsible. Like all principles, liberal neutrality is not absolute, but is widely held to be vitally important.

Tyranny does not come only in the form of a dictator or despot—basic rights and freedoms can be violated even in a democracy. In his 1859 book *On Liberty*, philosopher John Stuart Mill wrote of the possibility of a *tyranny of the majority*, in which a majority voting in a legitimate democratic election, or working through its duly appointed legislature, can deny essential rights to a minority.[28] Unfortunately, this is no mere theoretical possibility: this is how women, African Americans, and gays and lesbians were legally denied their moral rights to own property, vote, and marry throughout much of American history (and, in the case of same-sex marriage, continuing on to the day I write this, but perhaps not by the time you read it).

Before the Civil War started, when Maria Hill asked Cap to help implement the registration act, she said she was asking him "to obey the will of the American people."[29] But to Cap, that law was illegitimate because it denied heroes their basic rights of liberty, which cannot be denied by mere legislative action. When Sharon Carter argued that America was founded on the rule of law, Cap said, "no ... it was founded on breaking the law. Because the law was wrong."[30] Later, while drinking in a bar after Captain America was shot following his surrender, Bucky overheard a man angry that Cap was buried in Arlington National Cemetery, which is for "heroes ... not traitors." He continued, "Cap turned on his own people, he fought against the will of the American people ... he dishonored the uniform he wore." Bucky thought to himself, "I know what Steve would do here. He'd debate. He'd point out that just because a majority of people believe something doesn't mean it's right. He'd remind the room that a majority of the American people once supported slavery, too."[31] The tyranny of the majority serves as a reminder that essential principles, rights, and liberties are not subject to a democratic vote, but are guaranteed as a matter of justice and equality; this also helps to explain the importance of the freedoms and rights guaranteed in the Bill of Rights, which no legislature can simply vote away in pursuit of their policy goals (however worthy they may be).

As you can probably tell by now, the three principles we've been discussing are interrelated in many ways. In the most general terms, it's difficult to exercise one's liberty fully without an effective system of justice that protects the rights of all equally. Justice itself is meaningless without equality, or without the freedom to enjoy it. Finally, equality is an empty notion if it's not put into action through a system of justice that guarantees the freedom to live within it! Just like the three legs of a stool, each of these ideals is necessary to support the other two, regardless of how we may interpret and implement them—and even though we may disagree on how this is to be done.

Debating What We Disagree On While Recognizing What We Share

By focusing on the basic principles and ideals upon which America was founded, Captain America has been able to represent and inspire people of all political persuasions. This would be no surprise were he merely an empty shell or façade, a red-white-and-blue cipher on which people could impose their own values and beliefs. But as we've seen, Cap does stand for something: namely, the interrelated principles of justice, equality, and liberty. Not only does he represent these ideals in his words and actions, he both inspires other to follow his example and holds them to his standard— even when "them" means his own government. Captain America represents these core American values, and I believe that Americans—all of us— believe in them too.

But we seem to disagree on so much! How can this be if we share the same basic principles? As I said, we share a belief in the core ideals of justice, equality, and liberty, but we don't share the same ideas regarding how to interpret and implement them, including how to balance one against the others when they conflict. Nor should we! The positions we take on these details represent who we are: after all, they're derived from our individual characters and judgment. Just as judges who are equally experienced and knowledgeable about the law can come to different decisions in a hard case, so can we as Americans disagree on what our country should do in particular situations. Just as Captain America and Iron Man disagreed over superhero registration during the Civil War, Americans have disagreed about the trade-offs between liberty and security, not just since September 11, 2001, but since this country was founded!

As well as embodying core American principles and ideals, Captain America has also stood for the unity that, at its best, America represents: not just unity among people of different genders, races, ethnicities, and religions, but also between people of different political orientations and beliefs. After Cap's strength was artificially (and temporarily) boosted, Falcon felt inferior and broke off their partnership.[32] After Cap found him, he argued that any differences between them were less important than their similarities, especially their common mission:

> We are different—I don't deny it. There never have been and there never will be any two humans exactly alike. Everyone knows that—and yet, everyone distrusts differences. Variations seem threatening, because they're unfamiliar—because they indicate factors in life we know nothing about. Black/white ... young/old ... male/female ... and strong/less strong. Whichever side we're on, there's always another. If a person avoided everyone who was different from him, he'd avoid everyone—and obviously, that's not the way it works. Differences can be important—but the ones between you and me aren't! We both have the same goal: ending injustice! No matter how we each do it, we're united in that! Forget what sets us apart ... and remember what pulls us together![33]

Even in death, Captain America represented unity, as we see from the conclusion of the Falcon's eulogy at Cap's funeral soon after the end of the Civil War:

> Now. Look around you. Kind of amazing, isn't it? How we usually see the differences between us ... separated by nationality, by color, by religion ... and yet here we are all connected. Steve Rogers, the skinny blond-haired kid who grew up on the streets of New York ... showed us that the ideals of the American dream—the great melting pot that can bring out the best in each of us and bind us together—actually works! And he can keep teaching us that long after he's gone. By telling stories about him ... to our children ... to our grandchildren ... Steve Rogers, Captain America, will never die. This doesn't have to be a day of sadness. We can accept it as a gift of unity and hope. The kind of day Captain America lived for.[34]

Both passages, besides reminding us of the close friendship and bond shared by Captain America and the Falcon over the years, reinforce the fact that diversity and differences do not imply separation or opposition. As any leader knows, different beliefs, opinions, and perspectives contribute to better decisions—provided people work together to reach them in an environment of mutual respect.

One way of achieving that mutual respect is—you guessed it—by acknowledging our shared values and principles. For instance, Captain America met Vietnam veteran and conscientious objector Dave Cox at Peggy and Sharon Carter's family home in Virginia. After being attacked by the Serpent Squad, Cap came across Cox in his forest cottage; when the Squad found them, they tried to force Cox to tell them where Cap was. Not only did Cox refuse to fight back when attacked—staying true to his pacifist beliefs—but he also kept Cap's location secret until Cap could ambush the Squad himself.[35]

Years later, Cap ran into Cox again, at which point Cox remarked, "Weird how fate threw us together, wasn't it? Dave Cox, Vietnam vet and born-again pacifist—and Captain America, the greatest soldier who ever lived." Cap answered, "We're not that different, Dave." He continued:

> I think we're both motivated by the same hopes ... the same ideals. I sensed that about you the very first time we met. I'd encountered many other men who'd been changed by the horrors of war, who'd vowed to turn their backs on violence as a result of their experiences—but you had something those others lacked: a rare and powerful conviction. That conviction was put to the

test when you helped me and the Falcon against the first Serpent Squad. You could've made it easy on yourself by betraying me—but you held fast to your beliefs. You suffered at their hands without so much as lifting a finger in your own defense. You have your ways, Dave—and I have mine. But I've always felt that we were ... kindred spirits. Who knows? If I'd been born thirty years later, maybe I'd be standing in your shoes today.[36]

Despite their differences, Captain America recognized Dave Cox as an honorable man, a "kindred spirit," someone who shows conviction by maintaining his integrity under pressure. Cap was able to disagree with Cox while respecting his point of view, just as he acknowledged and respected the differences between himself and the Falcon. More important, Cap understood that he shared a common purpose with each man, which enabled them to work together towards it, even if by different means.

I believe this is the way to restore some measure of civility to our national discussion about the issues that concern and trouble us all. We need to focus on the principles and ideals we have in common in order to understand truly where we disagree—and then we can work on *that*. It doesn't help for each side in a debate in call the other side names, to exaggerate their opinions, to denigrate them as "stupid" or demonize them as "evil" when they simply disagree. Instead of debating policies on their merits against the background of their shared ideals and principles, people spend their time trying to define the terms of the argument and "control the narrative" to push their agenda, applying pseudo-military strategy to what should be a meeting of the minds. Extreme rhetoric may stir up the passions on each side—as we see from cable news personalities like Reed Broxton and his real-world analogues—but it does nothing to enhance mutual understanding and cooperation, and only pushes the sides farther apart and reduces the chances for constructive dialogue. Ironically, modern political discourse, in which each side characterizes itself as "good" and its opponents as "evil," displays simplistic black-and-white thinking more than Captain America ever has![37]

Disagreement does not have to mean opposition if people can recognize their shared basic principles and ideals. As we discussed in chapter 5 in the context of moral disagreement, two people can share exactly the same principles but disagree on how they understand them, balance them against each other, and put them into action. Every justice of the Supreme Court of the United States has sworn an oath to uphold this country's Constitution, but each one interprets the various clauses in it differently and considers some more important than others in specific circumstances. Sometimes this leads to split decisions, but even when two judges agree—or even when all nine of them agree—each may come to his or her opinion by unique reasoning (in which case they often write separate concurring opinions). The justices disagree on the specifics of the Constitution but they all agree on the document's central importance to this country and their responsibilities to it—and I see no reason why the rest of us can't do the same.

After Iron Man used the villain Mentallo's global mind control device to erase all knowledge of his secret identity—even from his friends and fellow heroes—Captain America accused him of overstepping his bounds. (No, really.) During one of their epic arguments, while Iron Man tried to downplay the harm he did (especially compared to the benefits), Cap argued that Tony "entered the minds of people who'd done nothing wrong and altered their life memories. You chose to control the way they think, and in doing so ... violated their freedom."[38] When Iron Man said Cap made him sound like Mentallo, Cap agreed:

> You two had a lot in common in that moment—as frankly, you did with a lot of men I've fought. Men who thought they had the right to have people think only the thoughts they approved of. You say what you did was okay. Ask yourself this: Would Mentallo's actions have been okay if he'd had a goal you thought was noble?

This is in line with previous ethical disagreements between Cap and Iron Man, in which Cap criticized Tony for using his ends—and his own brilliance—to justify his means while neglecting matters of right and wrong that Cap feels should take precedence. (Tony's concern over his secret identity getting into the wrong hands is deliciously ironic, though, given his more *laissez-faire* attitude during the Civil War.[39])

Later, however, after Cap faced a tragic dilemma of his own, he and Tony patched up their friendship (as they always do). As Cap explained:

> I still think you overstepped your bounds, Tony ... that your ends didn't justify the means as neatly as you say they did ... but I also think I tend to be a little judgmental sometimes ... particularly when it comes to issues of independence and personal rights. I'm not saying I condone your decision ... but I suppose I understand where you're coming from ... and that, all things considered, *we're still on the same side.*

I took the liberty of italicizing that last phrase because it makes my point so perfectly. While we as Americans often disagree on what this country should do and how it should do it, *we're still on the same side*—the side of justice, equality, and liberty. We're all trying to live by the principles that make this country great, and we disagree primarily on how to *keep* it great. Just like Captain America admitted to Iron Man, we often rush to judgment precisely because we lose sight of our common purpose. We're too quick to assume the other side is working against us rather when they're really working along a different path—a path that is often parallel to our own. If we can keep in mind what we have in common while disagreeing—respectfully and calmly—about the details, our national discussion will be more civil and constructive, enabling us to move forward in purposeful action rather than standing still in endless argument.

Now It's Our Turn

We're almost at the end, and at this point I would like to thank you for reading. If I did my job with this book, I will have given you a deeper appreciation of Captain America, whether you were a longtime fan, a new reader attracted by movies or animated series, or someone who never cared for superheroes much at all (until now!). I hope that my passion for the character—and my country—came through in my words as well as those I quoted from the decades of Cap's comic-book stories, which are due to the dozens of talented and devoted creators who have built the character up from Joe Simon and Jack Kirby's work in the early 1940s. But most of all, I hope you see the tremendous value Captain America has as a role model, both for personal virtue and judgment as well as for the kind of civilized discourse we as Americans need in order to tackle our many problems while respecting our founding ideals and principles.

The world we live in is constantly changing and we face new dilemmas and conflicts every day. But this does not mean we have to abandon the "old-fashioned" ethics and values that served us well in the past—we just have to find ways to apply them to our new problems. As Bucky told the Young Avenger Patriot after Cap's death following the Civil War:

> A while back, during that whole super hero Civil War, I remember reading some editorial ... Someone was saying Cap was in the wrong, out of step with the public ... that he needed to "find America," or some nonsense. And all I could think was, no ... America needs to find him.[40]

I wrote this book to show people that this is true, that Captain America's devotion to principle can provide a new way to look at our problems and work together to fix them.

I don't think this country is as divided as some people—including Captain America—say. Instead, I think we've forgotten how united we are, and once we remember that, the divisions that do exist will begin to heal. It will take work, of course—a *lot* of work. After all, we've got an entire political climate and media culture to fight back against. But as cliché as it may sound, if this book inspires just one person to try to understand people with different political views and engage them in a respectful, constructive exchange of ideas rather than a shouting match to score political points, then I will be happy. More important, we'll be on our way to a better America, one that can better serve the people within it as well as the rest of the world.

As a dying Cap said in *The Chosen*, "I'll gladly sacrifice my life if people will only understand that everyone has it in them to be a hero … that they can all be Captain America."[41] All it takes is the determination to be better and the judgment to decide how—in Aristotle's terms, to be excellent at what we want to do and who we want to be, and to work together to help create the society we want to live in. As a man replied when someone said that anyone could do what Cap does: "If we cared as much. And tried as hard."[42] No one needs super-soldier serum to do that.

Notes

1 *Captain America: Man Out of Time* #5 (2011).
2 Roger Stern, "Remembering Cap," in *Captain America: War & Remembrance* (2011).
3 *Tales of Suspense*, vol. 1, #75 (1966), "Thirty Minutes to Live!"
4 *Captain America*, vol. 1, #122 (1970).
5 *Captain America*, vol. 1, #134 (1970).
6 *Captain America*, vol. 1, #156 (1972).
7 It started in *Captain America*, vol. 1, #169 (1974) when the Committee to Regain America's Principles—note the acronym—started running ads accusing Cap of being a vigilante (about which Peggy Carter warned him in *Captain America*, vol. 1, #165, 1973). The Red Skull became a master of this tactic, manipulating the media against Cap time and time again, such as when he staged a movie about Captain America secretly intended to soil his image (as explained in *Captain America*, vol. 1, #263, 1981).

8 All of these people and events were discussed previously in this book.

9 *Captain America*, vol. 3, #13 (1999). Recall also his words after defeating the anti-nationalistic Flag Smasher: "There is nothing harmful about having a sense of national identity or ethnic heritage. America is made up of a multitude of different ethnic groups, each of which has had its own part to contribute to American culture. Be proud of your heritage, but never let that pride make you forget that beneath it all, we are all human beings and have the same wants and needs and deserve the same respect and dignity" (*Captain America*, vol. 1, #312, 1985).

10 *Civil War: Front Line* #9 (2006), "Embedded Part 9."

11 *Fear Itself* #1 (2011).

12 *Captain America*, vol. 6, #15 (2012). Cap discovers later in the issue that the Reed Broxton he heard was a robot impostor, but "his" words stayed with Cap nonetheless.

13 Ibid.

14 Other scholars have explored the parallels between superhero comics—especially Captain America's stories—and American history. In *Secret Identity Crisis: Comics Books & the Unmasking of Cold War America* (New York: Continuum, 2009), political scientist Matthew J. Costello focuses primarily on the classic Marvel characters (Cap, Iron Man, the Hulk, the Fantastic Four, and others) to explore their implications regarding the national identity of the United States during and after the Cold War (with an entire chapter devoted to the Marvel Civil War and the death of Cap afterwards). Also, in *Super-History: Comic Book Superheroes and American Society* (Jefferson, NC: McFarland, 2012), military historian Jeffrey K. Johnson takes a broader approach, looking at DC and Marvel (as well as smaller publishers) since the dawn of superheroes in 1938 through 2010. Finally, *Captain America and the Struggle of the Superhero: Critical Essays*, edited by Robert G. Weiner (Jefferson, NC: McFarland, 2009), is a collection of essays looking at Cap from a number of perspectives, including historical, political, and literary.

15 See the discussion of Everyman in the previous chapter.

16 *Captain America*, vol. 1, #103 (1968).

17 Psychologist Jonathan Haidt does a brilliant job exploring how this happens in his book *The Righteous Mind: Why Good People Are Divided by Politics and Religion* (New York, NY: Vintage Books, 2012). As I do in this chapter, Haidt also emphasizes understanding and empathy between political sides as one way to enhance civil discussion, but also stresses the difficulty of this, given the unconscious roots of our moral thinking.

18 For a popular account of justice by a philosopher, see Michael J. Sandel, *Justice: What's the Right Thing to Do* (New York, NY: Farrar, Straus and Giroux, 2009).

19 *Captain America*, vol. 1, #258 (1981).

20 This can be taken too far, of course, as in the case of vigilantes like the Punisher (whom Captain America confronted in *Captain America*, vol. 1, #241, 1980). Cap has always stood for justice over vengeance, such as when he had Sharon Carter taken off a SHIELD mission because he was afraid she wanted to avenge her ex-lover Agent Neal Taper, who died in a Philadelphia explosion set by the Winter Soldier. "I want justice for those people who died in Philadelphia, and I want answers," Cap told her. "You're looking for revenge" (*Captain America*, vol. 5, #9, 2005).

21 This idea is present in both Aristotle's *Nicomachean Ethics* (Book V) and *Politics* (Book III), although not stated anywhere nearly as succinctly as by modern writers. Aristotle describes it in terms of *proportionality*, an important element of justice that demands, for instance, that more serious crimes are matched with more serious punishments (and vice versa). In his discussion of fairness, Haidt finds that conservatives value proportionality more highly than liberals do (*The Righteous Mind*, pp. 212–213), an example of people with different political views holding the same value (fairness) but interpreting it differently.

22 Amartya Sen, "Equality of What?", collected in his *Choice, Welfare and Measurement* (Cambridge, MA: Harvard University Press, 1982), pp. 353–369.

23 Stefan Gosepath's entry on "Equality" in the *Stanford Encyclopedia of Philosophy* (http://plato.stanford.edu/entries/equality/) explores these variants of egalitarianism and more.

24 *Avengers*, vol. 1, #252 (1985).

25 This explains why Cap has so often shunned the reality-altering power of objects such as the Cosmic Cube (*Captain America*, vol. 1, #447, 1996, among others) and the Freedom Crystal (*Avengers Forever* #12, 2000); as he said when he refused the villainous Suprema's offer of cooperation and power, "Power—the evil that men have done—in its name!" (*Captain America*, vol. 1, #123, 1970).

26 *Captain America*, vol. 1, #273 (1982). For a similar speech made in his early days as an Avenger to his old enemy Baron Zemo, see *Avengers*, vol. 1, #6 (1964).

27 Although the idea can be found as far back as Plato and was perhaps expressed definitively by John Stuart Mill and Immanuel Kant, Ronald Dworkin gave an influential and succinct statement of liberal neutrality when he wrote that "political decisions must be, so far as it is possible, independent of any particular conception of the good life, or of what gives value to life" (*A Matter of Principle*, Cambridge, MA: Harvard University Press, 1985, p. 191). He expands on this, and also explains his theory of how justice, equality, and liberty intertwine, in his book *Sovereign Virtue: The Theory and Practice of Equality* (Cambridge, MA: Harvard University Press, 2000).

28 John Stuart Mill, *On Liberty* (New York, NY: W.W. Norton, 1859/1975), pp. 5–6.

29 *Civil War* #1 (2006).

30 *Captain America*, vol. 5, #22 (2006).

31 *Captain America*, vol. 5, #26 (2007). Then he thought, "But I'm not Steve," and proceeded to beat up everyone in the bar.

32 See note 8 in chapter 2 for more on Cap's temporary strength boost.

33 *Captain America*, vol. 1, #161 (1973).

34 *Fallen Son: The Death of Captain America* #5 (2007).

35 *Captain America*, vol. 1, #163 (1973).

36 *Captain America*, vol. 1, #293 (1984).

37 In *The Righteous Mind* (pp. 261–264), Haidt uses the term "Manichaean," deriving from the Middle Eastern philosophy Manichaeism that divided the world into clearly defined forces of good and evil, and which has been used to describe politicians accused of reducing complex issues to black and white.

38 All of the quotes related to this episode are from *Iron Man/Captain America Annual 1998*.

39 Also, recall from chapter 6 that Iron Man accused Captain America of hypocrisy when Cap questioned Tony's right to use his armor after the Siege of Asgard (*Avengers Prime* #1, 2010). Neither Cap nor Iron Man are as simple as they may seem at times, are they?

40 *Young Avengers Presents* #1 (2008). And Bucky's not the only one: as the Wasp once said to Captain America, "As far as I'm concerned, you don't need to conform to the world. We should all strive to be more like you" (*Avengers: Earth's Mightiest Heroes*, vol. 1, #8, 2005).

41 *Captain America: The Chosen* #6 (2008).

42 *Captain America*, vol. 4, #4 (2002).

Appendix
Why Are There Seven Volumes of Captain America and Five Volumes of Avengers?

If you looked up the endnotes and references to see where my comics source material came from, you undoubtedly noticed that most did say simply *"Captain America #268"* or *"Avengers #347."* Most of the comics cited in this book have volume numbers: to date, *Captain America* has had seven volumes, *Avengers* five, and *New Avengers* three. Here's a quick primer on the volumes of these main titles, the beginnings and endings of which usually coincide with major events in the Marvel Universe.[1]

Even though Cap debuted in *Captain America Comics* #1 in March 1941, our story starts with the **first volume of** *Avengers*, since it was in the classic issue #4 of that title (cover-dated March 1964) that Captain America was found in a block of ice and revived in the (then) present day. Later that year, Cap was awarded his own feature in *Tales of Suspense* #59 (November 1964), and starting with issue #100 (April 1968), *Tales of Suspense* was retitled as the **first volume of** *Captain America* (with Iron Man moving into his own book starting with issue #1 in May 1968).[2]

These long-running volumes of *Captain America* and *Avengers* lasted until 1996, reaching issues #454 and #402, respectively.[3] Both series ended when the Avengers (and the Fantastic Four) were apparently killed in a battle with the villainous Onslaught. As with most comics deaths, things were not what they seemed, and our heroes were "simply" shuttled into a pocket dimension. While they were there, the **second volumes of** *Captain America* **and** *Avengers* began under the banner "Heroes Reborn"—volumes you will notice are never cited in this book. ('Nuff said.)

After our heroes returned to the normal Marvel Universe (or Earth-616, as it's come to be known) the following year, the **third volumes of** *Captain America* **and** *Avengers* launched in early 1998. (A *Captain America: Sentinel of Liberty* series started thereafter, running parallel to volume 3 of Cap's main title, focusing on stories from earlier in his career and lasting twelve issues.) Volume 3 of Cap's title ended with issue #50 in February 2002, but after the three-issue *Captain America: Dead Men Running* miniseries, he returned in **volume 4 of** *Captain America* in June 2002 (starting with a story arc addressing the tragic events of September 11, 2001). Volume 4 ended with issue #32 in December 2004 during the "Avengers Disassembled" event—an event that, along with destroying Avengers Mansion and killing several key team members, also ended volume 3 of *Avengers* with issue #503 the same month. (The title had been renumbered at what would have been its five hundredth issue if the numbering had been continuous across all three volumes since issue #1 in September 1963.) Also, a *Captain America and the Falcon* title was introduced in the middle of *Captain America* volume 4's run and extended into the beginning of volume 5—as Jarvis would say, very untidy.

While **volume 5 of** *Captain America* began in January 2005, the *Avengers* title lay dormant for a while. Instead, the **first volume of** *New Avengers* debuted the same month, featuring Spider-Man and Wolverine (two of Marvel's most popular characters) as Avengers for the first time.[4] Both titles survived the Civil War amongst the Marvel heroes over the issue of super-hero registration, the subsequent death of Steve Rogers in issue #25 of his book, and Rogers' former sidekick Bucky Barnes taking on the mantle of Captain America. (Volume 1 of *Mighty Avengers* was also introduced following the Civil War, but Cap was not around until the end of its run and never featured significantly in it.)

After the Civil War ended and Steve Rogers died—or, as we say in comics, "died"—the Marvel Universe went through a turbulent period. First, after Iron Man took the helm of SHIELD following the Civil War, the alien race the Skrulls revealed their "Secret Invasion," which had begun years ago with the replacement of various key figures in the Marvel Universe. In the end, the Skrulls were defeated by Norman Osborn, formerly Spider-Man's foe the Green Goblin and then the head of the Thunderbolts, a team of reformed villains. Iron Man was blamed for letting the Skrulls invade and Osborn was given the keys to the kingdom, changing SHIELD to HAMMER and starting the "Dark Reign" in the Marvel Universe. (This included introducing his own team of Avengers—actually members of the Thunderbolts who adopted classic Avengers identities—who starred in their own title, *Dark Avengers*.)

Norman's next big plan was to attack Thor's home of Asgard, which had been floating above Broxton, Oklahoma, since Thor revived it following the last Ragnarok. This was known as the Siege of Asgard (although the miniseries was titled simply *Siege*), and it happened to occur at the same time as the revelation of what *really* happened to Steve Rogers: he was tossed back in time rather than killed. (Whew!) Cap's return to the present day in the *Captain America: Rebirth* miniseries coincided with the Siege—another lucky break, for he was able to lead the heroes in overthrowing Osborn once and for all.[5] The Dark Reign ended, and with it the first volumes of *New Avengers, Mighty Avengers*, and *Dark Avengers*.

After the Dark Reign ended, "The Heroic Age" began, bringing with it the **second volume of** *New Avengers*, a **fourth volume of** *Avengers* (a title not seen for five years), and the **first volume of** *Secret Avengers*, a new title. (*Mighty Avengers* and *Dark Avengers* would not return with second volumes until years later.) Steve Rogers was now running both SHIELD and the Secret Avengers while Bucky Barnes continued to serve as Captain America with the Avengers. The Age of Heroes was cut short, however, by a battle with the Midgard Serpent (who was Thor's uncle—never mind the biology) in the miniseries *Fear Itself*. During this event, Bucky Barnes was killed and Steve Rogers became Captain America once again (leaving the leadership of the Secret Avengers to Hawkeye). When Bucky died, volume 5 of *Captain America*—which, like *Avengers* #500 years prior, had returned to its cumulative numbering with #600—transitioned into *Captain America and Bucky* (telling tales from the past) with issue #620 and then a Captain America team-up book from #629 before ending altogether with issue #640. Meanwhile, **volume 6 of** *Captain America* was launched, starring Steve Rogers once again as the title character, although it only lasted nineteen issues before the next Earth-shattering event rocked the Marvel Universe.[6] Also, the **first volume of** *Avengers Assemble* was introduced, featuring a line-up familiar to those who saw the feature film *The Avengers* in 2012 (before changing up the line-up for each successive storyline).

Last but not least, after the *Avengers vs. X-Men* event, Marvel Comics relaunched many of its books and introduced new ones in its "Marvel NOW!" promotion. Most relevant for us, **volume 7 of** *Captain America* began, as well as the **volume 5 of** *Avengers* and **volume 3 of** *New Avengers*. (*Secret Avengers* also began a second volume, but Captain America has not been involved with that team as of this writing.) Also, the **first volume of**

Uncanny Avengers began, featuring a "unity" team composed of Avengers and X-Men in an effort to heal the divisions between the teams as well as between humans and mutants in general—dovetailing nicely with the focus on the book you are holding at this very moment!

The Watcher only knows what volume *Captain America* and the various *Avengers* titles are on as you read this, but I am confident that Cap will live in on comics, movies, and TV long after this book has changed the course of American history. (Fingers crossed on that last part.)

Notes

1 This appendix was inspired by a similar reading guide I included in *The Avengers and Philosophy: Earth's Mightiest Thinkers* (Hoboken, NJ: John Wiley & Sons, 2012), pp. 217–219, which covered all the various Avengers books and was titled "Why Are There Four Volumes of *Avengers*?" (As you can see, that's already out of date.)

2 By "first" I mean the first after his revival; also, his 1940s series was titled *Captain America Comics*, not simply *Captain America*. So there.

3 In the meantime, there was also a *West Coast Avengers* series (which was retitled *Avengers West Coast* in the middle of its run), but Cap was not a member of this team.

4 Volume 1 of *Young Avengers* also started around the same time, lasting twelve issues with minimal involvement with Captain America; volume 2 launched in 2013 and ended in 2014.

5 "Once and for all"—I actually managed to type that with a straight face.

6 Did I mention that Bucky didn't actually die (again)? He was secretly revived by SHIELD and now operates once again as the Winter Soldier, as he did before succeeding Steve Rogers as Captain America.

References

"Wait a minute, bub—this ain't nuthin' but funny books!"
—Socrates (rumored)

Well ... yes. Yes it is. But let me explain! I included full bibliographical details for academic books and journal articles in the notes to this book, but only the most basic details for the comics from which I drew and quoted, because they clearly made up the bulk of the citations. (You can't improve on the originals, I always say.)

Below you will find details for every individual comic I cited (not those for which only a long run or trade paperback collection is cited), listed in alphabetical order and then by volume and issue number. (For an explanation of the different volumes of the *Captain America* and *Avengers* titles, see the appendix.) The dates given for the comics are the cover dates; the actual release date was several months earlier. All the comics and trade paperbacks listed below are published by Marvel Comics (except one—see if you can find it!). In terms of creators, for the sake of space I've listed only the writers, pencillers, and inkers, but this is not to diminish the contributions of all the talented colorists, letterers, and editors—not to mention the artists who worked on the covers—who helped produce these great comics. (The writers are signified by a "w" and the pencillers and inkers together by an "a.") Also, I chose to omit the story titles except in cases in which more than one story appeared in the comic (such as oversized annuals and anniversary issues, as well as books like *Tales of Suspense*, which contained two stories, one of Captain America and one of Iron Man, in each issue).

The Virtues of Captain America: Modern-Day Lessons on Character from a World War II Superhero, First Edition. Mark D. White.
© 2014 John Wiley & Sons, Inc. Published 2014 by John Wiley & Sons, Inc.

I also indicate when the comic has been reprinted in a trade paperback or hardcover collection. I've abbreviated the *Marvel Masterworks* and *Essential* volumes that collect classic Marvel comics in color and black-and-white (respectively). As I finalize this book, these are the volumes available or solicited:

Marvel Masterworks: Captain America Vols. 1–7 (2003–2014), abbreviated as CA:MM1–7.

Essential Captain America Vols. 1–7 (2000–2013), abbreviated as CA:ESS1–7.

Marvel Masterworks: Avengers, Vols. 1–13 (2003–2013), abbreviated as A:MM1–13.

Essential Avengers, Vols. 1–9 (1998–2013), abbreviated as A:ESS1–9.

All other collections are given by their complete title and publication year. I make no guarantees that all will be in print as you read this—some are out-of-print as I write this! (Oops, there goes another one now.)

If my dear readers wish even more detail on the comics cited in this book, I suggest the following sources:

Captain America: Official Index to the Marvel Universe (2011) and *Avengers: Official Index to the Marvel Universe* (2011), which list an incredible amount of information about the main titles and some related miniseries.

Grand Comics Database (www.comics.org), a comprehensive online archive of comics information for all publishers, emphasizing bibliographic detail or story or character information.

Marvel Comics Database (http://marvel.wikia.com), similar to the Grand Comics Database but (obviously) focused on Marvel Comics and featuring character profiles and links.

A+X #4 (March 2013), "Captain America + Quentin Quire." Jason Latour (w), David Lopez and Alvaro Lopez (a). Collected in *A+X, Vol. 1: A+X = Awesome* (2013).

Age of Ultron #1 (May 2013). Brian Michael Bendis (w), Bryan Hitch and Paul Neary (a). Collected in *Age of Ultron* (2013).

Amazing Spider-Man #519 (June 2005). J. Michael Straczynski (w), Mike Deodato, Jr. and Joe Pimentel (a). Collected in *Amazing Spider-Man: New Avengers* (2005).

Amazing Spider-Man #537 (December 2006). J. Michael Straczynski (w), Ron Garney and Bill Reinhold (a). Collected in *Civil War: Amazing Spider-Man* (2007).

Amazing Spider-Man #538 (January 2007). Same as above.

Avengers, vol. 1, #4 (March 1964). Stan Lee (w), Jack Kirby and George Roussos (a). Collected in A:MM1 and A:ESS1.

Avengers, vol. 1, #6 (July 1964). Stan Lee (w), Jack Kirby and Chic Stone (a). Collected in A:MM1 and A:ESS1.

Avengers, vol. 1, #19 (August 1965). Stan Lee (w), Don Heck and Dick Ayres (a). Collected in A:MM2 and A:ESS1.

Avengers, vol. 1, #20 (September 1965). Stan Lee (w), Don Heck and Wally Wood (a). Collected in A:MM2 and A:ESS1.

Avengers, vol. 1, #21 (October 1965). Same creators as above. Collected in A:MM3 and A:ESS1.

Avengers, vol. 1, #25 (February 1966). Stan Lee (w), Don Heck and Dick Ayres (a). Collected in A:MM3 and A:ESS2.

Avengers, vol. 1, #26 (March 1966). Stan Lee (w), Don Heck and Frank Giacoia (a). Collected in A:MM3 and A:ESS2.

Avengers, vol. 1, #27 (April 1966). Same as above.

Avengers, vol. 1, #35 (December 1966). Stan Lee and Roy Thomas (w), Don Heck (a). Collected in A:MM4 and A:ESS2.

Avengers, vol. 1, #80 (September 1970). Roy Thomas (w), John Buscema and Tom Palmer (a). Collected in A:MM9 and A:ESS4.

Avengers, vol. 1, #81 (October 1970). Same as above.

Avengers, vol. 1, #113 (July 1973). Steve Englehart (w), Bob Brown and Frank Bolle (a). Collected in A:MM12 and A:ESS5.

Avengers, vol. 1, #211 (September 1981). Jim Shooter (w), Gene Colan and Dan Green (a). Collected in *Avengers: I Am an Avenger, Vol. 1* (2010).

Avengers, vol. 1, #213 (November 1981). Jim Shooter (w), Bob Hall and Dan Green (a). Collected in *Avengers: The Trial of Yellowjacket* (2012).

Avengers, vol. 1, #214 (December 1981). Same as above.

Avengers, vol. 1, #216 (February 1982). Jim Shooter (w), Alan Weiss and Dan Green (a). Collected in *Avengers: The Trial of Yellowjacket* (2012).

Avengers, vol. 1, #218 (April 1982). Jim Shooter and J.M. DeMatteis (w), Don Perlin and various inkers (a). Collected in *Avengers: The Trial of Yellowjacket* (2012).

Avengers, vol. 1, #220 (June 1982). Jim Shooter (w), Bob Hall and Dan Green (a). Collected in *Avengers: The Trial of Yellowjacket* (2012).

Avengers, vol. 1, #224 (October 1982). Jim Shooter and Alan Zelenetz (w), Mark Bright and various inkers (a). Collected in *Avengers: The Trial of Yellowjacket* (2012).

Avengers, vol. 1, #227 (January 1983). Roger Stern (w), Sal Buscema and Brett Breeding (a). Collected in *Avengers: The Trial of Yellowjacket* (2012).

Avengers, vol. 1, #228 (February 1983). Roger Stern (w), Al Milgrom and Brett Breeding (a). Collected in *Avengers: The Trial of Yellowjacket* (2012).

Avengers, vol. 1, #230 (April 1983). Roger Stern (w), Al Milgrom and Joe Sinnott (a). Collected in *Avengers: The Trial of Yellowjacket* (2012).

Avengers, vol. 1, #236 (October 1983). Same creators as above. Collected in *Spider-Man: Am I an Avenger?* (2011) and *Avengers: Absolute Vision, Book 1* (2013).

Avengers, vol. 1, #252 (February 1985). Roger Stern (w), Bob Hall and Joe Sinnott (a). Collected in *Avengers: Absolute Vision, Book 2* (2014).

Avengers, vol. 1, #258 (August 1985). Roger Stern (w), John Buscema and Tom Palmer (a).

Avengers, vol. 1, #260 (October 1985). Same as above.

Avengers, vol. 1, #268 (June 1986). Same creators as above. Collected in *Avengers: The Once and Future Kang* (2013).

Avengers, vol. 1, #270 (August 1986). Same creators as above. Collected in *Avengers: Under Siege* (2010).

Avengers, vol. 1, #310 (November 1989). John Byrne (w), Paul Ryan and Tom Palmer (a).

Avengers, vol. 1, #315 (March 1990). Same as above. Collected in *Spider-Man: Am I Am Avenger?* (2011).

Avengers, vol. 1, #318 (June 1990). Fabian Nicieza (w), Paul Ryan and Tom Palmer (a). Collected in *Spider-Man: Am I an Avenger?* (2011).

Avengers, vol. 1, #327 (December 1990). Larry Hama (w), Paul Ryan and Tom Palmer (a).

Avengers, vol. 1, #329 (February 1991). Same creators as above. Collected in *Avengers: I Am an Avenger* (2010) and *Spider-Man: Am I an Avenger?* (2011).

Avengers, vol. 1, #338 (September 1991). Bob Harras (w), Steve Epting and Tom Palmer (a).

Avengers, vol. 1, #340 (October 1991). David Michelinie and Scott Lobdell (w), Paul Abrams, Charles Barnett III, and Robert Jones (a).

Avengers, vol. 1, #345 (March 1992). Bob Harras (w), Steve Epting and Tom Palmer (a). Collected in *Avengers: Galactic Storm, Vol. 1* (2006).

Avengers, vol. 1, #346 (April 1992). Same as above.

Avengers, vol. 1, #347 (May 1992). Same creators as above. Collected in *Avengers: Galactic Storm, Vol. 2* (2006).

Avengers, vol. 1, #366 (September 1993), 1st story: "The First Rule!" Same creators as above.

Avengers, vol. 3, #7 (August 1998). Kurt Busiek (w), George Pérez and Al Vey (a). Collected in *Avengers Assemble Vol. 1* (2011).

Avengers, vol. 3, #8 (September 1998). Same as above.

Avengers, vol. 3, #12 (January 1999). Kurt Busiek (w), George Pérez, Al Vey, and Bob Wiacek (a). Collected in *Avengers Assemble Vol. 2* (2012).

Avengers, vol. 3, #23 (December 1999). Kurt Busiek (w), George Pérez and Al Vey (a). Collected in *Avengers Assemble Vol. 3* (2006).

Avengers, vol. 3, #25 (February 2000). Same as above.

Avengers, vol. 3, #45 (January 2002). Kurt Busiek (w), Manuel Garcia and Bob Layton (a). Collected in *Avengers Assemble Vol. 5* (2012).

Avengers, vol. 3, #48 (January 2002). Kurt Busiek (w), Kieron Dwyer and Rick Remender (a). Collected in *Avengers Assemble Vol. 5* (2012).

Avengers, vol. 3, #54 (July 2002). Same as above.

Avengers, vol. 3, #55 (August 2002). Kurt Busiek (w), Patrick Zircher and Scott Koblish (a). Collected in *Avengers Assemble Vol. 5* (2012).

Avengers, vol. 3, #59 (December 2002). Geoff Johns (w), Kieron Dwyer and Rick Remender (a). Collected in *Avengers: World Trust* (2010).

Avengers, vol. 3, #63 (March 2003). Geoff Johns (w), Alan Davis and Mark Farmer (a). Collected in *Avengers: Standoff* (2010).

Avengers, vol. 3, #67 (July 2003). Geoff Johns (w), Olivier Coipel and Andy Lanning (a). Collected in *Avengers: Red Zone* (2010).

Avengers, vol. 3, #70 (October 2003). Same as above.

Avengers, vol. 3, #75 (February 2004). Geoff Johns (w) and Scott Kolins (a). Collected in *Avengers: The Search for She-Hulk* (2010).

Avengers, vol. 3, #77 (March 2004). Chuck Austen (w), Olivier Coipel and Andy Lanning (a). Collected in *Avengers: Lionheart of Avalon* (2004).

Avengers, vol. 3, #84 (August 2004). Chuck Austen (w) and Scott Kolins (a). Collected in *Avengers: Once an Invader* (2004).

Avengers, vol. 4, #8 (February 2011). Brian Michael Bendis (w), John Romita, Jr. and Klaus Janson (a). Collected in *Avengers by Brian Michael Bendis, Vol. 2* (2012).

Avengers, vol. 4, #9 (March 2011). Same as above.

Avengers, vol. 4, #10 (April 2011). Brian Michael Bendis (w), John Romita, Jr., Klaus Janson, and Tom Palmer (a). Collected in *Avengers by Brian Michael Bendis, Vol. 2* (2012).

Avengers, vol. 4, #12 (June 2011). Brian Michael Bendis (w), John Romita, Jr. and Klaus Janson (a). Collected in *Avengers by Brian Michael Bendis, Vol. 2* (2012).

Avengers, vol. 4, #13 (July 2011). Brian Michael Bendis (w), Chris Bachalo and various inkers (a). Collected in *Avengers: Fear Itself* (2012).

Avengers, vol. 4, #16 (October 2011). Brian Michael Bendis (w), John Romita, Jr. and Klaus Janson (a). Collected in *Avengers: Fear Itself* (2012).

Avengers, vol. 4, #22 (April 2012). Brian Michael Bendis (w), Renato Guedes and Jose Wilson Magalhaes (a). Collected in *Avengers by Brian Michael Bendis, Vol. 3* (2012).

Avengers, vol. 4, #24 (May 2012). Brian Michael Bendis (w) and Daniel Acuña (a). Collected in *Avengers by Brian Michael Bendis, Vol. 3* (2012).

Avengers, vol. 4, #25 (June 2012). Brian Michael Bendis (w), Walt Simonson and Scott Hanna (a). Collected in *Avengers by Brian Michael Bendis, Vol. 4* (2013).

Avengers, vol. 5, #1 (February 2013). Jonathan Hickman (w) and Jerome Opeña (a). Collected in *Avengers, Vol. 1: Avengers World* (2013).

Avengers Academy #10 (May 2011). Christos Gage (w), Sean Chen and Scott Hanna (a). Collected in *Avengers Academy Vol. 2: Will We Use This in the Real World?* (2012).

Avengers Annual, vol. 1, #16 (1987). Tom DeFalco (w), various pencillers and inkers (a). Collected in *Avengers: The Contest* (2010), *Avengers: Legion of the Unliving* (2012), and *Avengers: West Coast Avengers—Zodiac Attack* (2012).

Avengers Assemble, vol. 2, #1 (May 2012). Brian Michael Bendis (w), Mark Bagley and Danny Miki (a). Collected in *Avengers Assemble by Brian Michael Bendis* (2013).

Avengers: The Children's Crusade #3 (January 2011). Allan Heinberg (w), Jim Cheung and Mark Morales (a). Collected in *Avengers: The Children's Crusade* (2012).

Avengers: Earth's Mightiest Heroes, vol. 1, #3 (February 2005). Joe Casey (w) and Scott Kolins (a). Collected in *Avengers: Earth's Mightiest Heroes* (2005).

Avengers: Earth's Mightiest Heroes, vol. 1, #4 (February 2005). Same as above.

Avengers: Earth's Mightiest Heroes, vol. 1, #8 (April 2005). Same as above.

Avengers: Endless Wartime (original graphic novel, 2013). Warren Ellis (w) and Mike McKone (a).

Avengers Forever #12 (February 2000). Kurt Busiek and Roger Stern (w), Carlos Pacheco and Jesus Merino (a). Collected in *Avengers Forever* (2011).

Avengers Prime #1 (August 2010). Brian Michael Bendis (w), Alan Davis and Mark Farmer (a). Collected in *Avengers Prime* (2011).

Avengers/Squadron Supreme Annual 1998 (July 1998). Kurt Busiek and Len Kaminski (w), Carlos Pacheco and various inkers (a). Collected in *Avengers Assemble Vol. 1* (2011).

Avengers vs. X-Men #3 (July 2012). Ed Brubaker (w), John Romita, Jr. and Scott Hanna (a). Collected in *Avengers vs. X-Men* (2012).

Avenging Spider-Man #5 (May 2012). Zeb Wells (w), Leinil Francis Yu and Gerry Alanguilan (a). Collected in *Avenging Spider-Man, Vol. 1: My Friends Can Beat Up Your Friends* (2012).

Captain America, vol. 1, #100 (April 1968). Stan Lee (w), Jack Kirby and Syd Shores (a). Collected in CA:MM2 and CA:ESS1.

Captain America, vol. 1, #101 (May 1968). Same creators as above. Collected in CA:MM3 and CA:ESS1.

Captain America, vol. 1, #103 (July 1968). Same creators as above. Collected in CA:MM3 and CA:ESS2.

Captain America, vol. 1, #110 (February 1969). Stan Lee (w), Jim Steranko and Joe Sinnott (a). Collected in CA:MM3 and CA:ESS2.

Captain America, vol. 1, #111 (March 1969). Same as above.

Captain America, vol. 1, #112 (April 1969). Stan Lee (w), Jack Kirby and George Tuska (a). Collected in CA:MM3 and CA:ESS2.

Captain America, vol. 1, #113 (May 1969). Stan Lee (w), Jim Steranko and Tom Palmer (a). Collected in CA:MM3 and CA:ESS2.

Captain America, vol. 1, #114 (June 1969). Stan Lee (w), John Romita and Sal Buscema (a). Collected in CA:MM4 and CA:ESS2.

Captain America, vol. 1, #115 (July 1969). Stan Lee (w), John Buscema and Sal Buscema (a). Collected in CA:MM4 and CA:ESS2.

Captain America, vol. 1, #117 (September 1969). Stan Lee (w), Gene Colan and Joe Sinnott (a). Collected in CA:MM4 and CA:ESS2.

Captain America, vol. 1, #122 (February 1970). Same as above.

Captain America, vol. 1, #123 (March 1970). Same as above.

Captain America, vol. 1, #130 (October 1970). Stan Lee (w), Gene Colan and Dick Ayers (a). Collected in CA:MM5 and CA:ESS3.

Captain America, vol. 1, #134 (February 1971). Same as above.[1]

Captain America, vol. 1, #155 (November 1972). Steve Englehart (w), Sal Buscema and Frank McLaughlin (a). Collected in CA:MM7 and CA:ESS3.

Captain America, vol. 1, #156 (December 1972). Same as above.

Captain America, vol. 1, #157 (January 1973). Steve Englehart and Steve Gerber (w), Sal Buscema and John Verpoorten (a). Collected in CA:MM7 and CA:ESS4.

Captain America, vol. 1, #161 (May 1973). Steve Englehart (w), Sal Buscema and John Verpoorten (a). Collected in CA:ESS4.

Captain America, vol. 1, #163 (July 1973). Steve Englehart (w), Sal Buscema, John Verpoorten, and Tony Mortellaro (a). Collected in CA:ESS4.

Captain America, vol. 1, #165 (September 1973). Steve Englehart (w), Sal Buscema and Vince Colletta (a). Collected in CA:ESS4.

Captain America, vol. 1, #169 (January 1974). Steve Englehart and Mike Friedrich (w), Sal Buscema and Frank McLaughlin (a). Collected in *Captain America and the Falcon: Secret Empire* (2005) and CA:ESS4.

Captain America, vol. 1, #176 (August 1974). Steve Englehart (w), Sal Buscema and Vince Colletta (a). Collected in *Captain America and the Falcon: Secret Empire* (2005) and CA:ESS4.

Captain America, vol. 1, #181 (January 1975). Steve Englehart (w), Sal Buscema and Vince Colletta (a). Collected in *Captain America and the Falcon: Nomad* (2006) and CA:ESS4.

Captain America, vol. 1, #183 (March 1975). Steve Englehart (w), Frank Robbins and Frank Giacola (a). Collected in *Captain America and the Falcon: Nomad* (2006) and CA:ESS4.

Captain America, vol. 1, #184 (April 1975). Steve Englehart (w), Herb Trimpe, Frank Giacola, and Michael Esposito (a). Collected in *Captain America and the Falcon: Nomad* (2006) and CA:ESS4.

Captain America, vol. 1, #198 (June 1976). Jack Kirby (w, a) and Frank Giacola (a). Collected in *Captain America and the Falcon: Madbomb* (2004) and CA:ESS5.

Captain America, vol. 1, #204 (December 1976). Same creators as above. Collected in *Captain America: Bicentennial Battles* (2005) and CA:ESS5.

Captain America, vol. 1, #206 (February 1977). Same creators as above. Collected in *Captain America and the Falcon: The Swine* (2006) and CA:ESS6.

Captain America, vol. 1, #215 (November 1977). Roy Thomas (w), George Tuska and Pablo Marcos (a). Collected in CA:ESS6.

Captain America, vol. 1, #217 (January 1978). Roy Thomas and John Glut (w), John Buscema and Pablo Marcos (a). Collected in CA:ESS6.

Captain America, vol. 1, #218 (February 1978). John Glut (w), John Buscema, Mike Esposito and John Tartaglione (a). Collected in CA:ESS6.

Captain America, vol. 1, #232 (April 1979). Roger McKensie (w), Sal Buscema and Don Perlin (a). Collected in CA:ESS7.

Captain America, vol. 1, #233 (May 1979). Same as above.

Captain America, vol. 1, #235 (July 1979). Roger McKensie (w), Sal Buscema and Jack Abel (a). Collected in CA:ESS7.

Captain America, vol. 1, #237 (September 1979). Chris Claremont and Roger McKensie (w), Sal Buscema and Don Perlin (a). Collected in CA:ESS7.

Captain America, vol. 1, #239 (November 1979). Peter Gillis (w), Fred Kida and Don Perlin (a). Collected in CA:ESS7.

Captain America, vol. 1, #241 (January 1980). Mike W. Barr (w), Frank Springer and Pablo Marcos (a). Collected in CA:ESS7.

Captain America, vol. 1, #243 (March 1980). Roger McKensie (w), Rich Buckler and Don Perlin (a). Collected in CA:ESS7.

Captain America, vol. 1, #244 (April 1980). Roger McKensie (w), Don Perlin and Tom Sutton (a). Collected in CA:ESS7.

Captain America, vol. 1, #245 (May 1980). Roger McKensie (w), Carmine Infantino and Josef Rubinstein (a). Collected in CA:ESS7.

Captain America, vol. 1, #249 (September 1980). Roger Stern (w), John Byrne (w, a), Josef Rubinstein (a). Collected in *Captain America: War & Remembrance* (2011), *Captain America Epic Collection: Dawn's Early Light* (2014), and CA:ESS7.

Captain America, vol. 1, #250 (October 1980). Same as above.

Captain America, vol. 1, #251 (November 1980). Same as above.

Captain America, vol. 1, #252 (December 1980). Same as above.

Captain America, vol. 1, #255 (March 1981). Same as above.

Captain America, vol. 1, #258 (June 1981). Chris Claremont and David Michelinie (w), Mike Zeck (a). Collected in *Captain America Epic Collection: Dawn's Early Light* (2014).

Captain America, vol. 1, #261 (September 1981). J.M. DeMatteis (w), Mike Zeck and Quickdraw Studios (a). Collected in *Captain America Epic Collection: Dawn's Early Light* (2014).

Captain America, vol. 1, #263 (November 1981). Same as above.

Captain America, vol. 1, #267 (March 1982). J.M. DeMatteis (w), Mike Zeck and John Beatty (a).

Captain America, vol. 1, #268 (April 1982). Same as above.

Captain America, vol. 1, #269 (May 1982). J.M. DeMatteis (w), Mike Zeck, John Beatty, and Josef Rubinstein (a).

Captain America, vol. 1, #270 (June 1982). J.M. DeMatteis (w), Mike Zeck and John Beatty (a).

Captain America, vol. 1, #273 (September 1982). David Anthony Kraft (w), Mike Zeck and John Beatty (a).

Captain America, vol. 1, #275 (November 1982). J.M. DeMatteis (w), Mike Zeck and John Beatty (a).

Captain America, vol. 1, #278 (February 1983). Same as above.

Captain America, vol. 1, #284 (August 1983). J.M. DeMatteis (w), Sal Buscema and Kim DeMulder (a).

Captain America, vol. 1, #285 (September 1983). Same as above.

Captain America, vol. 1, #286 (October 1983). Same creators as above. Collected in *Captain America: Deathlok Lives* (1993).

Captain America, vol. 1, #289 (January 1984). J.M. DeMatteis (w), Mike Zeck and John Beatty (a).

Captain America, vol. 1, #291 (March 1984). Bill Mantlo (w), Herb Trimpe and Jack Abel (a). Collected in *Captain America: Death of the Red Skull* (2012).

Captain America, vol. 1, #293 (May 1984). J.M. DeMatteis (w), Paul Neary and Ed Barreto (a). Collected in *Captain America: Death of the Red Skull* (2012).

Captain America, vol. 1, #294 (June 1984). J.M. DeMatteis (w), Paul Neary and Josef Rubinstein (a). Collected in *Captain America: Death of the Red Skull* (2012).

Captain America, vol. 1, #295 (July 1984). J.M. DeMatteis (w), Paul Neary and Brett Breeding (a). Collected in *Captain America: Death of the Red Skull* (2012).

Captain America, vol. 1, #298 (October 1984). J.M. DeMatteis (w), Paul Neary and Roy Richardson (a). Collected in *Captain America: Death of the Red Skull* (2012).

Captain America, vol. 1, #300 (December 1984). J.M. DeMatteis and Michael Ellis (w), Paul Neary and Dennis Janke (a). Collected in *Captain America: Death of the Red Skull* (2012).[2]

Captain America, vol. 1, #309 (September 1985). Mark Gruenwald (w), Paul Neary and Dennis Janke (a).

Captain America, vol. 1, #312 (December 1985). Same as above.

Captain America, vol. 1, #314 (February 1986). Same as above.

Captain America, vol. 1, #315 (March 1986). Same as above.

Captain America, vol. 1, #316 (April 1986). Same as above.

Captain America, vol. 1, #317 (May 1986). Same as above.

Captain America, vol. 1, #321 (September 1986). Same as above.

Captain America, vol. 1, #322 (October 1986). Same as above.

Captain America, vol. 1, #323 (November 1986). Same as above.

Captain America, vol. 1, #324 (December 1986). Mark Gruenwald (w), Paul Neary and Vince Colletta (a).

Captain America, vol. 1, #325 (January 1987). Mark Gruenwald (w), Paul Neary and Dennis Janke (a).

Captain America, vol. 1, #327 (March 1987). Mark Gruenwald (w), Paul Neary and John Beatty (a).

Captain America, vol. 1, #331 (July 1987). Mark Gruenwald (w), Paul Neary and Vince Colletta (a).

Captain America, vol. 1, #332 (August 1987). Mark Gruenwald (w), Tom Morgan and Bob McLeod (a). Collected in *Captain America: The Captain* (2011).

Captain America, vol. 1, #336 (December 1987). Mark Gruenwald (w), Tom Morgan and Dave Hunt (a). Collected in *Captain America: The Captain* (2011).

Captain America, vol. 1, #337 (January 1988). Same as above.

Captain America, vol. 1, #341 (May 1988). Mark Gruenwald (w), Kieron Dwyer and Al Milgrom (a). Collected in *Captain America: The Captain* (2011).

Captain America, vol. 1, #342 (June 1988). Same as above.

Captain America, vol. 1, #345 (September 1988). Same as above.

Captain America, vol. 1, #349 (January 1989). Same as above.

Captain America, vol. 1, #350 (February 1989), 1st story: "Seeing Red." Same as above.

Captain America, vol. 1, #350 (February 1989), 2nd story: "Resurrection." Mark Gruenwald (w), John Byrne and José Marzan, Jr. (a). Collected in *Captain America: The Captain* (2011).

Captain America, vol. 1, #355 (July 1989). Mark Gruenwald (w), Rich Buckler and Al Milgrom (a). Reprinted in *Fear Itself: Sin's Past* (one-shot) (June 2011).

Captain America, vol. 1, #377 (September 1990), 1st story: "The 100% Solution." Mark Gruenwald (w), Ron Lim and Danny Bulanadi (a). Collected in *Captain America: Streets of Poison* (1994).

Captain America, vol. 1, #390 (August 1991). Mark Gruenwald (w), Rik Levins and Danny Bulanadi (a).

Captain America, vol. 1, #401 (June 1992). Same creators as above. Collected in *Avengers: Galactic Storm, Vol. 2* (2006).

Captain America, vol. 1, #402 (July 1992), 1st story: "The Prowling." Same creators as above. Collected in *Captain America: Man & Wolf* (2011).

Captain America, vol. 1, #413 (February 1993). Same creators as above.

Captain America, vol. 1, #427 (May 1994). Mark Gruenwald (w), Dave Hoover and Danny Bulanadi (a). Collected in *Captain America: Fighting Chance – Denial* (2009).

Captain America, vol. 1, #428 (June 1994). Same as above.

Captain America, vol. 1, #439 (May 1995). Mark Gruenwald (w), Dave Hoover, Scott Koblish, and Danny Bulanadi (a).

Captain America, vol. 1, #443 (September 1995). Mark Gruenwald (w), Dave Hoover and Danny Bulanadi (a).

Captain America, vol. 1, #444 (October 1995). Mark Waid (w), Ron Garney and Mike Sellers (a). Collected in *Captain America: Operation Rebirth* (2011).

Captain America, vol. 1, #445 (November 1995). Mark Waid (w), Ron Garney and Scott Koblish (a). Collected in *Captain America: Operation Rebirth* (2011).

Captain America, vol. 1, #447 (January 1996). Mark Waid (w), Ron Garney and Mike Manley (a). Collected in *Captain America: Operation Rebirth* (2011).

Captain America, vol. 1, #450 (April 1996). Mark Waid (w), Ron Garney and Scott Koblish (a). Collected in *Captain America: Operation Rebirth* (2011).

Captain America, vol. 1, #452 (June 1996). Same as above.

Captain America, vol. 1, #454 (August 1996). Same as above.

Captain America, vol. 3, #1 (January 1998). Mark Waid (w), Ron Garney and Bob Wiacek (a). Collected in *Captain America: To Serve & Protect* (2011).

Captain America, vol. 3, #4 (April 1998). Same as above.

Captain America, vol. 3, #5 (May 1998). Mark Waid (w), Ron Garney, John Beatty, and Andy Smith (a). Collected in *Captain America: To Serve & Protect* (2011).

Captain America, vol. 3, #6 (June 1998). Mark Waid (w), Dale Eaglesham and Scott Koblish (a). Collected in *Captain America: To Serve & Protect* (2011).

Captain America, vol. 3, #7 (July 1998). Mark Waid (w), Dale Eaglesham, Andy Kubert, Scott Koblish, and Jesse Delperdang (a). Collected in *Captain America: To Serve & Protect* (2011).

Captain America, vol. 3, #13 (1999). Mark Waid (w) and Doug Braithewaite (a). Collected in *Captain America: Red Nightmare* (2011).

Captain America, vol. 3, #16 (April 1999). Mark Waid (w), Andy Kubert, Jesse Delperdang, and Joe Kubert (a). Collected in *Captain America: Red Glare* (2011).

Captain America, vol. 3, #17 (May 1999). Mark Waid (w), Andy Kubert and Jesse Delperdang (a). Collected in *Captain America: Red Glare* (2011).

Captain America, vol. 3, #24 (December 1999). Tom DeFalco (w), Ron Frenz and Jesse Delperdang (a). Collected in *Captain America: Land of the Free* (2013).

Captain America, vol. 3, #25 (January 2000). Dan Jurgens (w), Andy Kubert and Dan Green (a). Collected in *Captain America by Dan Jurgens: Volume 1* (2011).

Captain America, vol. 3, #31 (July 2000). Same as above.

Captain America, vol. 3, #32 (August 2000). Dan Jurgens (w) and Jerry Ordway (a). Collected in *Captain America by Dan Jurgens: Volume 1* (2011).

Captain America, vol. 3, #40 (March 2001). Dan Jurgens (w, a) and Bob Layton (a). Collected in *Captain America by Dan Jurgens: Volume 2* (2011).

Captain America, vol. 3, #41 (May 2001). Dan Jurgens (w, a) and Bob Layton (a). Collected in *Captain America by Dan Jurgens: Volume 2* (2011).

Captain America, vol. 3, #42 (June 2001). Same as above.

Captain America, vol. 3, #44 (August 2001). Same as above.

Captain America, vol. 3, #46 (October 2001). Same creators as above. Collected in *Captain America by Dan Jurgens: Volume 3* (2012).

Captain America, vol. 3, #47 (November 2001). Same as above.

Captain America, vol. 3, #48 (December 2001). Same as above.

Captain America, vol. 3, #49 (January 2002). Dan Jurgens (w), Juan Bobillo and Marcelo Sosa (a). Collected in *Captain America by Dan Jurgens: Volume 3* (2012).

Captain America, vol. 3, #50 (February 2002), 2nd story: "Keep in Mind." Kathryn Immonen (writing as Kathryn Kuder) (w) and Stuart Immonen (a). Collected in *Captain America by Dan Jurgens: Volume 3* (2012).

Captain America, vol. 3, #50 (February 2002), 3rd story: "To the Core." Dan Jurgens (w, a), Bob Layton and various cameo artists (a). Collected in *Captain America by Dan Jurgens: Volume 3* (2012).

Captain America, vol. 3, #50 (February 2002), 4th story: "Relics." Brian David-Marshall (w) and Igor Kordey (a). Collected in *Captain America by Dan Jurgens: Volume 3* (2012).

Captain America, vol. 4, #1 (June 2002). John Ney Reiber (w) and John Cassaday (a). Collected in *Captain America: The New Deal* (2003).

Captain America, vol. 4, #3 (August 2002). Same as above.

Captain America, vol. 4, #4 (September 2002). Same as above.

Captain America, vol. 4, #8 (March 2003). John Ney Reiber and Chuck Austen (w), Trevor Hairsine and Danny Miki (a). Collected in *Captain America: The Extremists* (2003).

Captain America, vol. 4, #11 (May 2003). Chuck Austen (w) and Jae Lee (a). Collected in *Captain America: The Extremists* (2003).

Captain America, vol. 5, #1 (January 2005). Ed Brubaker (w) and Steve Epting (a). Collected in *Captain America: Winter Soldier, Vol. 1* (2006).

Captain America, vol. 5, #3 (March 2005). Ed Brubaker (w), Steve Epting and Michael Lark (a).

Captain America, vol. 5, #5 (May 2005). Same as above.

Captain America, vol. 5, #9 (September 2005). Ed Brubaker (w) and Michael Lark (a). Collected in *Captain America: Winter Soldier, Vol. 2* (2006).

Captain America, vol. 5, #11 (November 2005). Ed Brubaker (w), Steve Epting and Mike Perkins (a). Collected in *Captain America: Winter Soldier, Vol. 2* (2006).

Captain America, vol. 5, #12 (December 2005). Ed Brubaker (w), Steve Epting. Michael Lark, and Mike Perkins (a). Collected in *Captain America: Winter Soldier, Vol. 2* (2006).

Captain America, vol. 5, #16 (May 2006). Ed Brubaker (w) and Mike Perkins (a). Collected in *Captain America: Red Menace, Vol. 1* (2006).

Captain America, vol. 5, #17 (June 2006). Same as above.

Captain America, vol. 5, #22 (November 2006). Same creators as above. Collected in *Civil War: Captain America* (2007).

Captain America, vol. 5, #25 (April 2007). Ed Brubaker (w) and Steve Epting (a). Collected in *The Death of Captain America, Vol. 1: The Death of a Dream* (2008).

Captain America, vol. 5, #26 (May 2007). Same as above.

Captain America, vol. 5, #35 (April 2008). Ed Brubaker (w), Butch Guice and Mike Perkins (a). Collected in *The Death of Captain America, Vol. 2: The Burden of Dreams* (2008).

Captain America, vol. 5, #600 (August 2009), 3rd story: "In Memorium." Roger Stern (w) and Kalman Andrasofszky (a). Collected in *Captain America: The Road to Reborn* (2010).³

Captain America, vol. 5, #612 (January 2011), 1st story: "The Trial of Captain America Part 2." Ed Brubaker (w) and Butch Guice (a). Collected in *Captain America: The Trial of Captain America* (2011).

Captain America, vol. 5, #615.1 (May 2011). Ed Brubaker (w) and Mitch Breitweiser (a). Collected in *Captain America: The Trial of Captain America* (2011).

Captain America, vol. 5, #616 (May 2011), 3rd story: "Must There Be a Captain America?" Ed Brubaker (w), Ed McGuiness and Dexter Vines (a). Collected in *Captain America: Prisoner of War* (2012).

Captain America, vol. 5, #616 (May 2011), 5th story: "Spin." Cullen Bunn (w) and Jason Latour (a). Collected in *Captain America: Prisoner of War* (2012).

Captain America, vol. 5, #619 (August 2011). Ed Brubaker (w), Butch Guice, Mitch Breitweiser, Chris Samnee, and Stefano Guadiano (a). Collected in *Captain America: Prisoner of War* (2012).

Captain America, vol. 6, #6 (February 2012). Ed Brubaker (w), Alan Davis and Mark Farmer (a). Collected in *Captain America by Ed Brubaker – Volume 2* (2012).

Captain America, vol. 6, #10 (June 2012). Same as above.

Captain America, vol. 6, #14 (September 2012). Ed Brubaker (w), Patrick Zirchner and Mike Deodato (a). Collected in *Captain America by Ed Brubaker – Volume 3* (2013).

Captain America, vol. 6, #15 (September 2012). Ed Brubaker and Cullen Bunn (w), Scot Eaton and Rick Magyar (a). Collected in *Captain America by Ed Brubaker – Volume 4* (2013).

Captain America, vol. 6, #19 (December 2012). Ed Brubaker (w) and Steve Epting (a). Collected in *Captain America by Ed Brubaker – Volume 4* (2013).

Captain America, vol. 7, #1 (January 2013). Rick Remender (w), John Romita, Jr. and Klaus Janson (a). Collected in *Captain America, Vol. 1: Castaway in Dimension Z, Book 1* (2013).

Captain America, vol. 7, #4 (April 2013). Same as above.

Captain America, vol. 7, #9 (September 2013). Rick Remender (w), John Romita, Jr., Klaus Janson, Scott Hanna, and Tom Palmer (a). Collected in *Captain America, Vol. 2: Castaway in Dimension Z, Book 2* (2013).

Captain America, vol. 7, #10 (October 2013). Rick Remender (w), John Romita, Jr., Klaus Janson, and Tom Palmer (a). Collected in *Captain America, Vol. 2: Castaway in Dimension Z, Book 2* (2013).

Captain America and the Falcon #3 (July 2004). Christopher Priest (w), Bart Sears and Rob Hunter (a). Collected in *Captain America and the Falcon, Vol. 1: Two Americas* (2004).

Captain America and the Falcon #4 (August 2004). Same as above.

Captain America and the Falcon #5 (September 2004). Christopher Priest (w), Joe Bennett and Jack Jadson (a). Collected in *Avengers Disassembled: Iron Man, Thor & Captain America* (2009).

Captain America and the Falcon #9 (January 2005). Christopher Priest (w), Joe Bennett and Jack Jadson (a). Collected in *Captain America and the Falcon, Vol. 2: Brothers and Keepers* (2005).

Captain America and the Falcon #14 (June 2005). Christopher Priest (w), Dan Jurgens and Tom Palmer (a). Collected in *Captain America and the Falcon, Vol. 2: Brothers and Keepers* (2005).

Captain America Annual, vol. 1, #13 (1994), 2nd story: "Symbols." Ron Marz (w), Rik Levins and Ricardo Villagran (a).

Captain America/Black Panther: Flags of Our Fathers #4 (September 2010). Reginald Hudlin (w), Denys Cowan, Tom Palmer, and Sandra Florea (a). Collected in *Captain America/Black Panther: Flags of Our Fathers* (2010).

Captain America: The Chosen #1 (November 2007). David Morrell (w) and Mitch Breitweiser (a). Collected in *Captain America: The Chosen* (2008).

Captain America: The Chosen #4 (December 2007). Same as above.

Captain America: The Chosen #5 (February 2008). Same as above.

Captain America: The Chosen #6 (March 2008). Same as above.

Captain America: Dead Men Running #3 (May 2002). Darko Macan (w) and Derek Hess (a).

Captain America: Man Out of Time #3 (March 2011). Mark Waid (w), Jorge Molina, Karl Kesel, and Scott Hanna (a). Collected in *Captain America: Man Out of Time* (2011).

Captain America: Man Out of Time #4 (April 2011). Mark Waid (w), Jorge Molina and Karl Kesel (a). Collected in *Captain America: Man Out of Time* (2011).

Captain America: Man Out of Time #5 (May 2011). Same as above.

Captain America/Nick Fury: The Otherworld War (one-shot) (October 2001). Peter Hogan (w) and Leonardo Manco (a).

Captain America: Reborn #6 (March 2010). Ed Brubaker (w), Bryan Hitch and Butch Guice (a). Collected in *Captain America: Reborn* (2010).

Captain America: Red, White & Blue (one-shot) (September 2002), 7th story: "… they just fade away …" Jeff Jensen (w) and Frank Quitely (a). Collected in *Captain America: Red, White & Blue* (2007).

Captain America: Sentinel of Liberty #1 (September 1998). Mark Waid (w), Ron Garney (w, a), and Dan Panosian (a). Collected in *Captain America: Sentinel of Liberty* (2011).

216 *References*

Captain America: Sentinel of Liberty #3 (November 1998). Mark Waid (w), Ron Garney (w, a), and Dan Green (a). Collected in *Captain America: Sentinel of Liberty* (2011).

Captain America: Sentinel of Liberty #6 (February 1999), 1st story: "Iron Will." Same as above.

Captain America: Sentinel of Liberty #7 (March 1999), 2nd story: "An Ending." Brian Vaughan (w), Steve Harris and Rodney Ramos (a). Collected in *Captain America: Sentinel of Liberty* (2011).

Captain America Theater of War: America the Beautiful (one-shot) (March 2009). Paul Jenkins (w) and Gary Erskine (a). Collected in *Captain America: Theater of War* (2010).

Captain America Theater of War: A Brother in Arms (one-shot) (June 2009). Paul Jenkins (w), John McCrea and various inkers (a). Collected in *Captain America: Theater of War* (2010).

Captain America Theater of War: Prisoners of Duty (one-shot) (February 2010). Kyle Higgins and Alex Siegel (w), and Agustin Padilla (a). Collected in *Captain America: America First* (2010).

Captain America Theater of War: To Soldier On (one-shot) (October 2009). Paul Jenkins (w), Fernando Blanco (a). Collected in *Captain America: Theater of War* (2010).

Captain America: Who Will Wield the Shield? (one-shot) (February 2010). Ed Brubaker (w), Butch Guice and Luke Ross (a). Collected in *Captain America: Two Americas* (2010).

Captain America's Bicentennial Battles (June 1976). Jack Kirby (w, a) and various inkers (a). Collected in *Captain America: Bicentennial Battles* (2005).

Civil War #1 (July 2006). Mark Millar (w), Steve McNiven and Dexter Vines (a). Collected in *Civil War* (2007).

Civil War #3 (September 2006). Mark Millar (w), Steve McNiven, Dexter Vines, and Mark Morales (a). Collected in *Civil War* (2007).

Civil War #4 (October 2006). Mark Millar (w), Steve McNiven and Dexter Vines (a). Collected in *Civil War* (2007).

Civil War #7 (January 2007). Mark Millar (w), Steve McNiven and various inkers (a). Collected in *Civil War* (2007).

Civil War: The Confession (one-shot) (May 2007). Brian Michael Bendis (w) and Alex Maleev (a). Collected in *Civil War: Iron Man* (2007).

Civil War: Front Line #9 (December 2006), 1st story: "Embedded Part 9." Paul Jenkins (w), Ramon Bachs and John Lucas (a). Collected in *Civil War: Front Line, Vol. 2* (2007).

Civil War: Front Line #11 (April 2007), 1st story: "Embedded Part 11." Same as above.

Civil War: War Crimes (one-shot) (February 2007). Frank Tieri (w), Staz Johnson, Tom Palmer, and Robin Riggs (a). Collected in *Civil War: War Crimes* (2007).

Daredevil, vol. 1, #233 (August 1986). Frank Miller (w) and David Mazzucchelli (a). Collected in *Daredevil: Born Again* (2010).

Fallen Son: The Death of Captain America #4 (July 2007). Jeph Loeb (w), David Finch and Danny Miki (a). Collected in *Fallen Son: The Death of Captain America* (2008).

Fallen Son: The Death of Captain America #5 (August 2007). Jeph Loeb (w) and John Cassaday (a). Collected in *Fallen Son: The Death of Captain America* (2008).

Fear Itself #1 (June 2011). Matt Fraction (w), Stuart Immonen and Wade von Grawbadger (a). Collected in *Fear Itself* (2012).

Fear Itself #5 (October 2011). Same as above.

Fear Itself #6 (November 2011). Same as above.

Fear Itself #7 (December 2011). Matt Fraction (w), Stuart Immonen, Wade von Grawbadger, and Dexter Vines (a). Collected in *Fear Itself* (2012).

Fear Itself #7.1 (January 2012). Ed Brubaker (w) and Butch Guice (a). Collected in *Fear Itself: Shattered Heroes* (2012).

House of M #1 (August 2005). Brian Michael Bendis (w), Olivier Coipel and Tim Townsend (a). Collected in *House of M* (2006).

Infinity Gauntlet #4 (October 1991). Jim Starlin (w), George Pérez, Ron Lim, Josef Rubinstein, and Bruce N. Solotoff (a). Collected in *Infinity Gauntlet* (2011).

Iron Man, vol. 1, #172 (July 1983). Denny O'Neil (w), Luke McDonnell and Steve Mitchell (a). Collected in *Iron Man Epic Collection: The Enemy Within* (2013).

Iron Man, vol. 1, #228 (March 1988). David Michelinie and Bob Layton (w), Mark Bright and Bob Layton (a). Collected in *Iron Man: Armor Wars* (2007) and *Captain America: The Captain* (2011).

Iron Man, vol. 4, #7 (June 2006). Daniel Knauf and Charles Knauf (w), Patrick Zircher and Scott Hanna (a). Collected in *Iron Man: Execute Program* (2007).

Iron Man, vol. 4, #12 (November 2006). Same as above.

Iron Man, vol. 4, #14 (January 2007). Same creators as above. Collected in *Civil War: Iron Man* (2007).

Iron Man/Captain America Annual 1998 (January 1999). Kurt Busiek, Roger Stern, and Mark Waid (w), Patrick Zircher and Randy Emberlin (a). Collected in *Iron Man: Revenge of the Mandarin* (2012).

Iron Man/Captain America: Casualties of War (one-shot) (February 2007). Christos Gage (w), Jeremy Haun and Mark Morales (a). Collected in *Civil War: Iron Man* (2007).

JLA/Avengers #2 (October 2003). Kurt Busiek (w) and George Pérez (a). Collected in *JLA/Avengers* (2008, published by DC Comics in association with Marvel Comics).

Marvel Spotlight, vol. 3, #9 (October 2006), "The Spotlight Interview with Ed Brubaker." No writer listed. Collected in *Captain America: Red Menace, Vol. 2* (2006).

Marvel Spotlight, vol. 3, #18 (June 2007), "Cap in Crisis: Steve Englehart's Captain America." Matt Adler (w). Collected in *Captain America: Red, White & Blue* (2007).

Marvel Spotlight, vol. 3, #18 (June 2007), "The Man Who Killed Captain America." Dugan Trodglen (w). Collected in *Captain America: Red, White & Blue* (2007).

Marvel Spotlight, vol. 3, #18 (June 2007), "Remembering 'Remembrance': Stern & Byrne Take Their Turn with America's Fighting Legend." Dugan Trodglen (w). Collected in *Captain America: Red, White & Blue* (2007).

Marvel Team-Up, vol. 1, #106 (June 1981). Tom DeFalco (w), Herb Trimpe and Mike Esposito (a).

Marvel Team-Up, vol. 1, #128 (April 1983). J.M. DeMatteis (w), Kerry Gammill and Mike Esposito (a).

Marvel Two-in-One #75 (May 1981). Tom DeFalco (w), Alan Kupperberg and Chic Stone (a). Collected in *Essential Marvel Two-in-One, Vol. 2* (2007).

Mythos – Captain America (one-shot) (August 2008). Paul Jenkins (w) and Paolo Rivera (a). Collected in *Avengers: Mythos* (2012).

New Avengers, vol. 1, #5 (May 2005). Brian Michael Bendis (w), Bryan Hitch and Danny Miki (a). Collected in *New Avengers: Breakout* (2006).

New Avengers, vol. 1, #6 (June 2005). Same as above.

New Avengers, vol. 1, #11 (November 2005). Same creators as above. Collected in *New Avengers: Secrets & Lies* (2006).

New Avengers, vol. 1, #15 (March 2006). Brian Michael Bendis (w) and Frank Cho (a). Collected in *New Avengers: Secrets & Lies* (2006).

New Avengers, vol. 1, #17 (May 2006). Brian Michael Bendis (w), Mike Deodato, Jr. and Joe Pimentel (a). Collected in *New Avengers: The Collective* (2007).

New Avengers, vol. 1, #21 (August 2006). Brian Michael Bendis (w) and Howard Chaykin (a). Collected in *Civil War: New Avengers* (2007).

New Avengers, vol. 2, #22 (April 2012). Brian Michael Bendis (w), Mike Deodato and Will Conrad (a). Collected in *New Avengers by Brian Michael Bendis Vol. 3* (2012).

New Avengers, vol. 2, #29 (October 2012). Brian Michael Bendis (w) and Mike Deodato (a). Collected in *New Avengers by Brian Michael Bendis Vol. 4* (2012).

New Avengers, vol. 3, #2 (March 2013). Jonathan Hickman (w), Steve Epting and Rick Magyar (a). Collected in *New Avengers, Vol. 1: Everything Dies* (2013).

New Avengers, vol. 3, #3 (April 2013). Same as above.

New Avengers: Illuminati, vol. 1, #1 (May 2006). Brian Michael Bendis (w) and Alex Maleev (a). Collected in *Road to Civil War* (2007).

Secret Avengers, vol. 1, #1 (July 2010). Ed Brubaker (w) and Mike Deodato, Jr. (a). Collected in *Secret Avengers, Vol. 1: Mission to Mars* (2011).

Secret Avengers, vol. 1, #7 (January 2011). Same creators as above. Collected in *Secret Avengers, Vol. 2: Eyes of the Dragon* (2012).

Secret Avengers, vol. 1, #12.1 (June 2011). Nick Spencer (w), Scot Eaton and Jaime Mendoza (a). Collected in *Fear Itself: Secret Avengers* (2012).

Secret Avengers, vol. 1, #21 (March 2012). Warren Ellis (w), Stuart Immonen and Wade von Grawbadger (a). Collected in *Secret Avengers: Run the Mission, Don't Get Seen, Save the World* (2012).

Secret War #5 (December 2005). Brian Michael Bendis (w) and Gabrielle Dell'Otto (a). Collected in *Secret War* (2009).

Siege #2 (April 2010). Brian Michael Bendis (w), Olivier Coipel and Mark Morales (a). Collected in *Siege* (2010).

Siege #4 (June 2010). Same as above.

Steve Rogers: Super-Soldier #1 (September 2010). Ed Brubaker (w) and Dale Eaglesham (a). Collected in *Captain America: Steve Rogers – Super Soldier* (2011).

Steve Rogers: Super-Soldier #2 (October 2010). Same as above.

Steve Rogers: Super-Soldier #3 (November 2010). Same as above.

Strange Tales, vol. 1, #114 (November 1963), 1st story: "The Human Torch Meets ... Captain America!" Stan Lee (w), Jack Kirby and Dick Ayers (a). Reprinted in *Captain America*, vol. 1, #216 (December 1977), and collected in *Marvel Masterworks: The Human Torch Vol. 1* (2006), *Essential Human Torch Vol. 1* (2003), and CA:ESS6.

Tales of Suspense, vol. 1, #59 (November 1964), 2nd story: "Captain America." Stan Lee (w), Jack Kirby and Chic Stone (a). Collected in CA:MM1 and CA:ESS1.

Tales of Suspense, vol. 1, #72 (December 1965), 2nd story: "The Sleeper Shall Awake!" Stan Lee (w), Jack Kirby and Frank Giacoia (a). Collected in CA:MM1 and CA:ESS1.

Tales of Suspense, vol. 1, #74 (February 1966), 2nd story: "The Final Sleep." Same as above.

Tales of Suspense, vol. 1, #75 (March 1966), 2nd story: "30 Minutes to Live!" Stan Lee (w), Jack Kirby and Dick Ayers (a). Collected in CA:MM1 and CA:ESS1.

Tales of Suspense, vol. 1, #81 (September 1966), 2nd story: "The Red Skull Supreme!" Stan Lee (w), Jack Kirby and Frank Giacoia (a). Collected in CA:MM1 and CA:ESS1.

Tales of Suspense, vol. 1, #91 (July 1967), 2nd story: "The Last Defeat!" Stan Lee (w), Gil Kane and Joe Sinnott (a). Collected in CA:MM2 and CA:ESS1.

Tales of Suspense, vol. 1, #95 (November 1967), 2nd story: "A Time to Die—A Time to Live!" Stan Lee (w), Jack Kirby and Joe Sinnott (a). Collected in CA:MM2 and CA:ESS1.

Thor, vol. 1, #390 (April 1988). Tom DeFalco (w), Ron Frenz and Brett Breeding (a). Collected in *Thor Epic Collection: War of the Pantheons* (2013).

Thor, vol. 3, #11 (November 2008). J. Michael Straczynski (w), Olivier Coipel and various inkers (a). Collected in *Thor by J. Michael Straczynski Vol. 2* (2009).

Truth: Red, White & Black #6 (June 2003). Robert Morales (w) and Kyle Baker (a). Collected in *Captain America: Truth* (2009).

Truth: Red, White & Black #7 (July 2003). Same as above.

Ultimates, vol. 1, #12 (November 2003). Mark Millar (w) and Bryan Hitch (a). Collected in *The Ultimates: The Ultimate Collection* (2010).

Uncanny Avengers #3 (March 2013). Rick Remender (w) and John Cassaday (a). Collected in *Uncanny Avengers, Vol. 1: The Red Shadow* (2013).

Uncanny Avengers #9 (August 2013). Rick Remender (w) and Daniel Acuña (a). Collected in *Uncanny Avengers, Vol. 2: Ragnarok Now* (2013).

Uncanny Avengers #10 (September 2013). Same as above.

Uncanny X-Men, vol. 1, #268 (September 1990). Chris Claremont (w), Jim Lee and Scott Williams (a). Collected in *X-Men Visionaries: Jim Lee* (2002) and other places.

Wolverine Origins #18 (2007). Daniel Way (w) and Steve Dillon (a). Collected in *Wolverine Origins: Our War* (2008).

Wolverine/Captain America #2 (April 2004). R.A. Jones (w) and Tom Derenick (w, a). Collected in *Wolverine/Captain America* (2012).

X-Men vs. Avengers #4 (July 1987). Tom DeFalco and Jim Shooter (w), Keith Polland and various inkers (a). Collected in *X-Men Versus Avengers/Fantastic Four* (2011).

Young Avengers, vol. 1, #6 (September 2005). Allan Heinberg (w), Jim Cheung and various inkers (a). Collected in *Young Avengers* (2010).

Young Avengers Presents #1 (March 2008). Ed Brubaker (w), Paco Medina and Juan Viasco (a). Collected in *Young Avengers Presents* (2008).

Notes

1   Starting with this issue and lasting through *Captain America*, vol. 1, #222 (June 1978), the logo on the cover of the book read "Captain America and the Falcon," though the title in the indicia remained simply "Captain America," which is how I've listed it here (which corresponds with the sources cited at the beginning).

2   Who is this "Michael Ellis," you ask? For the answer, as well as the fascinating look behind the scenes of the creation of a comic story and a peek at an abandoned Steve Rogers storyline, see J.M. DeMatteis's blog post "The Mysterious Michael Ellis" at his blog: www.jmdematteis.com/2012/03/mysterious-michael-ellis.html.

3   I chose to keep the volume number of *Captain America* the same when the numbering reverted to its cumulative total with issue #600. To me it seems more confusing to have the volume number go backwards with a new issue, and it helps keep the issues in chronological order when sorted by volume number before issue number.

Index

Abel, Jack, 209, 210
Abrams, Paul, 205
Abu Ghraib, 105
Acrobat, xi
Acuña, Daniel, 206, 220
Adler, Matt, 218
Agent 9 (SHIELD), 125–126
Agent 13 (SHIELD), *see* Carter, Sharon
AIM (Advanced Idea Mechanics), 155, 156, 159, 176
Alanguilan, Gerry, 207
Alexander, Larry, 142
"American dream versus American reality," xi, 98, 150–153, 162, 173–174
American ideals, xi, 86, 96, 111, 117, 134, 145–146, 153, 154, 162, 181–194; *see also* equality; justice; liberty
American Idol, 172
Anderson, Bryan (Sergeant), 53, 70, 83
Andrasofszky, Kalman, 214
anger, *see* righteous indignation
Annas, Julia, 23
Anscombe, G.E.M., 24
"Anti-Cap," 84, 116–117, 124, 148–149, 169, 180

Ant-Man, *see* Pym, Henry "Hank"
Appiah, Kwame Anthony, 43, 102, 103
Aristotle, ix, xi, 13–16, 46–47, 49, 57, 67, 78, 194, 196
Arp, Robert, 42, 138
Arlington National Cemetery, 83, 188
Arthurian legend, 80, 91
Asgard, ix, 66, 174, 200
Atlantis, 65, 147
Augustine, St., 167
Austen, Chuck, 206, 213
Avengers, vii, viii, 30, 46, 47, 49, 52–53, 61, 74, 80, 83, 106, 176, 180, 199–200
  adventures of, 1, 7, 32, 33, 51, 65, 66, 92, 93–94, 96, 97, 110, 115, 122, 153, 154–155, 170
  killing, code against, 88–89, 127–129
  leadership of, 62, 69, 136
  responsibility for, 62–63
Avengers (comics series), vii, viii, xi, 198–201
Avengers, The (2012 film), viii, xiv, 200
Avengers Academy, 1
Avengers Assemble (comics series), 200
Avengers charter, 113, 158, 176

The Virtues of Captain America: Modern-Day Lessons on Character from a World War II Superhero, First Edition. Mark D. White.
© 2014 John Wiley & Sons, Inc. Published 2014 by John Wiley & Sons, Inc.